The Star-Entangled Banner

The Star-Entangled Banner

ONE HUNDRED YEARS OF AMERICA IN THE PHILIPPINES

SHARON DELMENDO

RUTGERS UNIVERSITY PRESS
New Brunswick, New Jersey, and London

LIBRARY OF CONGRESS CATALOGING-IN-PUBLICATION DATA

Delmendo, Sharon, 1964–
The star-entangled banner : one hundred years of America in the Philippines / Sharon
Delmendo.
p. cm.
Includes bibliographical references and index.
ISBN 0-8135-3410-0 (alk. paper) — ISBN 0-8135-3411-9 (pbk. : alk. paper)
1. United States—Relations—Philippines.   2. Philippines—Relations—United
States.   3. United States—Foreign relations—20th century.   4. United States—
Foreign relations—2001–   5. Philippines—Colonization—History.
6. Nationalism—Philippines—History.   7. Nationalism—United States—
History.   8. Imperialism—History.   I. Title.
E183.8.P5 D45 2004
959.9'03—dc22

                                                                    2003018873

British Cataloging-in-Publication data record for this book is available from the British
Library

Manufactured in the United States of America

Kalayaan Kayamanan ng Bayan

Freedom is the treasure of the nation

For our daughters, Kalayaan "Kylie" and Kayamanan "Kaya" Raguso, and the hope that someday they will find their own way to Inang Bayan

Contents

LIST OF ILLUSTRATIONS

ACKNOWLEDGMENTS

IN LARGE PART, this book grew out of a yearlong teaching-research grant as Fulbright Professor of American Studies, hosted by De La Salle University in Manila. I must acknowledge the support and collegiality of the faculty in the literature department at La Salle, especially Isagani R. Cruz and Marge Evasco, as well as Alex Calata, executive director of the Philippine-American Educational Foundation, and the officers and staff of the U.S. Embassy, without whose help I would not have been able to attend the commemorative events of July 4, 1996, and June 12, 1998.

I owe thanks for the generosity of many people and organizations in both the Philippines and the United States for materials and information pertaining to the Balangiga Bells. In the Philippines I owe particular thanks to Eva Brillo of the Thomas Jefferson Information Center, the Cultural Affairs Office of the U.S. Embassy in Manila, and Bob Couttie and Rolly Borrinaga of the Balangiga Research Group. In the United States, I am grateful to the Wyoming State Archive; Sgt. Jeff Bohn and Sgt. Stacy Vaughn of the Public Affairs Office at Warren Air Force Base; Richard Kolb, executive editor of *VFW* Magazine; Kay at the *Casper (Wyo.) Star-Tribune;* Bishop Hart of the Diocese of Cheyenne; Jim Helzer, Sylvester Salcedo, and Wyoming state representatives E. Jayne Mockler and Jeff Wasserburger. Jayne Mockler, Sylvester Salcedo, Jim Zwick, Enrique de la Cruz, and Eric Brietbart also graciously provided me with some of the illustrations.

My thanks to Johns Hopkins University Press for permission to reprint chapter 4, originally published in the *Journal of Asian American Studies* (October 1998); to the University of Hawaii for permission to reprint an earlier version of chapter 3, originally published in *Literary Studies East and West* (winter 1996); to the Ateneo de Manila University Press, for giving permission to reprint another version of chapter 3, originally published in *Geopolitics of the Visible: Essays on Philippine Film Cultures* (2000); and to UCLA for permission to reprint a much earlier version of chapter 1, originally published in *AMERASIA* (summer 1998).

I would also like to acknowledge the support I received from my home institution, St. John Fisher College, to bring this project to fruition, including travel expenses and a Fulbright grant in the Philippines, and especially from Diane Lucas and the interlibrary loan staff, who were patient, creative, and enthusiastic in tracking down dozens of obscure articles, microfiches, and fragile hard copies.

This book could not have been completed without the help and support of Tim Raguso, Margot Backus, Kate O'Connell, Shelley Reid, and Judy Edwards. It takes a village to raise a child and a "tribe" to publish a book. *Maraming salamat sa inyong lahat.*

The Star-Entangled Banner

"The Splendid Struggle for Independence"

PHILIPPINE AND AMERICAN (CO)CONSTRUCTIONS OF NATIONALISM

FOR MORE THAN a century, the United States and the Philippines have been bound together militarily, economically, and culturally in a dynamic that has profoundly shaped both countries' national self-definitions. This relationship illustrates the complexity of nation-building for both a country struggling into existence and one at the brink of imperial dominance and highlights the extent to which the construction of nationalism(s) is an inherently dialogic process.

At the moment of engagement with the Philippines, the United States was at a crossroads; the imperatives of expansion and empire put pressure on conventional understandings of the United States as equated with national self-determination and colonial resistance. Tracing this tension and its resolutions (however tenuous or contradictory) over the one-hundred-year relationship between the countries provides insight into American nationalism and is especially productive during the current "War on Terror," during the prosecution of which the United States has again framed military adventures abroad in terms of national mission and destiny.

On the other side of the Pacific, the meaning of the United States to the Philippines has long been vexed and contradictory. The United States has been (and remains) to the Philippines variously military oppressor and liberator, political model and antithesis, economic savior and enslaver; moreover, often it has been all of these things simultaneously. The expressions of Philippine nationalism(s) that emerge from within this context are instructive for understanding both the condition of postcoloniality in general and the fluctuations between pro- and anti-American sentiments within the Philippines.

Questions regarding competing nationalisms and the power of the concept of nationhood to fuel both international connections and aggression are particularly timely. In the last decade of the nineteenth century the United States increasingly embraced a nationalism requiring domination and territorial acquisition beyond the North American continent. In the first decade of the twenty-first century, the United States once again seems poised to return to the pursuit of empire. The debates around the second Gulf War eerily echo debates about the Spanish-American War, with both the government and the mainstream press insisting upon a definition of nationalism and patriotism centered on invasion.[1]

THE WARRANT TO INTERVENE: THE WAR ON TERROR AND THE NEW AMERICAN EMPIRE

The echoes of the United States' intervention in the Philippines are not only rhetorical and metaphorical; the most recent chapter of the uneasy U.S.-R.P. alliance is being written through the War on Terror. With the War on Terror many of the fraught definitions of nationalism that first emerged during the beginning of the United States' entanglement in the Philippines have reemerged as timely and crucial for articulations of American national identity.

The September 11, 2001, attacks on the United States signaled a paradigm shift in relations between the United States and the Philippine Republic, renewing an alliance that had been diminished by the termination of military bases a decade earlier. Many Filipino nationalists celebrated the 1991 abrogation of the lease agreements for the Clark and Subic Bay installations as the republic's long-awaited, definitive establishment of political and economic sovereignty—nearly a half century after officially obtaining political independence.[2] The U.S.-Philippine alliance on the War on Terror, in the form of bilateral military exercises targeting Islamic terrorist cells, has provoked a storm of controversy over incursions on national sovereignty, the two countries' economic relationship, and the renewal of a new American imperialism.

On September 26, 2001, two weeks after the terrorist attacks, Philippine President Gloria Macapagal-Arroyo officially announced the Philippines' alliance with the United States in the "International Counter-Terrorist Coalition" (Doronila 2001). That alliance targeted the Abu Sayyaf, an Islamic fundamentalist group the U.S. government has listed as "a satellite organization" of al-Qaida, stimulating bilateral military projects such as the "Balikatan" exercises in Mindanao (Boradora and Pablo 2002).[3]

Many Filipinos are literally as well as figuratively gun-shy about American intentions in the Pacific, especially those embodying a military presence in the Philippines. One concern is that U.S. military intervention in what is fundamentally a Philippine domestic issue encroaches on Philippine political sovereignty. Another Filipino apprehension concerns a renewal of American colonial intentions. Conrado de Quiros voiced many Filipinos' distrust of the ostensible U.S. partnership with the Philippine military against the Abu Sayyaf, writing, "Does it make sense that the American troops, fighting alongside the entire Armed Forces of the Philippines, have not cornered the Abu

Sayyaf the way the AFP [Armed Forces of the Philippines] alone did in but one month of operations there last year? . . . It's enough to make you think they do not want the Abu Sayyaf to disappear at all" (de Quiros 2002). Commenting on the U.S. military exercises in Mindanao, Randy David cautioned that the U.S. War on Terror lent itself to a neo-imperialist bent: "the crusade against global terrorism gives [the United States] flexibility in defining the extent of their intervention in a country's internal affairs. . . . Today it is the war against terrorism on multiple fronts that is giving America that warrant. . . . to interven[e] . . . in the affairs of other nations. . . . Its final objective will not simply be the security of America but its economic and political hegemony" (David 2002). Not mincing words, Luis Jalandon, representative of the National Democratic Front, denounced the United States as an "imperialist hyperpower" (Javellana and Nocum 2001).

Filipinos are not alone in identifying the U.S. War on Terror as marking a renaissance of American imperialism. A decade ago, the phrase "American empire" would not have appeared in mainstream political discourse. Today, there is an increasing consensus among foreign-policy critics about the United States' reemergence on the imperialist stage. "[C]olonialism is back," Lance Selfa (2002, 50) declared, and Michael Elliott (2002) blithely concurred, remarking, "Imperialism is back in vogue." Thomas Donnelly (2002, 165) considers the matter decided, writing, "The fact of American empire is hardly debated these days." And Josh London (2002, 81) sums up the critical consensus on twenty-first-century American imperialism: "Increasingly, on both sides of the political spectrum, imperialism has been acquiring a new intellectual legitimacy."

This millennial imperial resurgence is not a global one; it is a distinctly *American* phenomenon. Commenting on the "arriv[al . . . of] a new imperial moment," the *Washington Post*'s Sebastian Mallaby attests that "by virtue of its power[,] America is bound to play the leading role" (2002, 6). In 2002 *Wall Street Journal* features editor Max Boot published *The Savage Wars of Peace*, in which he surveyed the United States' long-standing history of "small wars" (that is, guerilla warfare, from the Spanish). Taking his title from Kipling's "The White Man's Burden," Boot defends the United States' imperial ventures, arguing that when administered well, "American rule can serve the interests of occupiers and occupied alike" (Boot 2002, 346). "Yes, there is a danger of imperial overstretch and hubris," Boot admits at the book's conclusion, entitled "In Defense of the Pax Americana," "but there is an equal, if not greater, danger of undercommitment and lack of confidence. America should not be afraid to fight 'the savage wars of peace' if necessary to enlarge the 'empire of liberty'" (352).

This critical consensus overtly identifies the imperialistic underpinnings of the War on Terror. In his 2002 Veterans Day speech at the White House,

George W. Bush averred, "As many veterans have seen in countries around the world, captive people have greeted American soldiers as liberators. And there is good reason. We have no territorial ambitions . . . We don't seek an empire. . . . We . . . have fought evil regimes and left in their place self-governing and prosperous nations" (Bush 2002a). Bush's official foreign policy in the War on Terror echoes the imperialist ideology of a century ago. The National Security Strategy of the United States (NSS), popularly known as the "Bush Doctrine," lays out the official U.S. policy in the War on Terror. The Bush Doctrine reviews "the great struggles of the twentieth century" and concludes that the "decisive victory for the forces of freedom" produced "a single sustainable model for national success: freedom, democracy, and free enterprise" (NSS 2002). The Bush Doctrine contends that it aims not "for unilateral advantage," but instead aspires to "extend the benefits of freedom across the globe" (NSS 2002). Bush affirmed this twenty-first-century reincarnation of the white man's burden in his 2002 State of the Union Address, declaring, "History has called America and our allies to action, and it is both our responsibility and our privilege to fight freedom's fight" (NSS 2002; Bush 2002b).

Like Teddy Roosevelt before him, Bush eschews labeling the U.S. agenda "imperialism"; but Bush's extension of American principles is the contemporary counterpart of Roosevelt's imperial expansionism. Bush's insistence that "we have no territorial ambitions . . . We don't seek an empire" hearkens back to the Teller Amendment, which sought to reassure those who feared the United States would enter the Spanish-American War with an eye to colonial annexation. The Teller Amendment explicitly forbade the United States' forcible annexation of Cuba, but by the end of the year, the United States had somehow acquired Puerto Rico, Guam, and the Philippines and had retained a permanent military base on Cuba. Outside the Bush administration, apologists for the imperial implications of the U.S. War on Terror also echo nineteenth-century colonial rhetoric. Sebastian Mallaby might have been writing in 1902 instead of in 2002 when he wrote, "Empires are not always planned. . . . The United States today will be [a] . . . reluctant imperialist" (Mallaby 2002, 6). Thomas Donnelly might have been an adviser for William McKinley when he wrote, "whether or not the United States intended to acquire an empire, it has somehow done so and cannot easily escape the consequences" (Donnelly 2002, 170). The current U.S. role in world affairs is deeply inflected by its experiences with colonialism—a colonial career inaugurated in the Philippines, prompting Kipling's "White Man's Burden."

The current U.S.-Philippine shoulder-to-shoulder alliance in the War on Terror manifests the resurgence of an imperial nationalism. The politico-economic debates surrounding Balikatan and its sibling exercises manifest the latest imbroglio of the more than century-long entangling alliance between the two nations, in which both countries seek to achieve the benefits of an officially disavowed neocolonial dynamic. While concerns about incursions on Philippine sovereignty present a powerful argument against a U.S. military presence, economics provide a powerful supporting factor. President Macapagal's early and emphatic support of the Bush agenda seriously damaged her popularity at home, but her administration has been compensated by a dramatic payoff in economic aid. In the wake of the military pullout in Clark and Subic Bay, "US assistance declined to exactly zero by 1994" (Lopez 2003). In 2001, just after Macapagal-Arroyo's declaration of allegiance with the Bush Administration, U.S. military assistance rose to seventeen million dollars, and a year later to over eighty-three million dollars, with additional assistance in trade policies and development projects. This constitutes the highest level of aid in a decade, bringing military aid almost to the same level as before the closure of the bases (Lopez 2003).[4] Such quid-pro-quo relations substantiate anxieties among Filipino nationalists about U.S. intentions to reestablish military bases by an economic end-run around the 1987 constitution.

In April 1809, outgoing President Thomas Jefferson wrote to incoming President James Madison about the possibility of annexing Cuba and advised Madison, "I would immediately erect a column on the Southernmost limit of Cuba. . . . [W]e should then . . . have such an empire for liberty as . . . has never [been] surveyed since the creation: and I am persuaded no constitution was ever before so well calculated as ours for extensive empire" (Jefferson 1809). In just eight years, Jefferson had moved from his admonition in his first inaugural address that the "essential principles of our Government" dictated "peace, commerce, an honest friendship with all nations, entangling alliances with none," to advocating "an empire for liberty" (Jefferson 1801). Many view the United States' debut as a colonial power in 1898 as a watershed moment in U.S. history. But almost from its beginning, the United States has evinced an ideological conflict between the repudiation of and surrender to the seductive power of imperialism. This conflict became not only a fundamental conundrum in American nationalism, but also, from its beginning, an integral conflict in Philippine national aspirations.

"WHICH SHALL IT BE: NATION OR EMPIRE?"

The United States' fraught engagement with colonialism defined the terms of its nationalist discourse during the late nineteenth century. In the period leading up to the Spanish-American War, long-standing tensions between isolation and expansion gave rise to polarized, competing definitions of nationalism, one avowedly imperialist, the other staunchly opposed to imperial expansion. The ideologies of Manifest Destiny and the "White Man's Burden" committed the United States to global expansion. In addition, the rationale of democratic tutelage, which was crucial to the United States' perception of its relationship to the Philippines, gave new meaning to American nationalism. Anti-imperialists also deployed nationalist ideology to argue that the forcible annexation of other countries was a betrayal of the most sacred nationalist principles. The Philippines became a central site where the United States worked out conflicting definitions of its own national identity.

During debates over the United States' role in the Philippines, a common rhetorical feature was the invocation of the United States' "national character," core values presumed to be quintessentially American. Proponents and opponents of U.S. imperialism argued that national values and history either required or forbade the forcible annexation of the Philippines. Such appeals to icons of American nationhood invoked a sense of national legitimacy. Anti-imperialists claimed that by forcibly annexing the Philippines, the United States had betrayed its national character. From their perspective, every American, whether or not interested in the Philippines per se, was obligated to oppose annexation as a matter of national honor. In 1900 Joseph Henry Crooker warned that colonialism had deluded the national polity with "[a] false Americanism [that] has captivated our reason and corrupted our conscience," declaring: "We have come as a people to the parting of the ways. Which shall it be: Nation or Empire? Shall we still continue loyal to the American ideal: a Nation of free individuals, who . . . rule themselves, and enrich the whole world by the powerful and beneficent example of a just and prosperous Republic? Or, shall we renounce our principles of equality and liberty and engage in conquest for commercial advantage, in colonial government . . . ? Let us look this imperialism squarely in the face and realize what it means. It means the surrender of American democracy" (Crooker 1984, 305–7).

Theodore Conley, a Kansan soldier fighting in the Philippines, saw the United States as already having taken the wrong turn in the "parting of the ways" Crooker described. Conley argued not only that the United States was betraying its own anticolonial heritage in forcibly annexing the Philippines, but that by so doing, Americans were betraying national history as well as the national character. He declared with disgust, "There is not a feature of the whole miserable business that a patriotic American citizen, one who loves to read of the brave deeds of the American colonists in the splendid struggle for American independence, can look upon with complacency, much less with pride. This war is reversing history. It places the American people and the government of the United States in the position occupied by Great Britain in 1776. It is an utterly causeless and defenceless war, and it should be abandoned by this government without delay. The longer it is continued, the greater crime it becomes" ("Soldiers' Letters" 1899, 320).

Anti-imperialists focused in particular on the Declaration of Independence as the repository of national values and thus the moral compass for the United States' actions in extracontinental territories. William Dean Howells invoked the iconic rhetoric of the United States' core democratic principles when he articulated the political platform of the American (Anti-Imperialist) League of New York, stating in October 1899, "We affirm the doctrines of the Declaration of Independence. We believe that all others, as well as we, are of right entitled to life, liberty, and the pursuit of happiness. . . . We adhere to the American idea that government derives its just powers from the consent of the governed. We are, therefore, opposed to the use of force in the extension of American institutions" (Howells 1899). In May 1902, Joseph K. Ohl called attention to the irony of the United States' betrayal of its national values as articulated in the Declaration of Independence when American colonial administrators banned the document in the Philippines: "It was discovered that there were being circulated among the Filipinos copies of the American Declaration of Independence. . . . One of the best officers, a man regarded as conservative and no extremist, told us *this was promptly suppressed*, and gave it as his opinion that the Declaration of Independence is '*a d——- incendiary document*'" (Flower 1902). Benjamin Flower responded with outrage, declaring, "If five years ago one of our statesmen had had the hardihood to predict that within a decade the Declaration of Independence would be officially suppressed as a treasonable document in a land over which the Stars and Stripes floated, he would have been promptly denounced throughout the length and breadth of the Republic as either insane or a shallow-brained alarmist" (Flower 1902). The fact that, unlike the U.S. Constitution, the Declaration of Independence has no force of law highlights the emotional power of national symbols. It is because "we the people" cherish the U.S. Declaration of Independence as articulating nearly sacred principles of American democracy, not because it has any actual legal power, that it played such a central role in the debates surrounding the annexation of the Philippines.

Anti-imperialists argued that Filipino "insurgents," by adhering to the United States' revolutionary and democratic national values, were in fact showing themselves to be "true" Americans. University of Chicago Professor Albert H. Tolman declared on August 5, 1899: "Thank God for the brave Filipinos. They are more true to American principles than the Americans themselves" (Zwick 1995). Colorado Congressman John C. Bell, who compared Emilio Aguinaldo to George Washington and Mark Twain, echoed the comparison (Hoganson 1998, 170; Twain 1992, 52).[5]

Proponents of American imperialism also appealed to the Founding Fathers as national icons. In rebuttal to anti-imperialists' accusations that imperialism betrayed the core democratic ideal of government by consent of the governed, "Imperialists . . . note[d] that Thomas Jefferson himself, who authored the consent doctrine [in the Declaration of Independence], later proceeded to govern Indians in the Louisiana Purchase without their consent" (Williams 1980, 819).[6] Expansionist advocate William Levere opined that

"holding the Philippines . . . would put American men in accordance with
Thomas Jefferson, expansionist par excellence" (Hoganson 1998, 173). The
New York Journal indicted William McKinley for his hesitation on annexing the
Philippines, claiming that "[George] Washington loved a good fight. . . . [but]
McKinley was no Washington" (Hoganson 1998, 93).[7] Significantly, it was not
the Founding Fathers' explicit comments on the prospect of American empire
that both pro- and anti-imperialists cited; instead, it was the Founding
Fathers' cultural capital, their power as national symbols, that was deployed in
the annexation debates.

Pro-imperialists argued that the physical struggle provided by expansion
was critical to the maintenance of a healthy national "constitution." The cult
of masculinity-cum-expansionism figuratively embodied in Teddy Roosevelt's
"The Strenuous Life" conflated masculinity, proved through the physical and
moral challenge of colonial domination, with national vigor.[8] Roosevelt gave
an anthropomorphized vision of American expansion when he asserted, "The
young giant of the West stands on a continent and clasps the crest of an ocean
in either hand. Our nation, glorious in youth and strength, looks into the
future with eager eyes and rejoices as a strong man to run a race" (Hoganson
1998, 159).[9] Pro-imperialists did not posit this model of nationalist masculine
vigor as being merely recreational; imperialist proponents feared that domestic peace had enervated American national manhood and contended that the
maintenance of national health (of both the individual body and the body
politic) depended upon the literal as well as figurative exercise of "Americanism." In "Manhood and Statehood," Theodore Roosevelt excoriated
the "flabbiness, [the] unhealthy softness" that the pacifist anti-imperialists
evinced—a "softness" that "meant ruin for this nation" (1926, 321). Imperialists argued that colonial expansion was not just a matter of the United States'
Manifest Destiny; it was a national life-or-death issue.

Opponents of American imperialism emphasized the threat to U.S. political sovereignty inherent in such rhetoric. Stanford University professor David
Starr Jordan argued that ultimately the conquest of the Philippines would,
paradoxically, lead to the subjugation of the United States: "if we govern the
Philippines, so in their degree must the Philippines govern us" (Zimmerman
2002, 339). Moorefield Storey, president of the Anti-Imperialist League, also
feared the conquest of the Philippines would undermine U.S. sovereignty. In
a 1897 speech to the Naval War College, Storey declared he could imagine
"no greater calamity to this country than a successful war, which should lead
us to enlarge our boundaries and to assume greater responsibilities. . . . [T]o
our present difficulties would be added . . . new regions which, unfit to govern themselves, would govern us" (340).

Thus the Philippines became the literal as well as figurative territory
through which various U.S. constituencies defined and defended the Ameri-

can nation. This polarization of American nationalism into pro- and anti-imperial camps remains a feature of American political life at times of international crisis. Across the Pacific, a fundamental ambivalence toward the United States as the Philippines' (former) colonial master has dominated Philippine constructions of nationalism since 1898, when Filipino nationalism first became associated with profound anti-Americanism. Filipino nationalism too became polarized between an anti-American strain and a covert but influential pro-American strain.

"Do Be My Enemy—For Friendship's Sake"

Philippine nationalism did not emerge solely in counterdistinction to U.S. imperialism but rather relied on the U.S. model of nationalism in multiple and vexed ways. In one of the earliest entangled ironies of the Philippine-American relationship, Filipinos appealed to American icons as a rhetorical strategy to avert colonialization. When the United States' intention to forcibly annex the Philippines became clear, Filipinos invoked American national icons in much the same terms as had American anti-imperialists. On August 31, 1900, Apolinario Mabini, prime minister and secretary for foreign affairs during the Philippine Revolution, wrote to American Gen. J. Franklin Bell: "The Filipinos hope that [their] fight [for independence] will remind the Americans of the struggle borne by their ancestors against the Englishmen for the emancipation of the colonies which are now the free States of North America" (Mabini 1900, 295).

While Filipinos invoked the United States' revolutionary past to shame the United States out of its territorial ambitions in the Philippines, they also invoked American national icons to legitimate an independent Philippine government. Comparing Filipino revolutionaries to "the American patriots of 1776," Sixto Lopez, secretary of the Philippine mission sent to the United States in 1898 to negotiate Philippine independence, asserted that "the Declaration of American Independence ought to be the charter of our own" (Lopez 1900). While such a statement could be interpreted as a cagey rhetorical maneuver, it went further, actually proposing that an independent Philippine government model itself on the United States.

The incongruous claiming of a Philippine independence dependent upon the United States also manifests itself in Emilio Aguinaldo's June 12, 1898, Declaration of Independence. Aguinaldo asserted the Philippines' political sovereignty by "solemnly declar[ing that] . . . th[e] Philippine Islands . . . are and have the right to be free and independent. . . . that, like all free and independent states, they have complete authority to declare war, make peace, establish commercial treaties, enter into alliances, regulate commerce, and execute all other acts and things incumbent upon independent states" (Aguinaldo 1898, 46–47). However, Aguinaldo compromised his declaration of Philippine independence by his beginning the above statement "under the protection of the mighty and humanitarian nation, North America" (46). In addition, Aguinaldo paid tribute to the United States in the new national flag, which arranged red and blue portions in conjunction with a white triangle containing an eight-rayed sun. "The colors blue, red and white, commemorate those of the flag of the United States of North America, in manifestation of our profound gratitude towards that great nation for the disinterested protection she is extending to us and will continue to extend to us," Aguinaldo explained (48). Aguinaldo's Declaration of Philippine Independence paradoxically asserts the Philippines' sovereignty while simultaneously presenting the Philippines as an American protectorate.

Aguinaldo's political flattery/indebtedness could be rationalized as the product of the historical moment: on June 12, 1898, after two years of war against Spain, one might argue that Aguinaldo still hoped to avoid the outbreak of war against the Americans. But this assertion of Philippine (in)dependence continued well after the archipelago gained official independence in 1946. In 1962, President Diosdado Macapagal made the date of Aguinaldo's declaration of Philippine independence his country's official Independence Day. Macapagal explained that July 4, the date of the United Sates' choosing, "celebrat[ed] . . . Philippine subjection to and dependence on the United States [and thus] served to perpetuate unpleasant memories" (de Ocampo 1971, 8). In his official presidential proclamation designating June 12 as Philippine Independence Day, however, Macapagal affirmed the act as "done in the City of Manila, this 12th day of May, in the year of Our Lord, nineteen hundred and sixty-two, and of the independence of the Philippines, the sixteenth" (Macapagal 1962, 81). Thus, even as he officially asserted 1898 as the definitive moment of Philippine independence, Macapagal actually dated Philippine Independence from 1946, not 1898. Even at the very moment that he designated June 12 as the appropriate Independence Day because of Filipinos' "natural and inalienable claim to freedom and independence," Macapagal explicitly affirmed Philippine independence as derived from the United States.

Anti-Americanism continues to provide the foundation for a major school of Filipino nationalism. Claro Recto, regarded in the Philippines as one of the most important nationalist historians, based his vision of Philippine nationalism on Filipinos' need to divest themselves of what he called "Our Lingering Colonial Complex." "We are afflicted with divided loyalties. We have not yet recovered from the spell of colonialism," Recto asserted in a 1957 speech (Constantino 1986, 86). "This self-delusion," he declared, "is one of the greatest stumbling blocks to the full realization of Filipino nationalism and the ultimate attainment of complete and real sovereignty" (Constantino 1969, 292).[10] Renato Constantino, also regarded in the Philippines as one of the seminal critics of nationalist criticism, shared Recto's conviction that the foundation of Filipino nationalism entails the rejection of the United States' continuing colonial influence, a tradition continued today by popular historian Ambeth Ocampo.[11]

While anti-Americanism provides the foundation for one school of Filipino nationalism, another school posits economic, political, and military cooperation with the United States as the means to Philippine prosperity. Because an explicitly pro-American position is targeted too easily as being anti-Filipino, pro-American nationalism tends to be obscured from the public view, occurring in closed-door political negotiations rather than being published in the mainstream newspapers. From 1909 (when the terms of the Treaty of Paris expired) to 1934 (when the Tydings-McDuffie Act provided for the framing of a constitution), Philippine leaders often adopted a forceful public stance demanding immediate and complete independence because this position was popular with voters at home, while in their negotiations with American officials they favored delayed independence and economic formulas that increased Philippine economic dependence on the United States.

The political activities of Manuel Quezon, president of the Philippine Commonwealth 1935–1944, and Manuel Roxas, the Philippines' first postindependence president, provide examples of this ambivalence over Philippine independence. Publicly, Quezon was a fervent advocate of immediate and absolute independence, famously declaring in 1923, "I prefer a government run like hell by Filipinos to one run like heaven by Americans" (Constantino 1994, 335–36). Yet Quezon favored legislation that deferred or gave no specific date for Philippine independence. In December 1913 and January 1914, Quezon met with Gen. Frank McIntyre, chief of the Bureau of Insular Affairs of the War Department, to discuss negotiations over Philippine independence. According to McIntyre, Quezon, then resident commissioner of the Philippines, favored legislation that would forestall independence without appearing to do so.[12]

Even when official independence was finally conferred, President Manuel Roxas was vehement in his support of American political and economic interests as necessary to the economic development of the nascent Republic. In his inaugural address on July 4, 1946, Roxas declared, "Our safest course . . . is in the glistening wake of America whose sure advance with mighty prow breaks for smaller craft the waves of fear" (Agoncillo 1990, 436). Roxas's reentrenchment of Philippine dependence on the United States at the very moment of the long-deferred "recognition" of Philippine independence is striking. Roxas's administration continued to be pro-American, as when on March 17, 1947, he "went to the people to explain the 'blessings' of American exploitation of the natural resources of the country and painted a dream picture of wealth, contentment, peace, and prosperity" (438). The "blessing"

of American development of Philippine natural resources was codified concretely in an amendment to the Philippine Constitution establishing "parity
rights," which allowed Americans equal standing with Filipinos in developing
natural resources. (And given the devastation wrought on the Philippines during World War II, it was likely that more Americans than Filipinos would be
economically equipped to begin development projects.) Roxas insisted that
Philippine prosperity was possible only through alliance with the United
States, urging the passage of the parity rights amendment with the declaration, "We have today our one big chance to convert our native land into an
ideal of democracy. Our one chance is to grow and industrialize to reach the
first rank of the nations of the world" (438).

The double-edged reliance on the United States for economic development in the Philippines continues today. U.S. economic aid continues to play
a significant role in the country, and, like most Third World countries, the
Philippines courts foreign capital to provide much-needed jobs. The economic impact of the United States' military withdrawal at the Subic and Clark
bases was a serious issue, although Olongapo City, the town near the former
Subic Bay installation, has made an impressive comeback. The former base
itself has been designated a Special Economic Development Zone to facilitate
foreign investment. In 1996, as debates concerning continuing American neocolonialism in the Philippines simmered around the meaning of July 4 as
"Philippine-American Friendship Day," Federal Express opened a hub for
deliveries across Asia in the Subic Bay development. On July 5, 1996, the
Subic Bay Metropolitan Authority (SBMA) ran a full double-page ad in the
Philippine Daily Inquirer to promote the former military base as a magnet for
international capital. SBMA Chairman Richard Gordon emphasized the economic development of Subic as a vehicle for manifesting Filipino nationalism.
"A stronger sense of nationhood is [Gordon's] dream for the Filipino," the ad
reads. "Chairman Gordon believes that self-reliance is the key to progress."
The irony of this statement, of course, is that its insistence on nationalistic
pride and self-reliance could not be realized without foreign capital and the
tourist trade—and the SBMA was courting foreign investors with great fervor
at the time. The headline "Celebrate Fifty Years of Liberation" underscores
Filipino reliance on American (economic, rather than political) liberation, as
the ad implicitly situates Philippine liberation in 1946 rather than in 1898. In
1898, American imperialists invoked the white man's burden to rationalize
Filipinos' figurative deliverance from benighted savagery. Today, USAID and
multinational corporatism offer to deliver the Philippines from Third World
economic backwardness. As the celebratory hoopla surrounding Subic Bay's
repackaging as an icon of Filipino nationalist pride suggests, despite the
Philippines' half century of putative independence, the United States contin-

ues to occupy a position at the center of Philippine economics and, hence, of Filipino nationalism.

The SBMA's conflicting investments in Filipino independence and foreign investment are representative of the stormy debates over the meaning of Philippine-American relations that came to a head in the summer of 1996. July 4, 1996, now observed as "Phil-Am Friendship Day," marked the fiftieth anniversary of the United States' formal recognition of Philippine independence. Throughout the summer of 1996, Philippine newspapers bristled with articles and editorials through which academics, politicians, journalists, and readers debated the relationship between Philippine independence and the United States' continuing cultural, political, and economic influence. The subject of Phil-Am friendship was a contentious one. Adrian Cristobal humorously articulated many Filipinos' ambivalence toward it by declaring, "Thy friendship oft has made my heart to ache. / Do be my enemy—for friendship's sake" (Cristobal 1996). On June 12, 1898, the date Filipinos now celebrate as Independence Day, Emilio Aguinaldo planted the seeds of contention by expressing the Philippines' "gratitude" to the United States and invoking its protection at the same time he asserted Philippine independence. Six months later, the Philippine-American War had begun and Aguinaldo was denouncing the United States for its duplicitous dealings with Filipino revolutionaries. The shift in Filipino attitudes toward U.S. involvement—from friendship to enmity, with the thinnest of lines separating the two—was recapitulated nearly a century later in debates over the meaning of Philippine-American friendship.

Axes of Nationalism

Even a cursory review of Philippine-American relations in the last century makes clear the need for a flexible, multivalent definition of nationalism. Certainly, in the two decades since the publication of Benedict Anderson's *Imagined Communities: Reflections on the Origin and Spread of Nationalism* a range of theorists have articulated varying definitions of nationalism based on different approaches to the relationship between citizens and the state. Commenting on the lack of a "widely accepted definition" of nationalism, Benedict Anderson notes that "it is hard to think of any political phenomenon . . . about which there is less analytic consensus" (Anderson 1996, 1). For some scholars (Anderson, Renan, and Gellner), nationalism is primarily a psychological construct; for some (Breuilly) it is primarily a political dynamic, while for others (Weber) it is "a community of sentiment"; and for still others (Hobsbawm) it is primarily defined simply by citizenship. Many scholars (Gellner, Hechter, Handler, Breuilly, Lloyd, and Nakpil) agree that nationalism is centrally concerned with the state, but they disagree as to exactly what the nation/state dynamic is.[13]

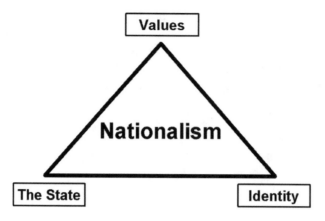

1. Axes of Nationalism.

Despite the regrettable tainting of the word *axis* by George W. Bush's "Axis of Evil," the figure of the axis nonetheless allows for a multivalent interplay between interrelated foci of nationalism. A tripartite framework to explore three integral axes—identity, values, and the state—allows for a mapping of nationalism that facilitates a nuanced reading of the psychological, sociological, and political strands in both Filipino and American nationalist constructions.

The tripartite axes model I present here offers a framework that is plastic enough to accommodate the various elements of nationalism other theorists have articulated and at the same time allows for the multivalent ways in which the various Filipino and American representatives, motivated by varying interests, produced differing models of nationalism. Nationalism is both an abstract and a concrete psychological/sociological/political phenomenon arising from the interplay of three integral axes.[14]

In the United States, the values axis includes such concepts as democracy, government by consent, the rights of the individual balanced against the needs of the state, etc. In the Philippines, a culture based more on interpersonal connections than individualism, national values include such concepts as *bayanhihan* (a cooperative endeavor/community development, something like a barn-raising)—for example, for Apolinario Mabini the goal of the 1896 revolution was "an independent nation [that] would bring about [a] condition of brotherhood, equality, contentment *(kaginhawaan)* and material abundance *(kasaganaan)*" (Sicat 1995, 420). Similarly, Ma. Teresa Sicat notes that for *Katipuneros,* national "unity was an experience of change in each Filipino's *loob*" (will, state of mind, heart) to facilitate "the redemption of Mother Filipinas" (420).

The second axis is the state. Carmen Guerrero Nakpil separates nationalist awareness from the formal state structure when she maintains, "Some countries become a nation and a state at the same time. We [Filipinos] have not been a state for one hundred years. But we have been a nation, bound by race, history, culture and aspirations for much longer" (Nakpil 1998, 230). As Nakpil points out, the nation and state do not completely overlap—one can have a nation without a state, and vice versa. In both the United States and the Philippines, some time before the outbreak of revolution, a group of individuals, breaking their personal affiliation and identification with the ruling colonial state, conceived of an independent state they would collectively construct. Thus both the United States and the Philippines have undergone a period of nationhood without statehood such as that described by Nakpil. Statehood, on the other hand, cannot exist for long (peacefully, at least) without a critical mass of popular support. As the People Power revolution of 1986 spectacularly demonstrated, when mainstream nationalist sympathies part ways over an extended period, the state cannot peaceably continue.

Whereas the state axis acknowledges the role of the state in institutionalizing nationalist sentiment, the identity axis provides for individuals' allegiance to the state. Benedict Anderson defines nationalism as an "imagined community" of individuals who consider themselves a sociopolitical collective.[15] Nationalism is the result of the politicization of a mass of people who collectively identify themselves with each other—when "I" becomes "we," and "we" becomes "we the people of ___." This language is explicitly codified in the U.S. Constitution, whose preamble proclaims, "We, the people of the United States, in order to form a more perfect union. . . ." Diosdado Macapagal, fifth president of the Philippine Republic (1961–65), articulated a similar conception of the nation's foundation in a politicized "we" when he declared, "a nation is born into freedom on the day when such a people, moulded into a nation by . . . a sense of oneness born of common struggle and suffering, announces to the world that it asserts its natural right to liberty and is ready to defend it with blood, life, and honor" (Macapagal 1986a, 76). Without "we, the (American/Filipino) people," the nation cannot exist, and without a state, that nation has no political force. José Rizal is commonly known as the "Father of Filipino nationalism" and the "First Filipino," not because he helped establish an independent Philippine state (in fact, he specifically and explicitly denounced the 1896 Philippine Revolution against Spain), but because he was instrumental in the creation of the conceptualization of "Filipino" as an ethnopolitical collective—as "a people," or, in the language of nationalism, "*the* people."

This study examines two nations—and nationalisms—variously defined and deployed by conflicting camps in both the United States and the Philippines across slightly more than a century. The model I have proposed, with its tripartite axes of values, identity, and the state, provides a framework for the examination of Philippine-American relations. Contending factions implicitly or explicitly invoked different senses of Philippine/American nationalism, foregrounding differing combinations of the three axes of nationalism to pro-mote differing and often conflicting nationalist visions. A reading of Philip-pine and American co-created nationalisms necessitates such a flexible model, which then allows for tracing contending factions' implicit or explicit fore-grounding of differing combinations of these three axes to establish two sep-arate but entangled nations.

SITES OF MEMORY: THE CONSTRUCTION
OF NATIONAL HISTORY

Nationalism is ultimately a kind of narrative, its present political values determined by its historical texts. In "DissemiNation: Time, Narrative, and the Margins of the Modern Nation," Homi Bhabha analyzes history as "the nation's writ," a narrative that codifies "the national will" (Bhabha 1990a, 310–11). Bhabha argues that national history is a complex combination of both forgetting as well as remembering: as an agent of state hegemony, the com-posers of national history have as their agenda not the simple recording of objective fact, but the fashioning of a narrative that will establish and preserve national interests. Bhabha's examination of nationalism as a historical phe-nomenon, wherein in the interests of the nation certain elements are remem-bered, others forgotten, calls attention to history—especially nationalist history—as a deliberately constructed palimpsest in which the national past is written and edited as a tool of political hegemony. These historical construc-tions have as their goal the invention of the nation. Renato Constantino made this point specifically in the Philippine context when he wrote in "A Sense of Nationhood" that "it is the task of the historian to weave particular events. . . . [so that h]istory . . . show[s] how a nation was born where previously there was none" (Constantino 1991, 3).

To understand the extent to which the Philippines and the United States constructed their national narratives through, against, and in collusion with one another, the chapters that follow each examine a different moment from representative eras of the Philippine-American century as a "site of memory": the space in which various purveyors of nationalism scripted, elided, amended, and encoded national narratives, crafting national history in the interests of developing or defending particular visions of the nation. Often these "sites" became the locus of conflicting national histories, in which the various par-ties contested opposing historical narratives, focused selectively on various elements while ignoring others, and promulgated or even fabricated historical errors in the interests of promoting particular versions of national character, protecting the national legacy, or defending the nation's legitimacy. Different factions contended for national legitimacy in transacting Philippine-Ameri-can relations, as each side established, contested, and undermined its own and the other's legitimacy through constructions of national history.

Chapter 1 reviews the ways in which José Rizal became a site of memory for both American and Filipino constructions of Filipino nationalism by investigating José Rizal's status as the Philippine national hero. Exploiting the identity axis, the United States promoted Rizal as the preeminent Filipino national hero because American colonial leaders chose Rizal as a national hero conducive to the American colonial agenda. This is a factor of which Filipinos are acutely aware, and the American colonial promotion of Rizal has threatened Rizal's preeminent position within the Filipino heroic pantheon. However, although there has been much debate among Filipino scholars about the United States' posthumous influence on Rizal as a national hero, there has been virtually no discussion of influence on Rizal during his lifetime. In fact, the United States had a significant impact on Rizal's contribution to the creation of Filipinos as a national polity. Rizal is revered as the "father of Filipino nationalism" in part due to a nationalist conceptualization that was influenced by the United States. Rizal helped to "father" Filipinos as an ethnopolitical collective through Los Indios Bravos, a pre-Katipunan organization whose name Rizal took from the spectacle of Native Americans performing in a Wild West show. In his recuperation of the *Indio,* a term derogatorily used to designate native Filipinos during the Spanish colonial period, Rizal transplanted to the Philippines the United States' ideological construction of Native Americans. Rizal's conceptualization of a symbolic fraternity between the American Indian and the Philippine Indio ironically prefigured the United States' export of the military tactics and racial attitudes developed through the U.S. Indian Wars to the Philippines in 1898. Thus the Wild West's Indio serves as a site of memory for contested nationalist narratives. A closer examination of Rizal as the preeminent Philippine national hero, as well as Rizal's politicizing of the Indio, both reveals that Philippine-American relations significantly antedated 1898 and demonstrates the ways in which U.S. and Philippine nationalisms invoked and manipulated each other in the interests of nation-building.

Chapter 2 explores the manipulation of the values axis in a popular children's book that representationally undermines Philippine aspirations for independence. In *The Brownies in the Philippines* (1904), the Brownies, elfish sprites who travel the world enjoying innocent adventures, encounter bestialized versions of Filipino revolutionaries who, in the book's various episodes, battle for their freedom. Although explicitly claiming to eschew the adult world of politics, profit, and violence, the Brownies carry the banner of "EXPANSION" into the Philippines, not only forecasting the pacification of the exotic but rebellious frontier, but even, in one episode, recasting the Americans as the besieged noncombatants helplessly enduring a fierce shelling by a Filipino foe, thus reversing the roles of aggressor and victim during the Philippine-American War. Thus *Brownies in the Philippines* rewrites Philippine revolutionary history to buttress American colonization. Author Palmer Cox added a new character to the Brownie company for their adventures in the tropics: the Brownie Photographer, who chronicled the band's exploits with the Eastman Kodak Company's newly introduced Brownie Box Camera. The symbiotic partnership between Cox's Brownies and the astoundingly popular Brownie Box Camera in the service of colonialism reveals the ideological partnership between photography, anthropology, and colonialism—a partnership that was similarly manifested in public exhibitions such as the 1904 St. Louis World's Fair. *Brownies in the Philippines* and live public exhibitions such as the Philippine Reservation at the 1904 World's Fair served the same ideological agenda: to proleptically impose the United States' pacification of the Philippines by bringing the Philippines within "the kodak zone," a metaphor Philippine-American War correspondent Frank Millet used to demarcate the lines between terra incognita and the territories Americans understood and, not coincidentally, claimed. Thus both *Brownies in the Philippines* and the St. Louis World's Fair worked to predict and, by so doing, secure American pacification of the Philippines while simultaneously promoting support of the United States' engagement in the Philippine-American War among the American populace at home.

Chapter 3 examines a complex manipulation of all three Axes of nationalism in the popular World War II film *Back to Bataan*. This film—a collaboration between Hollywood, the American military, and the government of the Philippine Commonwealth—revises Filipino history to establish Filipinos' neocolonial dependence on American leadership even before the official grant of Philippine independence. The film's central Filipino character is the putative grandson of Katipunan Supremo Andres Bonifacio. In the film, Bonifacio the younger refuses at first to let the Americans exploit the symbolic capital that is his grandpaternal legacy, but eventually he allows himself to become a figurehead for the American cause—a figurehead subordinated to American leadership as embodied in John Wayne, playing the role of a thinly veiled stand-in for Douglas MacArthur. The film's manipulation of Philippine national heroes as embodied in Andres Bonifacio provides a useful comparison to the American manipulation of Filipino nationalist heroic iconography in the case of José Rizal. The film's climax is the liberation of the American prisoners of war from a Japanese prison camp at Cabanatuan. *Back to Bataan* reconstructs Philippine revolutionary history not only to establish Filipino neocolonial dependence on America, but also to recuperate the United States' national honor tarnished in the defeats at Bataan and Corregidor and, ultimately, to pave the way for the triumphant global expansion of Pax Americana.

Chapter 4 focuses on Filipinos' grappling with the conundrum of their national history and its colonial heritage through the debates over the date to commemorate Philippine independence. A profound contradiction in Filipino nationalism concerns the question of whether the formation of the conceptual nation, or the formal establishment of a sovereign state, should mark the nascence of Filipino independence. The United States' overdetermination of Philippine nationalist history was demonstrated in Filipinos' concentration on 1996 as the fiftieth anniversary of the United States' official "recognition" of Philippine independence rather than on 1996 as the centenary of the Katipunan Revolution. The fact that issues relating to 1946, a noncentennial date, eclipsed attention to 1896, the ostensible focus of that year's centennial commemorations, demonstrates the United States' continuing dominance of Filipinos' nationalist consciousness. The spontaneous entanglement of the Philippine and American flags during the reenactment of the July 4, 1946, flag ceremony commemorating the transfer of political sovereignty provided an accidental symbol for contentions that the United States' colonial influence continues despite a half century of official independence, revealing the continuing tensions of the Philippine-American "special relationship."

Chapter 5 examines a contemporary formulation of Filipino nationalism linking the identity axis in relation to the reformation of the state in F. Sionil José's 1993 novel *Viajero*. Sionil José, the Philippines' most widely published and translated writer, is best known for the Rosales novels, a quintet focusing on the emergence of a Filipino nationalist protagonist who will devote himself to the *masa*, the Filipino people, at the expense of, and in repudiation of, the power and status inherent in alliances with the domestic elite and foreign (neo)colonizers. Sionil José presents the long-awaited nationalist champion in Salvador dela Raza ("Savior of the Race"), a Filipino expatriated during World War II and adopted and raised by an African American soldier. Dela Raza finally repatriates himself to the Philippines and makes the nationalist commitment Sionil José had constructed as the Rosales novels' goal. Throughout the Rosales novels and *Viajero,* various characters excoriate the United States for its colonization of the Philippines and its neocolonial influence decades after official independence. Thus, for Sionil José, as for Claro Recto and Renato Constantino, Filipino nationalism is, to some extent, necessarily anti-American. However, while on one hand *Viajero* explicitly denounces the continuing neocolonial dynamic, the novel ends by reasserting an identification with an alternate strand of American nationalism. Throughout the emergence and development of Filipino nationalism, Filipinos have simultaneously invoked and revoked particular strands of American nationalism. *Viajero* suggests that the question may not be one of how to repudiate the historical connections between the two nations but rather how to reimagine them.

The concluding chapter focuses on the Balangiga Bells, church bells allegedly taken by U.S. Marines during the Philippine-American War as war booty during a brutal scorched-earth campaign across Samar in retaliation for the "Balangiga Massacre." On September 28, 1901, Filipino "insurgents" launched a surprise attack on American soldiers that resulted in the largest number of Americans killed in action in a single encounter during the war and was at the time considered the worst American military defeat since Custer's Last Stand. Two church bells eventually came to reside at F. E. Warren Air Force Base in Cheyenne, Wyoming, as part of a memorial to the American casualties of the attack. The political controversy surrounding the bells illuminates the contending nationalist visions underlying American and Filipino opinions on the propriety of returning the bell(s) to the Philippines. For both sides, the bells are much more than simple components of a war memorial: they symbolize the rectitude of each nation's values and the moral legitimacy of their roles in the Philippine-American War. In the various arguments supporting or opposing the return of the bell(s), each side invoked nationalist icons in ways that recapitulate those made by pro- and anti-imperialist Americans as well as anti-American Filipinos in debates a century earlier. The striking similarity between the arguments made by contemporary Americans and Filipinos and those made by their predecessors a century ago demonstrates the enduring power of the identity axis of nationalism, as individual citizens a century apart demonstrate their personal and collective allegiance to the state axis through national symbols. The "battle of the bells," as one commentator dubbed the controversy, reenacts the Philippine-American War on a symbolic level a full century after the United States officially declared the hostilities of the "Philippine Insurrection" concluded.

The construction and deployment of both Philippine and American nationalisms have been more deeply knotted together, in a dynamic both more mutually indebted to and repudiating of each other, than has been acknowledged in the previous scholarship of our histories. The Philippine-American engagement has never been one of simple conquest or resistance, successful or not, but one of mutual cultural and ideological entanglement to a degree that as yet has not been adequately appreciated. An analysis of various moments along the historical spectrum of Philippine-American involvement allows us to see more clearly how various nationalist factors, and factions, compete and collude. Filipino and American nationalisms have been most intertwined, even mutually constitutive, at precisely the moment they appear most decisively to diverge.

CHAPTER 1

Cultural Constructions
of Nationalism

JOSÉ RIZAL, BUFFALO BILL, AND LOS INDIOS BRAVOS

IN HIS CLASSIC statement on nationalism, Ernest Renan pointed out the twin roles heroes play in constructing nationalism by connecting the individual within the national family/polity and connecting the national present with the past. The nation's "soul," Renan writes, "lies [partly] in the past, [and partly] in the present." On one hand, nationalism "is the possession in common of a rich legacy of memories; [on] the other [it derives from] present-day consent, the desire to live together, the will to perpetuate the legacy of memories that one has received in an undivided form. . . . The nation, like the individual, is the culmination of a long past of endeavours, sacrifice, and devotion. . . . A heroic past, great men, glory . . . this is the social capital upon which one bases a national idea. . . . 'We are what you were; we will be what you are'—is, in its simplicity, the abridged hymn of every *patrie*" (Renan 1996, 52). Renan's distillation of nationalism in the statement "We are what you were; we will be what you are" delineates the integral function heroes play in transmitting national values from the past to present generations. Heroes are critical components of the identity axis of nationalism. An individual's veneration of national heroes enhances the individual's sense of belonging to the national collective. By creating a sense of national kinship, heroes facilitate a person's internal allegiance to the nation, the awareness of citizenship and belonging to "the people," an element of what Benedict Anderson has called the "imagined community" that constitutes nationalism. Heroes also serve to unite the present (in the form of living individual citizens giving their allegiance to the state) with the past (in the form of national history). By creating a kinship bond with living citizens, heroes are a medium for transmitting the national heritage, an imagined place in the national family and its historical chronology.

Leon Maria Guerrero highlights the identity axis of Filipino nationalism in his 1984 study, as the title *We Filipinos* indicates. "Nations are known by the heroes they have," Guerrero declares. But national heroes, like national history, are constructed, fabricated: heroes are made, not born (Guerrero 1984, 67, 68). Heroes become "sites of memory" by being repositories of nationalist "social capital," in Renan's language, only because they are so fashioned.

"THE MAKINGS OF A HERO": JOSÉ RIZAL AND THE CONSTRUCTION OF PHILIPPINE NATIONALIST HAGIOGRAPHY

In this chapter I will undertake a closer examination of the U.S. impact on the role Filipino national hero José Rizal has played in Filipino nationalism, as defined by Rizal himself, by the American colonial regime, and by subsequent generations of Filipinos to demonstrate this book's fundamental theme regarding the imbrication of Philippine and American nationalisms. On the one hand, the United States promoted Rizal hagiography in apparent support of Philippine nationalism, but only because that particular strand of Philippine nationalism supported the American political agenda. On the other hand, Rizal found inspiration for his own conceptualization of Philippine nationalism through the United States. Through Rizal's establishment of an early nationalist organization, Los Indios Bravos, Rizal co-opted the image of American Indians in order to overthrow Spanish colonial hegemony over Filipino *indios*. Thus José Rizal and the U.S. government invoked each other at cross-purposes in the struggle to wrest the Philippines from one colonial master, on the one hand, and reestablish it under another colonial master, on the other.

The differing ways in which Rizal-as-national-hero have been constructed by both the Philippine and American governments—and Rizal's own integral role in defining Filipino nationalism—reveal the multivalent ways in which Filipino history and identity have been actively constructed by both Americans and Filipinos. Rizal is the national hero par excellence in the Philippines; his life epitomizes for Filipinos the great man's endeavors, sacrifice, and devotion. Rizal's heroic canonization has been partially compromised by the American colonial regime's promotion of Rizal as a national hero because U.S. colonial administrators considered him a figure amenable to the U.S. colonial agenda. While this issue has been a topic of much discussion among Filipino historians, the fact that Rizal himself was deeply influenced by the U.S. construction of its own nationalism has been ignored. Filipinos look to Rizal as the "First Filipino," the hero who defined Filipinos as a politico-ethnic people, the critical "we" that is foundational to nationalism. But Rizal's early conceptualization of the Philippine indio was an important prerequisite toward the ethnopoliticization of Filipino. Thus, contrary to traditional assumptions that Philippine-American history began with the Spanish-American/ Philippine-American Wars, the Philippine-American nationalist entanglement antedates 1898. Historical attention has focused on the United States' influence on Rizal after his death in 1896, ignoring the United States' influence on Rizal's anticolonial conceptualization of Philippine indios, which laid the foundation for his formulation of Filipino nationalism.

José Rizal: The First Filipino

It is difficult to overstate Rizal's centrality to Filipino nationalist identity. Leon Maria Guerrero underscores Rizal's significance for Filipino identity in the essay "Our Choice of Heroes," collected in the volume *We Filipinos,* one-third of which focuses on Rizal. Guerrero attests that Filipinos continue to define themselves as Filipinos through Rizal, as he articulates in the rhetorical question "Does it not reveal the character of our people that we have reserved our highest homage for the man of thought rather than the men of action, the man of peace rather than the makers of wars . . . ?" (Guerrero 1984, 70). Similarly, Ambeth Ocampo asserts that "Rizal shows us our potential for greatness" (Ocampo 1995, vi). Jovita Ventura Castro identifies Rizal as the "Father of Filipinas" (Castro 1992, 38–39).[1] The national veneration with which Rizal is regarded in the Philippines does not have even a close counterpart in the United States. In the Philippines, José Rizal is a secular saint. His face graces the most commonly circulated (one-peso) coin, his statue occupies a place of honor in every town plaza, and there is a compulsory college course entirely devoted to Rizal. The year 1996 saw a resurgence of Rizal hagiography; in addition to marking the centenary of the Philippine Revolution, 1996 was also the centenary of Rizal's martyrdom. Rizal often is referred to as the "First Filipino," a sobriquet that served as the title for Leon Maria Guerrero's biography of Rizal. Rizal's appellation as the First Filipino refers to Rizal's role in politicizing the term *Filipino* to denote those we now recognize as Filipino citizens, thus defining the Filipino people. But while Rizal helped claim *Filipino* for Philippine natives in the nineteenth century, in the twenty-first century Filipinos could come to be known as Rizalinos. Laguna Congressman Nereo R. Joaquin proposed a bill in the Philippine national legislature to rename the Philippines the Republic of Rizal ("Renaming of Philippines to Rizal Pressed" 1996). If the bill were passed, it would be a formal acknowledgment of Claro Recto's 1962 declaration that "A True Filipino Is a Rizalist" (Recto 1962, 2–5). On a figurative and potentially even a literal level, José Rizal gave a name to the Filipino people.

Yet even as Rizal's dominance of the Philippine national pantheon reached an apex in the movement to rename every Filipino a Rizalino, there has been for some time a movement to depose him as the preeminent national hero. In recent years, Rizal's role as *the* Philippine national hero has been challenged by many people and for many reasons. Some advocate replacing—or at least equating—the elitist Rizal with Andres Bonifacio, the "Great Plebeian" and founder of the Katipunan. Some question Rizal's status as the preeminent Philippine hero in spite of his repeated denunciations of the 1896 revolution, deciding it is ironic to celebrate Rizal as a hero of Philippine freedom when he repeatedly and explicitly advocated not Philippine independence from Spain, but rather full political assimilation into the Spanish empire.[2]

But of all the challenges to Rizal's preeminent position in the Philippine heroic pantheon, the most damning has been the issue of the U.S. role in Rizal's canonization. The issue of U.S. influence on Rizal is so troubling to Filipinos that even a century after Rizal's death, and a half century after the United States relinquished formal control over the Philippines, the question of the United States and Rizal dominates the major historical studies of Rizal. For example, three of the Philippines' leading historians, Leon Maria Guerrero, Renato Constantino, and Ambeth Ocampo, take up the issue of the American factor regarding Rizal in the introductory sections of their works. In *We Filipinos,* Guerrero attempts to debunk the U.S. role in Filipinos' veneration of Rizal, insisting, "We chose Rizal, spontaneously, unanimously, irrevocably. *Nor can it be said with complete truth* that Rizal became our national hero only because the Americans considered him the safest symbol of our nationalism, and therefore allowed, and even encouraged[,] his patriotic enthronization" (Guerrero 1984, 70; emphasis added). Constantino takes up the issue of Rizal as "An American-Sponsored Hero" in the second section of *Veneration without Understanding,* appearing before either "The Role of Heroes" or "The Concept of Filipino Nationhood." Ocampo opens his best-selling *Rizal without the Overcoat* with three essays on the United States' influence on Rizal. The first essay of the volume is "Was Rizal an American-sponsored Hero?"—not, significantly, "Why Rizal Is the National Hero," which appears as the book's fifth essay. Ocampo establishes the primacy of the issue of the U.S. sponsorship of Rizal on the first page of the first essay, flatly stating, "nothing strikes the Filipino psyche harder than the idea that Rizal was an American-sponsored hero" (Ocampo 1995, 2).

Despite the continuing primacy of the U.S.-Rizal issue, Filipino historians regard the U.S. influence on Rizal as being entirely posthumous; discussions of the American factor vis-à-vis José Rizal begin only after Rizal's execution by the Spaniards on December 30, 1896. There has been little discussion of Rizal's connection to the Spanish-American War, the Philippine-American War, or American colonialism during Rizal's lifetime. Rizal seems to have had little engagement with America, even if America actively promoted Rizal hagiography for its own colonial purposes. While it is true that the early American colonial regime encouraged Rizal's historiographical canonization, it is also true that Rizal was deeply influenced by America, and that the American influence played a significant role in Rizal's conceptualization of Filipino nationalism. A closer look at José Rizal's engagement with the United

States, both during his lifetime and in terms of the U.S. posthumous promotion of Rizal as national hero during the U.S. colonial era, will reveal the multivalence of the Philippine-American entanglement, both in terms of its length (antedating 1898 as the conventional starting point of Philippine-American history) and in terms of its complexity (Rizal's co-optation of a particular version of U.S. nationalism as the basis for his own version of Filipino nationalism during his lifetime, followed by the U.S. co-optation of Rizal's legacy for its own colonial purposes after his death).

Rizal As an American-Sponsored Hero

In *Insight and Foresight,* Renato Constantino reviews the American colonial regime's choice of Rizal as an acceptable national hero. "The public image that the Americans desired for a Filipino national hero was quite clear," writes Constantino. "They favored a hero who would not go against the grain of American colonial policy." "It was Governor William Howard Taft who in 1901 suggested to the Philippine Commission that the Filipinos be given a national hero. . . . [declaring,] 'now, gentlemen, you must have a national hero.' . . . In the subsequent discussion in which the rival merits of the revolutionary heroes were considered, the final choice—now universally acclaimed a wise one—was Rizal."[3] Charles Bohlen, one-time ambassador to the Philippines, described Taft's motivations more clearly: "Taft quickly decided that it would be extremely useful for the Filipinos to have a national hero of their revolution against the Spanish in order to channel their feelings and focus their resentment backward on Spain. But he told his advisers that he wanted it to be someone who really wasn't so much of a revolutionary that, if his life were examined too closely or his works read too carefully, this could cause us any trouble. He chose Rizal as the man who fit his model" (Constantino 1997, 29, 27–28, 28 n).[4]

American Gov. W. Cameron Forbes explained the basis for Rizal's desirability as a national hero in 1928: "Rizal never advocated independence, nor did he advocate armed resistance to the government. He urged reform from within, by publicity, by public education, and appeal to the public conscience" (Constantino 1997, 29).[5] Constantino cites several other

> factors [that] contributed to Rizal's acceptability to the Americans as the official hero of the Filipinos. In the first place, he was safely dead by the time the Americans began their aggression. No embarrassing anti-American quotations could ever be attributed to him. Moreover, Rizal's dramatic martyrdom had already made him the symbol of Spanish oppression. To focus attention on him would serve not only to concentrate Filipino hatred against the former oppressors, it would also mitigate their feelings of animosity toward the new conquerors against whom there was

still organized resistance at that time. . . . The Americans specially emphasized the fact that [Rizal] was a reformer, not a separatist. He could therefore not be invoked on the question of Philippine independence. He could not be a rallying point in the resistance against the invaders. . . . His name was invoked whenever the incapacity of the masses for self-government was pointed out as a justification for American tutelage. . . . The American decision to make Rizal our national hero was a master stroke. (29–30)

Ultimately, wrote Theodore Friend, Rizal won the American vote for "model hero" over "other contestants [because] Aguinaldo [was] too militant, Bonifacio too radical, Mabini unregenerate" (28).[6]

The American colonial regime's strategic canonization of Rizal not withstanding, however, Filipinos themselves canonized Rizal, even before his death. Sixto Orosa argues, "The Filipino people have been honoring Rizal as a national hero long before Taft came to the Philippines. If Rizal did not have the makings of a hero, if he did not deserve to be our national hero, one thousand executive orders of any governors-general would not have made him one" (Orosa 1961, 2). Reviewing the debate, Ambeth Ocampo concludes, "Although the Americans encouraged the hero worship of Rizal, the man was already a national hero to the Filipinos long before the Americans sponsored him as such" (Ocampo 1995, 3). Renato Constantino agrees, concluding that despite the American encouragement of Rizal hero-worship, "There is no doubt that we would have made Rizal one of our heroes even without American intervention" (Constantino 1997, 33). Thus, there is a curious ambiguity about the relationship between Rizal and the United States. Rizal stands trial in historical debates as a pawn of the American colonial regime, where his reputation is somewhat tarnished because the Americans promoted him, but is ultimately exonerated because Filipinos venerated him regardless.

Los Indios Bravos: Rizal's Conceptualization of Filipino Nationalism

During the Spanish colonial period, those we now call Filipinos were not, in fact, native Filipinos. The term *Filipinos* (synonymous with *insulares* or *Creoles*) referred to Spaniards born in the Philippines. The distinction between a *peninsulare* (a Spaniard born in Spain) and an insulare or "Filipino" was crucial; as Benedict Anderson describes it, the timing of one's birth decisively determined one's place in the colonial hierarchy: "It was nearly unheard-of for a creole to rise to a position of official importance in Spain. . . . Even if he was born within one week of his father's migration, the accident of birth in the [colony] consigned him to subordination—even though in terms of language, religion, ancestry, or manners he was largely indistinguishable from the

Spain-born Spaniard. There was nothing to be done about it: he was irremediably a *creole*" (Anderson 1991, 57–58).

Those we now call Filipinos were known then as indios. The Spaniards, peninsulares and insulares alike, discriminated against the indios. From the sixteenth through nineteenth centuries, peninsulares and insulares regarded indios as a "dusky race . . . very stupid and vicious, and of the basest spirits" (Anderson 1991, 59). As late as 1885, Franciscan friar Miguel Lucio y Bustamante maintained the unbridgeable racial and cultural gulf between the Spaniard and the indio, comparing the latter to a monkey and observing, "The monkey will always be a monkey however you dress him with shirt and trousers" (Agoncillo 1990, 121).[7]

Even in the late nineteenth century, Spanish colonialists used the term *indio* to emphasize the inferior status of Filipino natives. It was in the face of such attitudes that José Rizal, then traveling in Europe, took a decisive step toward a "Filipino" nationalist consciousness.[8] Rizal was an *ilustrado:* one of the Spanish-speaking upper class who went abroad to obtain the higher schooling denied to Philippine indios. Many of the ilustrados traveled around Europe and concentrated in Barcelona, where they began the Propaganda movement, which lobbied for Spanish reforms in the Philippines through the Propaganda journal *La Solidaridad.*[9] In 1889, Rizal visited the Exposition Universelle in Paris. "While attending the Paris Exposition of 1889, Rizal and his fellow Filipinos saw a Wild West show featuring Native Americans performing various skills on horseback. Impressed not only by their daring but also by the enthusiastic applause they received from the crowd, the Filipinos decided to form a mutual-aid association and call it *Los Indios Bravos.* Rizal himself had suggested the name, thinking to subvert the racist designation *indio* used by the Spaniards to refer to native Filipinos" (Rafael 1995, 149; see also Ocampo 1995, 121 and Ocampo 1999a, 1).

Rizal's formation of Los Indios Bravos represents a critical moment in the early stages of Filipino nationalism. Where the La Solidaridad organization/ journal worked primarily on formal political agendas, Los Indios Bravos focused on cultural issues (the identity axis of nationalism). Through Los Indios Bravos, Rizal turned the Spanish-imposed derogatory term into a term of pride and ethnic unity, asserting a Philippine ethnicity at a time when *Filipino* was still appropriated by the colonial masters. As E. San Juan Jr. notes, Rizal's aim "was to shape an image of the Filipino race as a community with a historical destiny"—the achievement of what Benedict Anderson, among other scholars, defines as the "imagined community" that is the foundation of nationalism (San Juan 1997, 24). If nationalism is, as Anderson proposes, a "radically changed form of consciousness," then Rizal's conceptualization of *indio* as a term of ethnic pride is an example of this radically changed consciousness: an oppositional reconceptualization of the colonial denigrating term (Anderson 1991, xiv). Many Filipino scholars point to La Liga Filipina as being Rizal's contribution to Philippine nationalism.[10] But Los Indios Bravos was an important prerequisite to the formulation of the concept of the Philippine Filipino and thus was foundational to La Liga Filipina. Whatever his position on the Revolution of 1896, it is in this sense, perhaps, that we can see José Rizal as a revolutionary.

Rizal's self-identification as an indio was not one he formulated only for the Los Indios Bravos group. Rizal went to his death identifying himself as an indio. At the Spaniards' trial that lead to his execution, Rizal "was ordered by the judge to sign the notification of sentence as required by law. [Rizal] declined. . . . When the document was shown him, he drew attention to the fact that he was incorrectly described as a Chinese mestizo (one of the aims of Spanish governmental publicity on the subject was to pretend that he was not even a real Filipino), saying that he was an *indio puro*" (Coates 1992, 311–12). The racial distinctions between peninsulares, insulares, mestizos (often, as in Rizal's trial, connoting mixed Chinese ancestry), and indios was a significant one, so much so that it became a point of political contention at Rizal's trial. The Spanish government's categorization of Rizal as a Chinese mestizo was not merely a racial slur; it was, as Coates points out, an attempt to compromise Rizal's political identity as "a real Filipino" (Coates uses the term in its contemporary sense). Rizal's retaliation by insisting that he was an indio puro was a political statement, an assertion of his ethnopolitical identity that was in itself a revolutionary declaration against colonial rule, as it reappropriated a Filipino identity at a time when *Filipino* had been appropriated by the colonizers. Rizal's adamant self-identification as indio puro was a precursory step to taking *Filipino* out of the hands of Philippine-born Spaniards and making it available to native-born Filipinos as the basis for a collective politicized identity.

The irony in Rizal's recuperation of *indio* from a term denoting colonial racial inferiority to an assertion of anticolonial nationalism is that Rizal's conceptualization of Indio Bravo was based on his admiration for American Indians. Insofar as Filipino scholars have noted consistently a contested engagement between Philippine and American nationalisms in and through the figure of José Rizal, Filipino scholars have freely acknowledged how American and Filipino nation-builders have competed over the meaning of the figure of Rizal. However, there has been little scholarly attention to the ways in which Filipino and American nationalist discourses were in competition from the first in Rizal's own nationalist formulation.

The significance of Rizal's conceptualization of the Filipino indio as based on the American Indian largely has passed without critical interrogation by Philippine historians. Leon Maria Guerrero writes in *The First Filipino: A Biography of José Rizal*: "In Paris . . . Rizal and his friends called themselves the indios bravos, transforming the traditional Spanish gibe into a badge of honor, for Rousseau with his myth of 'the noble savage' and James Fenimore Cooper with his Leatherstocking Tales had captured the imagination and the awe of Europeans for the plumed warriors of the prairies" (Guerrero 1977, 120). Guerrero relates this background to the Indios Bravos without irony; his tone here seems sincere in its admiration (from both Rizal's perspective and his own) for American Indians as "plumed warriors of the prairies." Ambeth Ocampo adopts a similarly blithe attitude toward the provenance of Los Indios Bravos in a 1999 essay:

> Rizal and his *barkada* [*group of close friends, here fellow Propagandists including Valentin Ventura, Marcelo H. del Pilar, and Mariano Ponce*] formed Indios Bravos in Paris. . . . During the Universal Exposition of 1889, Rizal and his *barkada* watched a "Buffalo Bill" or Western show. . . . The 1889 show had authentic American Indians doing all sorts of daredevil stunts in full costume. Rizal and friends were impressed; they remembered that they were *indios*, too, in Filipinas and decided to call themselves defiantly Indios Bravos. In some cases, "bravo" can be used as a synonym for "savage" or "*salvaje*," but the Indios Bravos chose the more positive meaning, a synonym for "valiant" or someone who can . . . fight bravely in battle. (Ocampo 1999a, 1)

Ocampo is renowned for his investigation (and often destruction) of historical myths. But he does not question the Wild West show, affirming the Wild West's "authentic American Indians" whose authenticity apparently was not compromised by the inherent theatricality of their performing in full costume. Vicente Rafael, too, relates the provenance of Rizal's naming of Los Indios Bravos, noting that Rizal and his fellow Propagandists were "impressed not only by [the Wild West show performers'] daring but also by the enthusiastic applause they received from the crowd" (Rafael 1995, 149). Filipino historians such as Guerrero, Ocampo, and Rafael all focus on Rizal's revolutionary act of self-naming, not on the spurious authenticity of the performance that inspired the name.

"AMERICA'S NATIONAL ENTERTAINMENT": THE WILD WEST'S SPECTACULARIZATION OF MANIFEST DESTINY

"Buffalo Bill's Wild West and Congress of Rough Riders," popularly known as the Wild West show, had become a phenomenal success during its European run touting itself as "America's National Entertainment" and disseminating Manifest Destiny as the narrative of U.S. nationalism. Manifest Destiny constructed American nationalism through the frontier—and, constitutively, the conquest of Native Americans. From the Revolutionary period, Americans had used the trope of the Indian to define a national territory distinct from England; for example, in his preface to *Edgar Huntly* (1799), novelist Charles Brockden Brown asserted that "the field of investigation opened to us by our own country, should differ essentially from those which exist in Europe," and concluded that "the incidents of Indian hostility, and the perils of the Western wilderness, are . . . suitable [for a distinctly American literature]; and for a native of America to overlook these would admit of no apology" (Brown 1887, 3–4). From the American Revolutionary period through the "closing" of the frontier in the late nineteenth century, Anglo-Americans posited Native Americans as both the foes and foils of U.S. nation-building. On one hand, Anglos imaginatively assumed a fabricated Indian identity to create a transformative space in which European settlers became distinctly and distinctively Americans. On the other hand, Anglo-Americans defined themselves and claimed the literal as well as figurative national territory through the conquering of Native American tribes. Thus the Indian functioned as both the muse and the enemy in the crucible of American identity formation. The Wild West's depictions of dramatic scenes of life on the American frontier featured vignettes of Indian attacks on white settlements and the settlers' rescue by Buffalo Bill, cowboys, and Anglo scouts. Audiences thrilled to sensationalized dramatizations of Indian warfare and admired Native American skills and dances but remained comfortably reassured that, ultimately, white settlement would win the day, the frontier, and the country. White audiences could safely admire the Indians' performances because the performances themselves reenacted Native Americans' subjugation to Manifest Destiny.

At the end of the nineteenth century Filipinos, too, would appeal to the figure of the Indian as the imaginative basis for separation from their colonial masters. Whereas U.S. discourses of expansion ultimately turned on the displacement/conquest of Native Americans by Anglo settlers, Rizal's construction of Los Indios Bravos turned on a notion of shared indigenous visibility through the assertion of a transnational Indian identity. José Rizal and his fellow Filipinos read the exhibitions of the show Indians' prowess and the defiance they displayed during the show's reenacted battles as demonstrations of anticolonial rebellion. Ironically, however, the ethnic fraternity Rizal conceptualized as a step toward Filipino nationhood redounded on Filipinos just a few years later, as the U.S. exported the policies and racial attitudes developed during the U.S. Indian Wars to the Philippines in the Philippine-American War. The sense of Filipino national identity Rizal helped create also laid the groundwork for the Philippine "insurrection," for having initiated a revolution to throw off one colonial master and having established their own government, Filipinos would not submit easily to colonial rule from another quarter.

The Wild West functioned as a site of memory for the construction of nationalism through the identity axis, focusing in particular on the Indian/

indio as the imaginative figure of nationalist identification. Both the Wild West and José Rizal made the figure of the Indian the repository of conflicting nationalist visions. Through the Wild West's Indians, Buffalo Bill and José Rizal located their national identities on opposite sides of the colonial dynamic: for Buffalo Bill, the Indian as antagonist, for Rizal, the Indian as protagonist. Each based his national vision on the heroizing of his chosen role: Buffalo Bill as champion of American expansionism, Rizal as anticolonial warrior. For both Americans and Filipinos, the formation of a national identity through the figure of the Indian was always a fantasy. While the stereotypically exotic figure of the Indian brave/"indio bravo," the "plumed warrior of the prairie" complete with plaited hair and buckskin, provided an imaginative foil for the conceptualization of both American and Filipino national identities, the figure of the Indian remained a kind of mental costume, something both Filipinos and Americans could imagine themselves *through,* not *as.* Anglo-Americans never seriously intended to "go native" any more than Filipinos did. For Filipinos as much as for Americans, the Wild West was an imaginative territory upon which nationalist conceptions of "the people" could be created. Through the figure of the Indian, the Wild West provided an imaginary landscape for the peopling of both the U.S. and Philippine national polities.

Thus, for both Anglo-Americans and Filipinos, the Wild West provided a site for the construction, dissemination, and contestation of imbricated nationalist identities. The Wild West show, and its constitutive image of the Indian brave, served as a site of memory in which a national narrative was asserted (by Anglo-Americans), simultaneously cooperated with and challenged (by the show Indians), and exported as a form of anticolonial rebellion and the foundation of a new national identity (by José Rizal and his fellow Propagandists). The Wild West functioned as a palimpsest, a performative narrative in which nationhood and historical hegemony were contested. The Wild West as a site of rhetorical struggle via the figure of the Indian—producing opposing U.S., Native American, and Filipino constructions and receptions of the Indian brave—prefigured the U.S. exportation of the Indian Wars across the Pacific following the "closing" of the frontier. The U.S. and Philippine nations' constructions of the Indian brave forecast the two countries' future military conflict: the United States, through the nationalist narrative of Manifest Destiny, constructed the figure of the Indian as subjected to colonial nationalism, while Filipinos constructed the figure of the "indio bravo" as a figure of anticolonial nationalism. These discursive artifacts of an early U.S./Philippine ideological entanglement antedate conventional perceptions of the U.S./Philippine historical entanglement starting in 1898; each country's national identity—expansionist on the U.S. side, emergent anticolonial on the Philippine side—led the two nations both to constitute themselves via the other and to oppose each other. The Wild West and its reception by Rizal evince a vigorous struggle for control over the power to name, define, and represent national protagonists and antagonists: the heroes, enemies, victors, and victims of nation-building.

A detailed excavation of the transcultural logic by which José Rizal became "the first Filipino" sheds light on the ways in which both Americans and Filipinos constructed national identity through the figure of the Indian: Americans through the conquering of the Indians, the national narrative the Wild West staged on a daily basis, and Filipinos through a sympathetic fraternal identification with the indio bravo, reclaiming an ethnopolitical identity as an important precursory step toward imagining a national identity. Ultimately, Filipino and later American constructions of an affiliation between American Indians and Philippine indios became directly related to one another as the United States, achieving the goal of winning the Indians' "wilderness," sought extracontinental "frontiers" to conquer and exported the ideology and tactics of the U.S. Indian Wars to the Philippines in the wake of the Spanish-American War. Thus this chapter demonstrates the ways in which transculturation and the identity axis played out in both American and Philippine cultural constructions of nationalism at the end of the nineteenth century.

Playing Indian in American Nation-Building

In Playing Indian, Philip Deloria outlines the ways in which Euro-Americans invoked, constructed, and manipulated Indian images and stereotypes to provide the foundation for what he calls the emerging nation's "key origin story." Deloria locates the beginning of this tradition in the Boston Tea Party (1773), in which Boston citizens assumed the guise of Indians to rebel against oppressive British colonial taxation. White constructions of "Indianness" provided American colonists with plastic notions of freedom, the warrior, rebellion, and an affinity with the land. Deloria argues that white constructions of Indianness underlie "the various ways Americans have contested and constructed national identities. . . . From the Boston Tea Party . . . [through] the next two hundred years. . . . Indianness provided impetus and [the] precondition for the creative assembling of an ultimately unassemblable American identity." By "playing Indians," Deloria asserts that Anglo-Americans achieved what D. H. Lawrence called a "'have-the-cake-and-eat-it-too' dialectic of simultaneous desire and repulsion," a dynamic Deloria posits "both juxtaposes and conflates an urge to idealize and desire Indians and a need to despise and dispossess them" (Deloria 1998, 2–4).

One example of American national identity forged through the "playing Indian" dynamic Deloria outlines can be found in Frederick Jackson Turner's classic speech on "The Significance of the Frontier in American History." Turner describes the nexus of American national identity as achieved through the investment in and subsequent divestment of a Native American lifestyle. For Turner, the frontier provided the environment in which Anglo-European settlers divested themselves of their previous ethnic/national identities and invested themselves in a distinctively American identity. This transformation of nationalist identity occurred through the process of figuratively going native:

> [The] wilderness masters the colonist. . . . It strips off the garments of civ-ilization and arrays him in the hunting shirt and the moccasin. It puts him in the log cabin of the Cherokee and Iroquois and runs an Indian palisade around him. Before long . . . he shouts the war cry and takes the scalp in orthodox Indian fashion. . . . [A]t the frontier the environment is at first too strong for the man. . . . Little by little he transforms the wilderness, but the outcome is not the old Europe, not simply the development of Germanic germs. . . . [H]ere is a new product that is American. . . . In the crucible of the frontier the immigrants were Americanized, liberated. (Turner 1893)

Turner argues that immigrants "transform . . . the wilderness" in the process of becoming Americans, but they must first transform themselves from white men into "orthodox Indian[s]." Turner's depiction of the immigrant's transmogrifica-tion to American is accomplished through the occupation of the Indian pal-isade, the putting on of hunting shirt and moccasin, the taking up of a tomahawk—as though these accoutrements of Native American life had been abandoned, almost deliberately so, to provide for the white man's use. Turner's depiction of "American development" achieves what Albert Memmi calls the paradigmatic colonial fantasy in which the colonizer rids the colony of the col-onized (Memmi 1965, 66). In Turner's fantasy of "American development," the natives appear to have obligingly abandoned the field for the white man's ben-efit in an implicit acknowledgment of the U.S. Manifest Destiny. Through metamorphosis into an imaginary Indian-hood, Turner implies what he cannot admit explicitly: that the settling of the frontier, and hence the defining estab-lishment of the American nation, is predicated on territorial acquisition at the expense of Native Americans.

Years before Frederick Jackson Turner's famous speech, the Wild West show spectacularly dramatized Turner's "frontier thesis," which claimed that American "history has been in a large degree the history of the colonization of the Great West" (Turner 1893). Like Turner's frontier thesis, Buffalo Bill's Wild West predicated the triumph of American nationalism on the territorial conquest of the Great Plains and, concomitantly, its American Indian nations. For Buffalo Bill, as for Turner, the frontier was the arena through which America defined itself.

The Wild West was an enthusiastic proponent of Manifest Destiny, but it reinserted Native Americans into the frontier. Turner fantasized an absence of

Indians as active opponents of the march of American nationalism. The Wild West did the opposite, dramatizing Native Americans' opposition to white settlement. That was the point: the thrill of the show was in the sensational-ized dramatizations of the Indian Wars. The Wild West and Turner approached America-as-frontier through opposite channels: Turner denied Native Amer-ican dispossession and genocide; the Wild West spectacularized it within a fan-tasy that safely reenacted the power struggle between Anglos and Indians, assuring the audience of the ultimate triumph of Anglo-Americanism. But both achieved the same end result: the American nation constituting itself through westward expansion.[11]

The Wild West canonized white scouts (especially Buffalo Bill) and soldiers as the heroes and cast white settlers as its innocent protagonists and the Indian braves José Rizal so admired as the antagonists. By presenting the white settlers as the victims, Native Americans as the attackers, and white scouts such as Buf-falo Bill as the rescuers, the Wild West portrayed the Indian Wars as essentially defensive wars: the wars against the Great Plains tribes were not wars of aggres-sive conquest; quite the opposite, they were merely rescue operations aimed at defending peaceful Anglo settlers victimized by Indian "savages." Richard White has made this same point, observing that the Wild West's "spectacles presented an account of Indian aggression and white defense; of Indian killers and white victims; of, in effect, badly abused conquerors. . . . To achieve . . . [a] 'kingdom won without the guilt / Of studied battle,' Americans had to transform conquerors into victims. . . . We, these stories say, do not plan our conquests. . . . We just retaliate against barbaric massacres" (White 1994, 27).[12] By portraying the Indian Wars as defensive campaigns, the Wild West has its ideology both ways. On one hand, its active promotion of Manifest Destiny implicitly entails territorial aggression: Anglo-American expansion moved ever westward, and Native Americans could either recede, assimilate, or die, but since Anglo-American expansion was destined by a kind of presumptive divine land charter, it was not something to feel guilty about.[13] On the other hand, if there was any guilt to be attributed, it lay with the Native Americans, since they were the aggressors making war against peaceful farmers, women, and children. The cloaking of expansionist aggression with a manufactured air of innocence, necessitating a "defensive" war, was so ideologically effective that it was invoked again for the Philippine-American War. Americans constituted Filipino hostilities against the United States as an "insurrection" on the grounds that the Philippines was American territory—and insurrections are, by definition, domestic rebellions against an established government. Thus the Wild West's depiction of Indian aggression against innocent whites prefigured the U.S. official military policy in the Philippines a few years hence.

As ideologically compelling as generic scenes of Indian attacks and assaults on various scenes of white settlement were, the Wild West did not stop with such formulaic dramatizations. One of the Wild West's claims to authenticity derived from the show's reenactments of actual events. The Wild West constructed reenactments of Custer's Last Stand (the battle at the Little Big Horn) and the Battle of Summit Springs, among other historical events, as being paradigmatic moments of American national history. While the representation of real events was one key element in the show's realism, another was having real veterans of the events depicted populate the dramatis personae. The Wild West's American Indian performers, with their spectacular (and spectacularized) feats of equestrian skill and "authentic" cultural performances constituted a key element of the show's entertainment value and, more important, in the presumptive realism that conferred a significant portion of the show's ideological value.[14] The show Indians provided a crucial part of the Wild West's putative authenticity because the show Indians, like Buffalo Bill, were real representatives reenacting rather than enacting events that really happened.[15] The importance of the Wild West's Indian performers, in other words, was the fact that they were real Indians performing reenactments of real events, more than (or at least as much as) their skill at riding, warfare, or dancing. Even the show's portrayal of Native Americans' bravery, horseman- and marksmanship serviced the show's ideological message; as L. G. Moses observes, the show's Indians had to be "portrayed as worthy adversaries, for how else could the showmen-entrepreneurs like Cody validate their prowess in battle?" (Moses 1996, 8).

The participation of Native Americans in the Wild West was so integral to the show that they were always on display, even when they were not performing in the show itself. The show's Native American performers were always "on"; they were encouraged to wear their costumes offstage and were photographed as ethnic curiosities in Venetian gondolas or riding in automobiles (see Kasson 2000, 89, 194). By conspicuously appearing in costume outside the arena, "these men and women in blankets and feathers were a walking advertisement for the show, and the fact that they appeared the same whether on- or offstage seemed to endorse the Wild West's claims to authenticity and its view of history," notes Kasson (162). The show Indians' offstage appearance in costume demonstrates their theatrical overdetermination: they were always a dramatized display, even while ostensibly viewers rather than viewees.

The show Indians' sightseeing also had a political agenda. Both Buffalo Bill and the U.S. government encouraged the Wild West's Native Americans' offstage tours to impress upon them the overwhelming scope and strength of white society, thus convincing them of the hopelessness of Native American resistance to white encroachment. John Burke, Bill Cody's partner in the Wild West, made this point in 1894, boasting "the Indians who have traveled with Buffalo Bill are firmly convinced of the white man's power and of the hopelessness of the Indian's trying to cope with it. They have done more in the

interests of preserving peace than all the school educated Indians in the country" (Kasson 2000, 195). The show's Native American performers were
expected to disseminate this inculcated hopelessness back home, a point so
significant that in 1890 Acting Commissioner of Indian Affairs Robert Belt
hoped the returning show Indians' tales would help avert the crisis building
over the Ghost Dance Movement (Moses 1996, 105). The Wild West played
the issue of cultural assimilation in conflicting ways. On one hand, through
exposing the show Indians to white culture abroad and thus convincing
Native Americans of the inevitability of their culture's extinction, the Wild
West waged an indirect campaign for Native Americans' compulsory assimilation with white "civilization." Simultaneously and paradoxically, however, by
highlighting Native American "savagery" to titillate white audiences and
underwrite the show's promotion of Manifest Destiny, the Wild West undermined the Native Americans' assimilation into white culture.

Through their careful and deliberate construction of the Wild West show's
scenes of frontier conflict and, just as important, its claims to historical
authenticity, William Cody and his partners made the Wild West a medium for
the dissemination of American nationalism clothed as popular entertainment.
The show was deliberately constructed to promote a nationalist script: the triumph of Manifest Destiny across the Great Plains, the "winning [of] a wilderness" that Frederick Jackson Turner equates with "American history" (Turner
1893). In its early versions, the Wild West claimed to "report" events from the
Indian wars still in active contest on the Great Plains, but through the 1880s,
as the balance of power shifted to Anglo-America, the Wild West likewise
shifted from ostensible reportage to dramatic entertainment—without, however, making the change clear to its audience. While in the early 1880s the
Wild West could claim with some legitimacy that it was reporting "history in
the making"—that is, events whose outcomes were still undecided—the ultimate outcome (conquest of the Native American tribes) was not in any real
doubt. The Wild West's significance as popular entertainment was in its dissemination of a national history it created rather than, as it claimed, simply
related. Its audience was threefold: the domestic Anglo-American audience
who embraced the spectacle of the taming of the frontier and its "savage"
aboriginals as the "story of America"—that is, the narrative of the national
"us"; the Native Americans who performed in the Wild West but were
induced to be an ancillary audience to the spectacle of the subjugation they
themselves (re)enacted; and a European audience that had, previous to this
point, looked down upon the United States for failing to produce a distinctively "American" spectacle. Even Mark Twain, who excoriated imperialism
in the Philippines as an abuse of American nationalism (see Twain 1992b),
endorsed the Wild West as "a purely and distinctively American . . . exhibition," one which would dispel European (especially British) snobbery about

the U.S. inability to produce a national exhibition of which Americans could be proud (Kasson 2000, 72).[16] Touted as "America's National Entertainment," the Wild West disseminated American nationalism-cum-expansionism not only at home but also abroad; Twain's endorsement was for the Wild West's European tour, which started in 1887 and included the five-month engagement in Paris (1889) that so impressed José Rizal (41).

While portraying the United States to the world, the Wild West also portrayed the world coming to the United States. The show celebrated American extracontinental territorial aggrandizement, enlarging its acts to exhibit as war trophies representatives of newly conquered territories. William Cody made the show's increasingly global scope explicit by marketing his show as "Buffalo Bill's Wild West and Congress of Rough Riders of the World." Cody originated the name "Rough Rider," establishing a moniker Teddy Roosevelt would popularize in Cuba, and within a year of the Battle of San Juan Hill, "detachments from Roosevelt's Rough Riders" were reenacting the Cuban incident in the Wild West. More than just theatrically reenacting the Spanish-American War, Cody volunteered for active duty, grandly describing "How I Could Drive Spaniards from Cuba with 30,000 Indian Braves," going so far as to claim that by fighting on the side of the United States, Native Americans could retaliate for the injuries to Native American peoples because "Spain sent the first white man to America" (Kasson 2000, 249, 251).[17] The Wild West quickly featured representatives from the Spanish-American War's territorial acquisitions. The 1899 Wild West program included a picture of Negroid Filipinos, ranging from an old man to young boys in the foreground, with a small hut and palm trees in the background, and this caption: "Strange People from Our New Possessions. Families of Porto Ricans, Sandwich Islanders and Filipinos." By 1900, Filipinos were performing in the Wild West (253).

In 1893, a promotional poster for "Buffalo Bill's Wild West and Congress of Rough Riders of the World" depicted a befeathered Native American warrior with the caption "An American" (Kasson 2000, 199). As Joy Kasson notes, Cody increasingly advertised his show with an international flair: in addition to Filipinos and other "Strange People from Our New Possessions," the Wild West advertised the participation of other "national types," including "Cossacks, Mexicans, and Arabs" in the show. In its Congress of Rough Riders of the World, the Wild West invoked two distinct and interwoven strands of U.S. nationalism at the cusp of the closing of the frontier and, not coincidentally, the U.S. emergence as a world power. The Wild West's domestic component affirmed the successful domestic conquest of the Native American tribes, which the show, like Frederick Jackson Turner, depicted as *the* narrative of American nationalism. The show's international component, on the other hand, promoted extracontinental Manifest Destiny, as the participation of Cubans, Filipinos, Mexicans, and "Porto Ricans" demonstrates. But all participants were not ideologically equal within the Wild West's "Congress." The show's inclusion of an American Indian warrior as "an American" did not depict Indians as equal citizens in the American democracy; rather, the show's narrative portrayed Native Americans as antagonists, and Indians' inclusion under the rubric of "American" was as a conquered people, as was the case for Cubans, Filipinos, and Puerto Ricans, as the phrase "Our New Possessions" highlights. The Wild West's Congress of Rough Riders, then, did not imagine a quasi-legislative body of equal partners in a global democracy; it depicted the United States as a global master, conquering rebellious peoples at home and abroad and exhibiting them as living trophies for the entertainment of their racial superiors. By performing in such a context, the show's ethnic performers reconfirmed, with every performance, their territorial subjugation. This was particularly true of the Wild West's Filipinos in the promotional photo to advertise the show, since the Negroid islanders featured in the photograph were not actually performers in the show. The Filipinos, then, were promoted strictly as war trophies for a war that had just begun; by using the photo as an advertisement for the Wild West, Buffalo Bill was not promoting his actual show but instead was promoting Manifest Destiny across the Pacific. The fact that Filipinos joined the Congress of Rough Riders and were used as a promotional image for the Wild West foretold Filipinos' eventual conquest, predicting for them a fate analogous to the show Indians'.

The Wild West's dramatization of "representative" events of U.S. national history aimed at the identity axis of nationalism. Through the show's reenactments of scenes of Anglo-Native American conflict, the Wild West constructed a national narrative in which, as Joy Kasson argues, "historical events seemed to become personal memory, and personal memory was reinterpreted as national memory" (2000, 7). One key aspect of the Wild West's performance entailed circus-type feats of riding and showmanship exhibited by the show's Native American performers as well as white performers such as Annie Oakley, which the audience consumed as entertainment but with which the audience did not identify (that is, such demonstrations were "for us," not "about us"). On the other hand, the show's sensationalized representation of "our" national life activated the audience's identification with the national "imagined community"; through watching such scenes as the Indian attack on the Deadwood coach or the battle at the Little Big Horn, the white audience experienced the drama as something that happened to "us." Thus the Wild West promulgated a nationalist narrative that dictated the relational terms in the imperialist dyad: the show interpellated the Anglo audience as the conquerors, and the show's Native American and other performers from "Our New Possessions" as the conquered. By taking the show abroad, William Cody exported the Wild West's expansionist national narrative to an international audience. But while Cody and his partners deliberately con-

structed the Wild West to disseminate a particular brand of American nationalism abroad, that nationalist narrative was open to interpretation and adapta-
tion by others during the show's international run.

The Wild West's dissemination of a carefully constructed national narrative also activated José Rizal's sense of national identity. Rizal and his *ilustrado
compadres* were forced to go abroad for education and cultural opportunities
that they, as indios, were denied by the Spaniards in the Philippines. Impressed
by the Wild West show Indians, Rizal identified with them, not with the
show's white performers. The Wild West Indians' evident bravery and skills as
well as "the enthusiastic applause they received from the crowd" created for
Rizal the image of the Indian as a laudatory ethnic identity, leading Rizal to
see in the show Indians an ethnic fraternity through which Filipino indios
could recuperate the pejorative connotations imposed by Spanish colonialism
(Rafael 1995, 149).

But it is important to note that it was the *image*, not the reality, of the
American Indian as a proud warrior on which Rizal based his recuperation of
the Philippine indio. In May 1888, Rizal had traveled fairly extensively
through the United States, crossing the country from San Francisco to New
York, passing through Colorado, Utah, Nebraska, Illinois, and New York and
writing about his impressions of the land and its people. He did not record
actually meeting any Native Americans, although he "saw an Indian, garbed
half-European and half-Indian, leaning against a wall" on May 7 and noted in
his diary "What I observed in Chicago was that every tobacco shop had a . . .
different . . . statue of an Indian" (Ocampo 1999b, 1999c). These fleeting
observations of American Indians—the live man leaning against a wall and the
carved men posted outside tobacco shops—made little impression on Rizal;
indeed, the flat, abbreviated descriptions Rizal gave them made the "real"
Indian and the "fake" (that is, carved) ones sound remarkably similar. Rizal
scholars have not reported that Rizal wrote in his diaries or letters any impressions of the Wild West's Native Americans, but his naming Los Indios Bravos
in their honor clearly indicates the depth to which the Wild West Indians
impressed him. Rizal focused on the spectacularization of the American Indians' martial and equestrian skills, their portrayal of bravery and exoticism, not
the implicit message of their performance: their role as the whites' enemy,
destined to defeat. It was the Indian as performed, not the real American
Indian Rizal saw in Nevada, that formed for Rizal the critical identity connection between American Indians and Philippine indios.

But the show Indians were not simply stooges for the Wild West's ideological campaign. Native Americans seized what agency they could from
Anglo-American fabrications of Indianness. "It would be folly to imagine that
white Americans blissfully used Indianness to tangle with their ideological
dilemmas while native people stood idly by, exerting no influence over the

resulting Indian images," Philip Deloria writes. "Throughout a long history of Indian play, native people have been present at the margins, insinuating their way into Euro-American discourse, often attempting to nudge notions of Indianness in directions they found useful. As the nineteenth and twentieth centuries unfolded, increasing numbers of Indians participated in white people's Indian play, assisting, confirming, co-opting, challenging, and legitimating the performative tradition of aboriginal American identity" (Deloria 1998, 8).

For the Wild West's Native American performers, the show was one of the few available sites for challenging the dominant historical narrative in whose creation they were also participating. In exhibiting Native Americans as war trophies, the Wild West made colonial conflict spectacularly visible. Although the Wild West included Native Americans solely as antagonists and, ultimately, the defeated foe, the show's Native American performers had their own ideas about their role in the show. The inherent duality of their performance was made explicit when performers seized occasional moments to either mock the Anglo-European audience's naive reception of the Wild West's various depictions of "authentic" Native American practices, or to declaim, and therefore reclaim, their side of the history. For example, the show Indians deliberately undermined the much-touted authenticity of the Indian performances by having Sioux perform Omaha dances (Kasson 2000, 212). And at the end of the 1892 Glasgow run, Kicking Bear stayed in the arena after the performance's end. "The interpreter reported that he was recounting in Lakota his deeds of valor," asserting "his own version of his history" (191). Thus, although the Wild West's show Indians daily reenacted their own disenfranchisement by Anglo-Americans, they also used the show to subvert the historical and nationalist hegemony their presence helped validate. In *Wild West Shows and the Images of American Indians,* L. G. Moses observes that a "major conflict [developed] between Wild West shows and Indian-policy reformers" over "a struggle to determine whose image of the Indians would prevail" (1996, 5). This struggle was not limited to whites; the show Indians also actively contested the stereotypes they simultaneously enacted.

Thus the Wild West was not only a site of memory for a particularly crafted version of U.S. national history; it was also a site of (re)presentation, in which multiple levels of "truth," "realism," identity politics, and "authenticity" were played out and played against one another. While Europeans who watched the show may have unproblematically identified with the conquering Anglo-Americans, Rizal and his comrades clearly identified with the Native Americans as the heroes of the show. Even though the Indians lost the show battles, Rizal and his Filipino compatriots, who themselves had been subjected to colonial rule, saw the Native Americans as the heroes. In *Imperial Eyes,* Mary Louise Pratt utilizes the concept of transculturation, a term that describes "how subordinated or marginal groups select and invent from materials transmitted to them by a dominant . . . culture. While subjugated peoples cannot readily control what emanates from the dominant culture, they do determine to varying extents what they absorb into their own, and what they use it for" (1992, 6). Pratt defines transculturation as a process by which subjugated peoples assert some agency against their subjugators, and Rizal's recuperation of the indio to overturn the Spanish denigration of Philippine natives provides a clear example of this dynamic. Rizal's recuperation of the Filipino indio through Los Indios Bravos was an act of anticolonial nationalism that engages the Wild West's contested imaginary frontier and sides with the show Indians and the vanquished tribes they represented. While one might interpret Rizal's admiration for the show Indians as "indios bravos" as a naive misreading of their ideological position in the show, precisely the opposite was true. Rizal's identity as a Philippine indio, on the eve of a career of anticolonial activism, led him to construct an imagined fraternity between American Indians and Philippine indios because of their similar positions within their respective colonial orders. Although the "indios bravos" after whom Rizal named his nationalist organization were, even at the moment Rizal saw them, recapitulating their subjugation by an imperialist power, Rizal took from them the inspiration to engage in his own struggle to wrest Filipinos' ethnopolitical identity from their colonial oppressors.

Indian Wars in the Philippines

José Rizal's adoption of the image of the American Indian as a model for recuperating the Philippine indio is a clear example of transculturation, but the implications of the Indian/indio connection Rizal constructed reveals how multivalent the transcultural dynamic was. The United States, conversely, transplanted the policies, military tactics, and racial attitudes it had developed toward Indians to the Philippine indios.

While José Rizal employed the Indian/indio connection as a powerful symbol for the establishment of Filipino nationalism, the U.S. government used the same figurative ethnic fraternity as the basis for Filipinos' conquest. Eighty-seven percent of the generals serving in the Philippine-American War and "all of the four military governors of the Philippines between 1898 and 1902 (Wesley Merritt, Ewell Otis, Arthur MacArthur, and Adna Chaffee) had seen extensive Indian service" (Williams 1980, 828–29). Brig. Gen. Henry Lawton, who led the campaign in Cavite, had also begun his military career in the Civil War but had gained fame during the Indian Wars as the man who "captured the legendary Geronimo" (Miller 1982, 70). (Ironically, Lawton met his death at the hands of the Filipino Gen. Lucerio Geronimo on December 18, 1899, during a skirmish in Southern Luzon [98].) These American veterans transplanted the tactics of the late American Indian Wars to the

Philippines and translated the insurgent Filipino indio into an Indian to be dealt with as the various Native American tribes had been. Col. Jacob Smith, a veteran of Wounded Knee, opined that "because the [Filipino] natives were 'worse than fighting Indians,' he had already adopted the appropriate tactics that he had learned fighting 'savages' in the American West" (94–95). Gen. Henry Lawton agreed. Both he and Gen. Samuel Young "were seasoned Indian fighters who knew how to deal with savages and who would 'pursue the rebel Filipinos just as they relentlessly pursued the Modocs and Apaches in the triumph of civilization'" (97).[18] Lawton engaged Filipino forces at Cavite on June 10, 1899. Although Lawton's military success was doubtful, American newspapers such as the *San Francisco Call* again engaged in the preemptive construction of history, triumphantly relating the story on June 12, 1899, under the headline, "Success of the Moment against Filipino Braves" (71–72). The *Boston Journal* defended Gen. J. Franklin Bell's *reconcentrado* policy (that is, confining natives in a small concentration camp and practicing a scorched-earth policy outside the camp in order to cut insurgents' lines of support), declaring that Filipinos lost little in having their houses destroyed; being only "structures of straw and branches, only a little more elaborate than Indian wigwams," the journal concluded that Filipinos might "profit by compulsory removal from abodes that long use and neglect have made unwholesome" (209). The *Boston Journal* conveniently forgot that American humanitarian outrage against "Butcher" Weyler's reconcentrado policy had been a major factor in the United States' involvement in the Spanish-American War (Pratt 1993, 398C).[19] Theodore Roosevelt repeatedly drew parallels between fighting Indians and Filipinos. On April 18, 1889, he wrote, "Expansion . . . [is] precisely parallel between the Philippines and the Apaches and Sioux," and he asserted the "doctrine I preached in my Winning of the West" was equally applicable in the Philippines (Williams 1980, 825–26). All in all, the American military, political, and journalistic translation of Filipino "indio" to "Indian" could be summed up in the *Kansas City Times*' interview of an American soldier in the Philippines who explained the Americans' "adapt[ation] of [the] old frontier adage. . . . 'the only good Filipino is a dead one. Take no prisoners; lead is cheaper than rice'" (Miller 1982, 179–80).

In basing Los Indios Bravos on a sincere, if perhaps uninformed, admiration of Native American Indians, José Rizal, of course, did not know the violence with which the perceived similarity between Filipino indios and American Indians would rebound on his countrymen. Ironically, the national identity Rizal helped found became one of the fundamental bases for Filipinos' refusal to accept the United States as another colonial master, thus leading to the Philippine-American War in which American attitudes and tactics toward "fighting Injuns" would devastate large portions of the Philippine archipelago. Had Rizal had more familiarity with America's history of domestic imperialism, perhaps he would have realized the more dangerous ramifications of the indio/Indian connection. In 1889, the same year he founded Los Indios Bravos, the United States' propensity for imperialistic aggression was very much on Rizal's mind, and he analyzed the United States' territorial ambitions in the Pacific in an essay entitled "The Philippines a Century Hence." While Rizal's admiration for American Indians was a positive factor in his conceptualization of early Filipino nationalism, he voiced well-founded fears that America posed a serious threat to the incipient Philippine nation. While he understood the United States was a potential imperialist threat to the Philippines, Rizal failed to see the implication of recasting indios as Indians. By focusing on the Wild West Indians' anticolonial rebellion rather than the show's ideological end point, Rizal failed to see the show's Indians as predictors of Filipino indios' fate should the U.S. realize the imperialist ambitions Rizal outlined in his essay.

"Filipinas dentro de cien años" was published in the Propagandist journal *La Solidaridad* from September 1889 through early February 1890. The essay has two main parts. In the first part Rizal warns the Spanish colonial regime that revolution was almost inevitable if it did not treat the Philippines more fairly. In the second half of the essay, Rizal's analysis of global imperialism at the close of the nineteenth century results in his hypothesis that the United States might annex the Philippines. If the Philippines did manage to separate from Spain, by either peaceful or forcible means, Rizal understood too much about global imperialism at the end of the nineteenth century to be confident that the islands would be able to elude simply trading one imperial master for another. As the age of global imperialism came to a close, Rizal wrote, the great imperial powers—England, Germany, France, Holland, China—were grasping at the few remaining conquerable lands while they fought to retain those they already held.

Global imperialism in the East had provided an almost irresistible temptation to the nations of the West; as Rizal wrote, "the example is contagious, [and] covetousness and ambition are among the strongest vices" facing any industrializing country. Greed lured nations that had not previously joined the imperialistic race to snatch some of the few remaining lands. But the race belonged to the strong, and with the main European powers preoccupied in Africa or in holding their existing possessions, Rizal concluded that only the United States might be strong enough to enter the fray at this comparatively late date: "Perhaps the great American Republic, whose interests lie in the Pacific and who has no hand in the spoliation of Africa may some day dream of foreign possession. This is not impossible, for . . . Harrison manifested something of this sort in the Samoan question. But the territory of the States [is not] congested with inhabitants. . . . North America would be quite a troublesome rival, if she should once get into the business" (Rizal 1992, 287).

Rizal was right on nearly every count. America *did* have interests in the Pacific; the United States annexed Hawaii in 1898, and more territories would provide materials and markets for a rapidly expanding industrialism. It may have been true, relatively speaking, that "the territory of the [United] States [was not yet] congested with inhabitants," but in 1889, when Rizal wrote his essay, the frontier was only a year away from being declared "closed." Anglo America feared that Manifest Destiny was running out of territory rapidly. The apprehension that Manifest Destiny would end as westward settlement halted at the Pacific shore was a more critical factor than the actual population density; indeed, as Richard Slotkin notes, "As a purely material entity, the Frontier was far from closed [in 1890]. More public land would be taken up and brought into production between 1890 and 1920 than during the supposed heyday of the western frontier in the decades that followed passage of the Homestead Act (1862)" (Slotkin 1992, 30). The fear that the United States was running out of "free land" was, so to speak, groundless. It was the frontier's ideological value, representing the opportunity for boundless expansion, that gave the closing of the American frontier an ominous prospect. As I have shown in the introduction, advocates of American imperialism insisted that continuing colonial expansion was necessary to the maintenance of the national health. Imperialists cast the conquest of new territories as a critical venue for the exercise and triumph of collective masculine vigor as a crucial antidote to the indolence and feminizing effects of industrialization and national peace. The American frontier was officially declared closed by the 1890 U.S. Census, and by 1893 Frederick Jackson Turner mourned the passing of the frontier, declaring that its closing represented the end of an era that defined American nationalism. For Turner, the answer to the problem posed by the loss of the frontier was to take Manifest Destiny beyond the United States' continental boundaries: Turner "drew hope from the current call for a more assertive foreign policy, for an interoceanic canal, for enhanced sea power, '*and for the extension of American influence to outlying islands and adjoining countries*'" (Drinnon 1980, xiv; emphasis added). Although Turner did not specifically identify the Philippines as the United States' next "frontier," at roughly the same period and for roughly the same reasons, Frederick Jackson Turner and José Rizal, on their respective sides of the Pacific, saw a similar progression for U.S. expansionism.

Concluding his meditations on a Philippine revolution against Spain and another country—probably the United States—taking the Philippines over, Rizal predicted, "These and many other things may come to pass within something like a hundred years." Rizal severely underestimated the acuity of his own analysis; the revolution against Spain came a mere six years after the publication of his essay, and America's acquisition of the Philippines came only two years after that. Rizal was wrong, too, in his hope that the taking of colonies being "contrary to [America's] traditions" would stop the United States from acquiring the Philippines (Rizal 1992, 287). During his dealings with American representatives, in 1898 Emilio Aguinaldo bluntly asked American General Anderson "if the Philippines were to become 'dependencies' of the United States, to which the commander responded that in 120 years his country had yet to establish any colonies. 'I have studied attentively the Constitution of the United States and I find in it no authority for colonies, and I have no fear,' Aguinaldo concurred"—and was misled exactly as the Americans had intended (Miller 1982, 41–42). Aguinaldo, like Rizal, hoped that America's history as a postcolonial nation would prevent the United States from taking colonies of its own. For Rizal, this hope remained hypothetical because he did not live to see 1898. Aguinaldo staked the sovereignty of the First Republic on his faith in America's anticolonial foundation, and lost.

In "The Philippines a Century Hence," Rizal alludes to the racial prejudices of the Spanish colonial regime that designated as inferior indios with their "rather brown skins and faces with somewhat wide nostrils" (Rizal 1992, 277). Rizal rejects such attitudes, insisting "law has no skin nor reason nostrils" (278). But such declarations had little effect in the face of the racial prejudices of the time, and Rizal decries indios' internalization of colonial racism: "they [indios] were lowered in their own eyes, they become ashamed of what was distinctively their own, in order to admire and praise [w]hat was foreign . . . their spirit was broken and they acquiesced" (265). The Spaniards derided Philippine indios not only for their dark skin but also for their uncivilized, "savage" nature, the two factors, of course, being presumably indivisible. The ilustrados' acquisition of the markers of civilization—European clothes, education, mastery of several European languages—had little impact on Spanish attitudes toward indios. In the Wild West Indians, Rizal saw physiological features resembling indios': the "rather brown skins," the "somewhat wide nostrils," sculpted cheekbones, brown eyes. Rizal's admiration for the show Indians probably was influenced by his intuition of a racial confraternity between Indians and indios as well as by the show Indians' displays of equestrian and martial prowess. Imagining himself and his fellow indios as Indios Bravos probably had as much to do with imagining indios as being valiant *brown* warriors as it did imagining them valiant warriors: in declaring an imagined brotherhood with American Indians, Rizal turned the visual markers of his race into markers of racial pride rather than of racial inferiority, as the Spanish term connoted. Through Los Indios Bravos, Rizal healed the racial pride that Spanish colonialism had wounded and thus began the process of challenging indios' "acquiescen[ce]" to colonial subjugation.

The irony of Rizal's choice of the name Los Indios Bravos after seeing a speciously "authentic" show of Indian bravery is that Filipinos, too, would, only a few years hence, be displayed in similarly "authentic" exhibitions as a demonstration of the U.S. pacification of exotic, "savage" Filipinos. The exhibition of Indian prowess in the Wild West shows sought to firmly assert that Native Americans were no longer a threat to white settlement; similarly, the purpose of "ethnic" exhibits of Filipinos at the 1904 St. Louis World's Fair was to visually confirm the pacification of the Philippines and its exotic, unruly inhabitants as the expected outcome of the U.S. Manifest Destiny. Both the Wild West and the World's Fair functioned as sites of memory to proleptically inscribe the defeat of native peoples into history before that defeat was assured.

CHAPTER 2

Marketing Colonialism

LITTLE BROWN BROTHERS IN THE KODAK ZONE

ON JULY 4, 1902, U.S. President Theodore Roosevelt officially declared the Philippine-American War to be at an end. Roosevelt's declaration came more as a result of Americans' declining support for the war, especially following well-publicized accusations of American war atrocities, than because Filipino military resistance had actually ceased. (Filipino hostilities would in fact continue for several more years.) In 1903, William McKinley made his famous statement about assimilating the Philippines as the United States' God-given duty. After consulting the Almighty, McKinley decided that "there was nothing left for us to do but take them [the Philippines] all, . . . and uplift and civilize and Christianize them," and having made this decision, McKinley finally "slept soundly." "The next morning," McKinley continued, "I sent for the Chief Engineer of the War Department (our map maker) and told him to put the Philippines on the map of the United States . . . and there they are, and there they will stay" (de la Costa 1965, 219).

In this chapter, I will examine the "Philippine Reservation" of the 1904 World's Fair and the 1904 children's book *Brownies in the Philippines,* two American representations of Filipinos during the critical period marking the transition from the U.S. war for territorial acquisition to "peacetime" colonial administration. Both served a function similar to that of Buffalo Bill's Wild West: invoking the frontier as an imaginative territory for the renegotiation of American national identity through dramatized confrontations with and pacification of the savage aboriginal Other. The Wild West proleptically relegated Native American political sovereignty to the national past. Early colonial representations of Filipinos similarly identified Filipino natives with an atavistic prehistory that naturalized Filipinos' colonization by locating them at both the spatial and temporal periphery of American nation-building. Like Roosevelt's claim of American victory in the Philippines, both the 1904 World's Fair and *Brownies in the Philippines* imposed "pastness" (that is, historical closure) on a struggle that had not yet concluded. These popular cultural sites of memory cast the moment of American victory decisively into the past, where it could be comfortably revisited as history. As with McKinley's cartographic extension of the United States to incorporate the Philippines, both the World's Fair and *Brownies* brought into being a new and expanded American identity through quasi-official visual representations that ostensibly documented—but in fact helped to create—the pacification of the Philippines.

The previous chapter outlined the way in which Buffalo Bill's Wild West literally and figuratively made history through its dramatization of American nation-building on the frontier. Ultimately, the Wild West constructed the American frontier as an imaginative space, as L.G. Moses noted in his study of Wild West shows: "*The West,* the centuries-old term for the Anglo-American frontier, was a place beyond the horizon that could ignite the imaginations of vicarious explorers. Instead of a geographical expression, the West became, in the imaginations of Americans stranded in the cities and towns of the late nineteenth century, a wild region inhabited by even wilder humans, some white and brown, but most red" (Moses 1996, 4).

Richard Slotkin made the same point, observing that "in 1893 the Frontier was no longer a geographical place. . . . Its significance as a mythic space began to outweigh its importance as a real place" (Slotkin 1992, 61). The frontier, then, became an imaginative space in which and through which Americans defined themselves through conquest. From the earliest settler days on the U.S. eastern seaboard, Anglos had imagined the frontier both as free land available for conquest, and a bewildering, chaotic wilderness. Civilization transformed the wilderness into land that Anglo-Americans could understand and settle; the conceivable coincided with the conquerable.

This conflation of exploration and territorial conquest continued westward across the U.S. mainland and made the transpacific leap to the Philippines in 1898. In 1899, Frank D. Millett, a war correspondent for *Harper's Weekly* during the Philippine-American War, wrote:

> Few persons had more than a very hazy idea as to the geographical position of the Philippines until the exhilarating news of Dewey's victory brought out the atlases. . . . [T]he geographical position of [Manila] and of the group of islands of which it is the metropolis was about as vague in most minds as the situation of the last discovered irrigation area in Mars. . . . The reading public in the United States had more or less knowledge of the Hawaiian islands and of both Micronesia and Polynesia. . . . The Philippines, however, remained outside the kodak zone. (Vergara 1995, 1)

Millett's definition of the "kodak zone" makes explicit the ideological dynamic of the frontier. The frontier demarcated the boundary between the imaginable and the inconceivable in the American public consciousness, but did so within a context of territorial acquisition. Within the kodak zone,

Americans could identify geographical location, but, more important, they could conceptualize social, political, and cultural reality. Outside it, the Philippine frontier was alien to the point of being extraterrestrial. Millet's statement reveals a geographical curiosity, causally linked to imperial acquisition, that Americans of the period felt toward exotic locales.

Millet's use of the kodak zone as a metaphor for the extracontinental tropical frontier was not coincidental; by the late nineteenth century, photography had been mobilized in the service of U.S. imperialism both at home and abroad. World fairs and expositions offered visitors a kind of imaginary travelogue of exotic territories, as well as domestic cultural and industrial progress, through exhibits set up as a series of tableaux pitting primitivism against progress, superstition against science, savagery against discipline. These tableaux celebrated the ideology of Anglo-American racial and cultural superiority triumphing over nonwhite peoples. The expositions' ethnological exhibits became favorite subjects for photographic souvenirs. Photography itself, ostensibly a mechanical reproduction of an empirical fact, lent a presumptive reality to such souvenirs, giving visitors a factual confirmation of an exhibit's reality. Photographs of the living exhibits captured, both literally and figuratively, the essence of each display: its ideological import, not its ostensibly accurate representation of the day-to-day life of the exhibits' participants in their home environments.

Buffalo Bill's Wild West disseminated U.S. expansionism through the venue of popular entertainment. The Wild West's marketing of its nationalist agenda—initially, the United States defined as a nation through its conquest of American Indians and, later, the annexing of "strange peoples" representing newly acquired territories—sold the Anglo-American populace on expansionism as a constitutive part of American nationhood, an ideological accomplishment all the more effective because of the Wild West's success in making its audience personally identify with the show's ideological narrative of "winning a wilderness."[1]

Like the Wild West, world fairs and expositions increasingly displayed "strange peoples" from exotic lands in ethnographic exhibits. Such exhibits reveal tourism's partnership with imperialism: by exhibiting exotic peoples as living curiosities, contained and displayed to satisfy the audience's voyeuristic appetites, ethnographic exhibits figuratively brought the world to the United States in a metaphoric demonstration of the States' benevolent assimilation. Many exhibition layouts were designed to chart the progression from nonwhite primitivism to the triumph of Anglo-American/European civilization, as manifested in lavish monuments to the latest industrial and cultural developments. The effect of touring the exposition was significantly different from the effect of attending a Wild West performance. In the Wild West, those in the audience were passive receptors, the performers the active agents—the actors—of the show; in the expositions, ethnic peoples were contained in their exhibits, while the audience members were the active participants. By physically walking through the exhibits, tracing the ideological progression from primitivism to civilization, the typical visitor directly if unconsciously experienced the triumph of imperialism. Moreover, visitors to the exposition were able to interact with those displayed in ethnographic exhibits. However, while the modes of the audience's experience differed—the audience of the Wild West essentially passive, the fair attendee more active—the effect was the same: both experienced a sense of personal participation in the expansionist drama, the identity axis of nationalism activated through the visitors' sense of belonging to the national polity for which and through which such spectacles were constructed.

CREATING THE KODAK ZONE AT HOME: THE PHILIPPINE RESERVATION AND THE 1904 ST. LOUIS WORLD'S FAIR

The 1904 St. Louis World's Fair was part of a succession of world expositions celebrating the host country's "progress in all fields—not only in industry, trade, and transportation, but also in the arts, sciences, and culture" (Corbey 1993, 339). This rather abstract celebration of modern nationalism, however, inevitably developed into a promulgation of expansionism and imperialism.[2] Like other world's fairs of the early twentieth century, the St. Louis fair promoted the racial superiority of the American Caucasian race by celebrating the scientific, agricultural, manufacturing, commercial, and cultural achievements of the host country, in sharp contrast to the exhibitions of exotic and backward native peoples, including Native Americans, "Patagonian giants," African pygmies, Japanese Ainu aborigines, Canadian Kwakiutl Indians, and over one thousand Filipinos.[3] The fair's various exhibits, whether of domestic or exotic natives, encoded the ideology of the display: tableaux carefully crafted to promulgate a nationalist campaign in which progress was a euphemism for industrialization and colonialism.

The St. Louis fair was held to commemorate the Louisiana Purchase centenary, and a major ideological focus of the fair was the celebration of U.S. domestic expansionism and its extension to the newly acquired Philippines. One of the official publications of the exposition made the point explicitly, declaring that "the time is coming when the purchase and retention of the Philippine Islands will seem as wise to our descendants as does the Louisiana Purchase seem to us who live today" (Rydell 1984, 167). The Indian School Building, celebrating the civilization of the Native Americans, lay directly across Arrowhead Lake from the Philippine Reservation. The proximity of the Indian and Philippine exhibits, in addition to labeling the Philippine exhibit a reservation, linked the domestication of American Indians and Filipino

Indios. W. J. McGee, the head of the fair's anthropology department, asserted that "the Indian School Building . . . was 'designed not merely as a consummation, but as a prophecy; for now that other primitive peoples [that is, Filipinos] are passing under the beneficent influence and protection of the Stars and Stripes, it is needful to take stock of past progress as a guide to the future" (167). These statements clearly demonstrate the fair's construction as a site of memory, as the fair was deliberately fashioned to naturalize the annexation of the Philippines into the putatively linear history of Manifest Destiny. The Louisiana Purchase was already so far back in the American historical memory as to be ancient; to most Americans, it was hard to conceptualize the lands included in the Louisiana Purchase as not being a part of the United States. The acquisition of the Philippines was just one more step in the "natural" progression of American nationalist expansionism.

The Philippine Reservation was the keystone in the 1904 St. Louis World's Fair. It was one of the most popular, if not the most popular, of the St. Louis exposition's attractions; in fact, 99 percent of the fair's attendees visited the reservation (Rydell 1984, 170). Through well-staged visual tableaux, the reservation drew millions of curious Americans to vicariously experience the terra incognita of the Philippines and preached the gospel of Manifest Destiny in the United States' new tropical territory. The fair's object was to achieve the same effect for the Philippines that it had for the Louisiana Purchase: to naturalize the territorial acquisition of the Philippines so that the archipelago seemed to have been always already a part of the United States. The Philippine Reservation's tableaux of Filipinos moving from savagery to civilization attempted to shape the future of the American polity by visually bringing the Philippines in the present moment under the imagined aegis of the U.S. national past.

Popular support for the American colonial project in the Philippines had taken a beating owing both to the unexpected length of the Philippine-American War and to increasing reports of American war atrocities, which cast doubt over the putatively benevolent assimilation of the Philippines. The Philippine Reservation resuscitated popular support for the U.S. colonial administration of the Philippines now that the war had, at least by U.S. decree, been won. The American government realized the fair's potential for buttressing popular support for the government's colonial agenda and gave active support to the Philippine Reservation. Although by the early twentieth century other world fairs routinely included ethnic villages, Robert Rydell notes that the St. Louis fair "was . . . unique in having the full support of the federal government at the outset" (Rydell 1984, 168). William Howard Taft, civil governor of the Philippines during the early American colonial administration, supported the project because, he stated, "Filipino participation [in the fair] would be a very great influence in completing pacification and in bringing

Filipinos to improve their condition" (168).[4] The 1904 fair's ideological campaign to establish Filipino incapacity for political sovereignty and, therefore, the necessity of American colonial rule, was aimed at Filipinos as well as Americans. As the *Portland Oregonian* reported, "The Filipinos themselves learned from the St. Louis experience that they were not ready for self-government" (178). It is unclear why the Filipino participants of the ethnological exhibits would have learned from that experience in and of itself the lesson of Filipino incapacity for political sovereignty; it is likely that, like the Wild West's show Indians, the experience of being exhibited as racial and cultural curiosities, as well as the impression caused by the sheer numbers of visitors who came to see the ethnological exhibits and their relative material well-being, inculcated in the exhibition Filipinos a sense of cultural inferiority and hence, presumably, political inferiority. Thus the Philippine Reservation served the American colonial agenda on two levels: first, by creating a visual display emblematizing the triumph of American colonial improvement to millions of American visitors and, second, by inculcating in the exhibition's Filipino subjects a sense of American cultural and racial superiority. In other words, like the Wild West's show Indians, the exhibitions promulgated American imperialist ideology to both the exhibition audience and the exhibition subjects themselves. Thus the political and ideological affiliation between the American Indian and Filipino indio José Rizal had conceptualized became fully realized in the St. Louis fair's Philippine Reservation as Philippine indios and American Indians were cast as twin objects of a triumphalist imperial gaze.

The cover of a "Philippine Exposition" promotional brochure suggests the process of the colonial transformation of the Philippine savage: from the front cover photograph of a scowling native with exotic headdress to the disciplined Philippine scout standing at attention on the back cover.[5] The front cover of the brochure proclaims that the Philippine Exposition is "BETTER THAN A TRIP THROUGH THE PHILIPPINE ISLANDS." From the American government's perspective, it was indeed better than a trip through the Philippine Islands. Since the Philippines had not yet been completely pacified, a trip through the islands was a dangerous proposition. At the Philippine Reservation, on the other hand, millions of Americans could see Philippine natives contained, displayed, and laid out not only for easy inspection but also, more important, in carefully constructed tableaux of American colonial success ranging from "wild tribe" exhibits displaying exaggerated demonstrations of Filipino "savages" such as the "Bontoc headhunters" to the "Visayan Homestead," where Filipinos demonstrated their potential for civilization through a musical performance that culminated in a rousing rendition of the "Star Spangled Banner" (Stevens 1903, 146, 163). The Philippine Reservation brochure iconized the success of the U.S. civilization project in the transformation of the wild Filipino with his surly expression and outlandish headdress to the

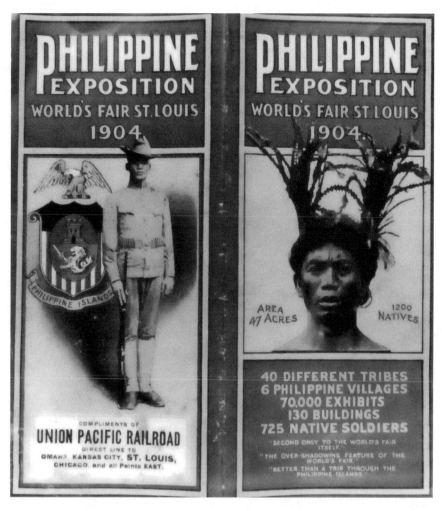

2. A promotional brochure touting the Philippine Exposition at the 1904 St. Louis World's Fair as "BETTER THAN A TRIP THROUGH THE PHILIPPINE ISLANDS." Photo courtesy of Eric Breitbart.

pseudo-military discipline of the Philippine constabulary, powerfully but economically asserting the domestication of the Filipino savage into a self-policing subordinate to American rule.

The verisimilitude of the St. Louis fair's ethnic villages reflects this period's growing fascination with the visually empirical and scientific in the service of imperialism. Several critics have noted the simultaneous, and ideologically linked, emergence of photography and imperialism during the nineteenth century.[6] At its foundation, photography's ideology of capturing its subject lent itself naturally to the colonial project. Citing Susan Sontag, Raymond Corbey explains: "'There is an aggression implicit in every use of the camera' . . . and taking pictures was indeed another means of taking possession of native peoples and their lands" (Corbey 1993, 362).[7] Photography was seen as objective, even clinical. "Because it was mechanical, photography was believed by many during this period to be a direct reflection of nature and reality, evidence in support of facts," writes Joanna Scherer, but those facts were highly suspect; the "invention [of photography] was aimed at replacing reality" (Scherer 1992, 33). The careful structuring of images of ethnic peoples and their containment, literal and figurative, in exhibitions such as the 1904 Philippine Reservation, created more than reflected reality. Photography's putative realism engendered what Vicente Rafael in his study of American photographs of Filipinos calls "an alibi of objectivity" through which "a photograph seems only to record what is in front of it while masking intentions" (Rafael 2000, 77).

Photography played a significant role in both the experience and promotion of the St. Louis fair and the fair's promulgation of American colonialism of the Philippines. Eric Breitbart states, "It is impossible to separate the photographs of the Filipinos at the 1904 fair and the organization of the Philippine Reservation from contemporaneous discussions, both in Congress and in the press, about Filipinos' suitability for self-government" (Breitbart 1997, 53). Brietbart argues that the ideological effect of the St. Louis photographs allowed photography to substitute for firsthand experience (9). The mechanical eye of the camera became a substitute for the human eye; the photograph became the eyewitness to the highly structured, staged/framed, ideologically loaded reality recorded by the camera's ostensibly objective mechanism. In the carefully staged presentation of the Philippines' various natives, the Philippine Reservation putatively offered fairgoers an imaginative travelogue of the Philippine archipelago in which each exhibit of natives functioned as a kind of colonial snapshot of the Philippine environment and peoples. Both the symbolic freezing of Filipino culture in the various exhibits and the freezing of Filipinos into photographed mementoes of the fair served to present Filipino natives as quaint holdovers from a barbarous past rather than as active agents in an ongoing struggle for their own future.

Laura Wexler describes in detail the popularity of photographs of ethnic peoples exhibited at the 1904 fair. Photographs of ethnic peoples were so popular and lucrative a business that fair officials strictly controlled the number and character of professional photographers authorized to take commercial photographs at the fair.[8] The newly introduced Brownie camera was the exception to this tight control of commercial photography. To promote the new Brownie Box camera, Eastman Kodak

> set up a company building on the [1904 St. Louis] fairgrounds. Hand-held cameras didn't need permits from the fair's press office, and were

exempt from other restrictions that made amateur photography so difficult at the 1893 Chicago fair, so amateur shutterbugs . . . could walk
around the fairgrounds snapping pictures to their hearts' content, posing
with the exotic Bagobos . . . or taking pictures of native dances. Photographs also gave people a chance to take home personalized, visual souvenirs, extending the fair's influence far beyond the millions of visitors
who passed through its gates. (Breitbart 1997, 45)

The Brownie Box camera, which helped popularize amateur photography for
the general populace but was especially marketed to children, helped facilitate
the figurative conquest of the frontier as an imaginative space. Just as the West
came to operate both literally and figuratively in the American imagination,
Millet sees the kodak zone as both a literal and figurative frontier. As with the
West, where a literal territory awaiting conquest provided a figurative page on
which American history would write itself, the Philippines' purported availability for conquest opened up the area simultaneously as an imaginative space
in which American identity could be re-envisioned. That renegotiation bol-
stered imperial claims to the Philippines. The kodak zone was the space in
which terra incognita became known and therefore claimed. Conceptualization entailed appropriation. The Philippine Reservation offered visitors to the
St. Louis Fair the opportunity to get to know the Philippines through its
natives and impose themselves upon a fabricated Philippine landscape, photographically capturing the strange people from our new possession. Thus the
kodak zone was a site where knowledge, consumption, and imperialism
coalesced in the linked interests of anthropology, colonialism, and tourism.

Bringing the Philippines into the Kodak Zone

As the United States was emerging as a colonial power, Palmer Cox
founded his own empire in popular culture through his Brownies series, in
which fey folk explored the world on the behalf of millions of American
youngsters whose geographical curiosity outstripped their opportunities for
literal travel. Over a twenty-year period, Cox published a series of Brownies
books detailing the Brownies' adventures "At Home," "Through the Union,"
"Abroad," and, in the only book that focuses on a single foreign country, "In
the Philippines." Cox described his Brownies as "imaginary little sprites . . .
[who] sport while weary households sleep, and never allow themselves to be
seen by mortal eyes."[9] Like fairies, gnomes, and elves, Cox's Brownies inhabit
an otherworldly plane but visit the human world. Cox parlayed the myth of
the Brownies into thirteen books, several serializations for both juvenile and
adult periodicals, and a popular play that ran for over five years throughout the
United States and Canada. Cox's Brownies series was so phenomenally popular that, in addition to making its author a rich man from the book royalties

alone, it enabled Cox to become one of the first copyrighted merchandisers for the emerging American consumer culture. Cox made a fortune licensing the Brownies to advertise over forty commercial products: everything from stove polish, to nails, to candy, to Ivory soap and Lion coffee (Cummins 1973, 101; Face 1999, 24). The Brownies became their own cottage industry, as Brownies merchandise featured the sprites on everything from children's games and toys to wallpaper, scarves, and stationery ("Palmer Cox" 1924; also Morgan 1996, 5536). However, the most famous Brownies commercial product was the Brownie Box camera.

Kodak's Brownie Box camera marketed amateur photography to American middle-class children. Eastman Kodak introduced the first box camera in 1900. Although the camera is sometimes said to be the namesake of its technical creator, Frank Brownell, Eastman aggressively marketed the Brownie Box camera through Palmer Cox's Brownies. Multicolored pictures of Brownies adorned the Brownie Box camera box itself (see figure 3). A full-page advertisement from the December 1900 issue of *St. Nicholas Magazine* (where Palmer Cox published many of his Brownie stories) bears the legend "Any school-boy or girl can make good pictures with one of the Eastman Kodak Co's Brownie Cameras," beneath which cluster half a dozen Brownies, including the easily recognizable Uncle Sam, the Policeman, and the Dude (see figure 4). An April 1902 Kodak advertisement depicts a young girl propping a Brownie Box camera on a desktop to take a picture of a Brownie, who poses perhaps a foot away (see figure 5). As in *Brownies in the Philippines,* photographic agency is plastic; the Brownies are both the agent and the subject of exploration-cum-photography, and with the Brownie Box camera, the Kodak advertisements implied, child photographers could overcome Cox's injunction against Brownie-human contact—indeed, the one-dollar price of a Brownie Box camera appeared to include a Brownie (or perhaps several) willing to pose for its owner to practice his or her picture-taking skills and/or to assist with technical tasks that might be challenging to the young photographer, such as changing the camera's film.

The Brownie Box camera represented a surprising symbiosis between two giants in popular culture merchandizing. While Palmer Cox jealously guarded his copyright to the Brownies image, he allowed the Eastman Kodak company to use the Brownie image without paying royalties. Conversely, Cox invented a new Brownie character whose function was to take pictures of the Brownie band's various adventures with—what else?—a Brownie Box camera. *Brownies in the Philippines* was the first Brownies offering to be published after the introduction of the Eastman camera, and Cox drew the Brownie Box camera into the series and made the Brownie photographer a central character.

The Brownie Photographer is a significant character: through him, Cox offered his juvenile audience all the ideological benefits of tourism without

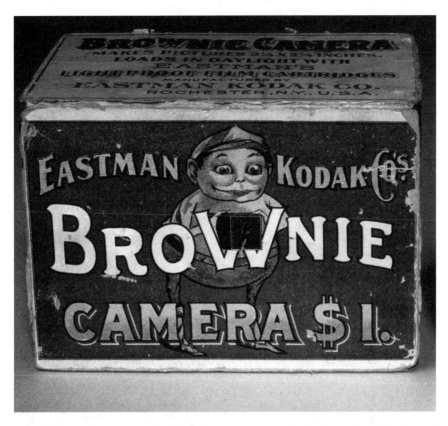

3. A full-page advertisement for the Brownie Box camera in the December 1900 issue of *St. Nicholas Magazine,* where Palmer Cox published many of his Brownie stories. Photo courtesy of the George Eastman House.

the inconvenience of actual travel. Thanks to his ever-present Brownie Box camera, the Brownie Photographer allowed Cox's juvenile fans to imaginatively insert themselves as conquering heroes in a carefully staged colonial frontier, just as thousands of adults did with their own trusty Brownie Box cameras in St. Louis. Like each separate exhibit on the Philippine Reservation, each chapter in *Brownies in the Philippines* presented a different tableau of Philippine reality. *Brownies in the Philippines* functioned as a print version of the Philippine Reservation. Through its pseudo-travelogue of the Philippine archipelago, *Brownies in the Philippines* presented a literary version of the St. Louis fair's ethnic villages. By offering homebound Americans the opportunity to vicariously capture native Filipinos in ostensibly authentic tableaux of colonial pacification, *Brownies in the Philippines* extended the nationalist project undertaken by the Philippine Reservation into the realm of children's literature.

4. In this 1900 Kodak advertisement, Brownies help young photographers load film, wind the key, and perform other maintenance on their Brownie Box cameras. Photo courtesy of the George Eastman House.

In the context of the Philippines, as the metaphor of the kodak zone reveals, getting to know a landscape was indivisibly joined with taking possession of it. Tourism was not merely travel for the sake of entertainment and/or education. The transition from uncharted territory to charted territory signaled not just an epistemological shift: the shift from terra incognita to known terrain signaled colonial domination. Putting the Philippines on Americans'

5. In the "Girl with a Brownie" 1902 Kodak advertisement, youngsters are offered the opportunity to practice their picture-taking skills with an obliging Brownie as their subject. Photo courtesy of the George Eastman House.

cognitive map secured the Philippines' position on the U.S. map as a territorial possession.

Palmer Cox's Brownies were point men for the simultaneous exploration and possession of the colonial frontier. Cox considered his Brownies altruistic, harmless, and disinterested in such concerns of the adult world as politics or profit; however, through "open[ing] up a new continent of faery into which the young entered by the millions," as one anonymous Cox biographer wrote, *Brownies in the Philippines* participated in the colonial enterprise through the fictional "mapping" of the United States' newest acquisition ("Palmer Cox," 1924). The putative purpose of *Brownies in the Philippines* is the entertainment of America's youngsters through the Brownies' amusing adventures abroad. But the real adventure of *Brownies in the Philippines* is imperial adventurism, the spectacle of the mythical Brownies innocently exploring the Philippines in a way that justifies and naturalizes American colonial pacification.

As a work of popular culture, *Brownies in the Philippines* reveals the organic connection between colonial domination and commercial development through its commodification of the tropical Other. The engagement with the Philippines in American popular culture demonstrates both the American fascination with the exotic territorial unknown and its conquest through exploration and photographic reification. *Brownies in the Philippines* enacts the convergence of the popularization of photography with the ideological construction of nationalism through the coded medium of juvenile fantasy. Millet's designation of the Philippines as "outside the kodak zone" is not an inconsequential metaphor. Photography developed concomitantly with the new science of modern anthropology, and both formed an ideological alliance with imperialism. As a mechanism of the imperial eye, photographs both created and witnessed colonial constructions of Filipino savagery, thus rationalizing the need for colonial control. In *Brownies in the Philippines*, Cox introduced two new characters to the Brownie band: the Rough Rider, based on staunch imperialist Teddy Roosevelt, and the Brownie Photographer, whose photographs bring the Philippines within the kodak zone.[10] Both characters were integral to the book's promotion of colonial ideology. The Rough Rider is the most central character in the book, often serving as the symbol for American expansionism across the archipelago. The Rough Rider enacts feats of colonial subjugation, which the Photographer both witnesses and disseminates through pictures. By chronicling the Brownies' adventures with the newly introduced Kodak Brownie Box camera, the Photographer lends a specious realism to the Brownies' adventures, strengthening the book's covert promotion of the colonial ideology that was similarly manifested—and likewise photographically chronicled—in the 1904 St. Louis World's Fair.

While the Brownies books usually feature a series of relatively disconnected adventures, *Brownies in the Philippines* follows an implicit plot that makes a case for American colonial rule. Cox portrays Filipino natives as embodiments of the racial stereotypes of the day and metaphorizes them as animals, thereby covertly advancing the American colonial agenda. In the course of the Brownies' ostensibly innocent, happy-go-lucky adventures through the Philippines, they map and pacify the wild, rebellious natives of the United States' newly acquired tropical territory. Because it is a children's book, produced for the entertainment as well as the edification of a juvenile audience, *Brownies in the Philippines* explicitly renounced the political motivations of the adult world. This self-conscious disavowal of ideological intentions ironically makes the book's ideological agenda more effective because it is a story—not, at least overtly, history—although I will argue that Cox's 1904 construction of a fictional Philippines is very much an act of creating history. Serialized in the *New York Herald* in 1903 and appearing in book form in 1904, *Brownies in the Philippines* was published after the United States' official declaration that the Philippine-American War had been (successfully) concluded. Like the St. Louis World's Fair, *Brownies in the Philippines* serves to naturalize the U.S. possession of the Philippines, making the new territory seem ancient in the American national memory. This was a particularly challenging task because Filipino insurgency continued despite official U.S. declarations that the Philippine-American War was over.

In its covert treatment of the Philippine-American War, *Brownies in the Philippines* repeatedly invokes and revokes Filipinos' nationalistic aspirations and simultaneously provides through its metaphors the ideological underpinnings for an American nationalism structured in contrast to and premised on the impossibility of a meaningful Filipino nationalism. U.S. policy at the time required the Philippine-American War to be over, to be history. *Brownies in the Philippines* invokes Philippine history in order to impose closure on it, to make it a narrative of past events rather than ongoing rebellion. But as we will see, Cox reveals anxieties about the "overness" of the Philippine-American War that he cannot quite conquer through the Brownies' amusing antics. *Brownies in the Philippines* operates as a site of memory both in what it reveals and what it obscures in its attempt to make history.

Although according to Cox's mythology the Brownies are innocent of any political agenda, Cox establishes his collusion with American imperialism in the very first illustration of *Brownies in the Philippines*. A gallery of the chief Brownie characters, including the Uncle Sam Brownie, the Rough Rider, the Dude, and the Policeman, appears at the top of the book's first page. These figures, respectively symbolizing the American nation, its presidential executive, industry, and penal control, form a panoply in support of American "EXPANSION." The book portrays the Brownies as stand-ins for American colonial agents, both subduing Filipino natives and insisting on America's determination to stay the colonial course, despite (here, comic) native opposition. The Brownies, whose name supposedly derives from their brown skin, ironically play the part of Anglo-Saxon conqueror to Filipino natives, who, in Cox's portrayal, do not even quite obtain human status. The Brownies boast a remarkably diverse democracy for the time, including among their band non-white characters such as the "Red Indian" and "the Chinaman." Their (relative) ethnic diversity notwithstanding, the Brownies literally carry the banner of expansionist ideology, with its equal ties to capitalist exploitation and racism. The Brownies simultaneously explore and claim a new colonial territory by implicitly disenfranchising Filipinos, popularly known as America's "little brown brothers." The significance of the ethnically heterogeneous Brownies' confrontation with Filipino "brownies" is that it is through the process of imperial domination that the United States' increasingly diverse ethnic groups unify into a coherent body politic in opposition to a racialized savage Other.

Although the Brownies' band is made up of characters representing several different countries, critics regard their mix as manifesting a definitively American democratic character. Cox's main characters were largely identified by visual cues denoting nationality, profession, or ethnicity—for example, the Dude, the Sailor, the Fisherman, the (American) Indian, the Cop, the China-man, Uncle Sam, the Eskimo, etc. Although Cox took the idea for the

6. Flanked by the Rough Rider and the Policeman, the Uncle Sam Brownie hefts Old Glory flying the expansionist banner.

Brownies from Scottish folklore, the Brownies' diversity, combined with their nonhierarchical society, caused many critics to see the Brownies as a metaphor for American democracy and diversity. Despite the existence of such characters as an Uncle Sam Brownie, a John Bull Brownie, a Policeman Brownie, and even a King Brownie, the band had no political leader.[11] Critics hailed the Brownies as a particularly American democracy. As an article in the July 25, 1924, *New York Times* put it, the Brownies "presented, in their own terms, the American Scene, as HENRY JAMES would have called it" ("Palmer Cox" 1924). As recently as the 1970s, critics still saw in the Brownies a positive embodiment of American democracy. Roger Cummins observes, "the world of the Brownies not only is utopian but embodies characteristics commonly associated with the American dream. . . . [T]he Brownies believe in working for the common good while retaining their individuality, and their efforts result in felicity: the Brownies embody the American dream of combining individualism with the idea of good society" (Senick 1991, 76). David Kunzle adds, "Even disregarding its internationalism, we can view the pluralistic, unstratified, leaderless Brownie society as a miniature ideal democracy, the kind towards which the United States was supposedly striving and, in the belief of many, nearly if not actually achieving" (Kunzle 1975, 455).

While critics commonly lauded Cox for creating in the Brownies a working idealization of American democracy, they also hailed Cox's relatively liberal stance on ethnic diversity. Again, critics affirmed the Brownies' ethnic diversity as being distinctively American and positive. Karin Face remarks that the Brownies' ethnic diversity "reflect[ed] the immigration patterns in America at the time," and Wayne Morgan makes the same point (Face 1999, 24; Morgan 1994, 28). The Brownies' ethnic diversity did not simply provide ethnic variety for variety's sake; it was an integral asset in the success of their democracy. Roger Cummins asserts, "Through the Brownies a child learned that it was possible for a group of disparate members . . . to live together in harmony. . . . The very differences among the Brownies constitute a major source for the gaiety and happiness of the band" (Cummins 1973, 112). The presentation of "the Brownie American and the Brownie Chinaman . . . as equal and compatible partners in improving and exploring the world" was relatively liberal for the time (Kunzle 1975, 456).

But there were telling limits to the Brownies' much-touted diversity. The Brownies were all male, and the ethnic group most tellingly absent from the band was African Americans. Likewise, Filipinos are not represented within the group, although Cox introduced two new characters in *Brownies in the Philippines*. It would have made sense to add a Filipino Brownie to the band in the course of their adventures across the archipelago; however, as I will be arguing throughout this chapter, Cox perceived Filipinos—and African Americans for that matter—as "other," outside the bounds of what it was possible to bring together in a happy egalitarian community. For Cox, neither Negroes nor Filipinos attained the status of other humans and thus did not qualify for Brownie status. The exclusion of a Filipino Brownie reveals the lie in the American benevolent assimilation of the Philippines. The previous chapter outlined the ways in which the American Indian provided prefabricated stereotypes for the transplantation of imperialist attitudes and policies from the U.S. mainland to the Philippines. As *Brownies in the Philippines* illustrates, African Americans provided the other main source of already established visual and cultural/racial stereotypes that justified Anglo-American colonial rule in the Philippines.[12]

Colonial Encounters with "Faces Dark with Sun and Crime"

One of Cox's primary rules prohibited Brownies from interacting with humans, so one would not expect the Brownies to meet native Filipinos during their adventures. It is hard to promote colonial ideology, however, without any natives to colonize. In *Brownies in the Philippines*, Cox breaks his rule prohibiting contact with humans, thereby implying that Filipinos are not, in fact, human.

Cox negotiates this problem of Brownie/human contact in two different ways. In many episodes, he creates animal stand-ins for native Filipinos, an examination of which will follow. He also in two episodes depicts Filipinos as Negroid humans, a group that was, within the racist ideology of the time, outside the purview of the strictly human. There is an ethnic group of Filipinos with African features. Named *Negritos* by the Spaniards for their black skin, they are now often referred to as Aetas and generally live on Luzon and some islands in the Visayas, including Negros, but they are a small ethnic minority. In

Brownies in the Philippines' imaginative travelogue, the *only* native Filipinos the Brownies meet are Negroid; the Brownies do not encounter a more ethnically typical Filipino or indio, much less the more Europeanized Tagalogs or Visayans (see figure 8).[13] The probability that visitors would encounter a tribe of Negritos in their travels through the Philippines is real but slight. The chances that, in two encounters with native Filipinos, both times the natives would be Negritos, of whom there were only thousands total, as opposed to indios or mestizos, of whom there were millions, are highly unlikely. Given Cox's dedication to researching lands abroad to achieve geographical and cultural realism in his books—to the extent of making the long journey to the Philippines to do research—his racial selectivity in his depiction of native Filipinos is ideologically significant. The Wild West demonstrated a similarly selective representation of "the" Filipino: the "Strange People from Our New Possessions" photograph used as a promotional picture for the Wild West featured a group of Negroid natives, presumably Negritos, against a tropical background of palm trees and a nipa hut. This photograph was particularly significant because the men pictured were not performers in the Wild West. Their purpose was to represent Filipinos, not to represent performers in the show.

In both the book and comic strip versions of *Brownies in the Philippines,* Cox portrayed Filipino natives as stereotyped Negroes with thick lips, broad noses, wooly hair, comically surprised expressions, and grass skirts, thereby playing on popular racist stereotypes of Africans and African Americans. (These stereotypes, deployed specifically in the context of the American colonization of the Philippines, were depicted in May's 1899 political cartoon for the *Detroit Journal,* "THE WHITE MAN'S BURDEN." See figure 9.) In two episodes, the Brownies encounter Negroid Filipinos whom Cox implicitly presents as being typical Filipino natives. In portraying the typical Filipino as black, Cox evokes a racist argument for subjugation: the dusky of skin were savage, childlike, literally un(en)lightened, morally and mentally regressive, and thus in need of control by the more morally and mentally evolved, enlightened whites.

The fourth chapter relates the Brownies' encounter with the natives from the Visayan region. On the island of Romblon, the Brownies decide

> A native chief to serenade,
> In hopes the music they possessed
> Would serve to soothe the savage breast,
> And cause, perhaps, his heart of stone
> To melt into a softer tone. (Cox 1904, 22)

The Brownies choose music that is allegedly universal in its appeal.

> Said one: "The sweetest airs we find
> So popular with humankind,
> We'll play, as lightly as a feather

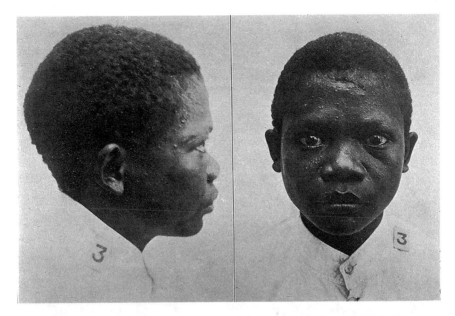

7. Negrito from Bataan Province, Luzon. Photo courtesy of Enrique de la Cruz.

In solo parts, then all together,
And with a crash that's sure to bring
Applause from every living thing." (22)

The Brownies' Romblon serenade, then, is a musical version of "E Pluribus Unum," which they anticipate will not only draw "applause from every living thing" but also, more important, "soothe the savage breast" of the Romblon natives. The serenade here is in the service of native pacification. Cox's description of the Rombloños portrays the natives as "dusky souls" who are, by nature, savagely simplistic: "nothing could those men delight / Except, perhaps, a feast or fight" (26). Although the Brownies assert that they will play a symphony made up of all "the sweetest airs we find / So popular with humankind," what they actually play for the Romblon natives, according to an accompanying illustration, is "Hail to the Chief." Their serenade is not an appeal to a universal appreciation for music, but an assertion of the U.S. government as embodied in its chief executive. In the illustration depicting the Brownies' performance of "Hail to the Chief," the Rough Rider Brownie— added to the band in this book—plays, literally, a central position in this musical indication that the power of the United States is advancing into the Philippines. As the Rough Rider Brownie was based on the current U.S. president, Teddy Roosevelt, the Brownies' rendition of "Hail to the Chief," in which the Rough Rider Brownie occupies a front-and-center position, is particularly significant.[14]

8. Portrait of Emilio Aguinaldo, a "civilized" Filipino.

Cox depicts the Rombloños' reception of the Brownies' serenade on page 27. Although Cox ascribes a putative realism to the scene by locating the Rombloños in a realistically drawn nipa hut, the Rombloños themselves, their "dusky souls" manifested by dusky faces, and their look of comic astonishment when confronting the Brownies' well-intentioned musical offering, are pure imperialist fantasy (see figure 11). In fact, the resemblance between the Negroid Filipino in "THE WHITE MAN'S BURDEN" political cartoon and Cox's portrait of the Rombloños is remarkable. Cox's Rombloños are the more

9. "The White Man's Burden," an 1899 political cartoon in the *Detroit Journal*. Image courtesy of Jim Zwick.

comic—contemptibly so—because they do not appreciate the Brownies' benevolent intentions. Although the island's birds were delighted by the Brownies' symphony, the chief and his followers misinterpret the Brownies' serenade as "an insult of the deepest dye," and hail rotten eggs and dead rats down upon the Brownies' hapless heads (Cox 1904, 28). The Rombloños' retributive "hail" of eggs and dead rats is not only a protest against the Brownies' cacophonous musical offering; it is a direct repudiation of a metaphorical invasion.[15]

In the book's eighteenth episode, Cox again employs stereotypes of African Americans to underscore the barbarity and otherness of the Filipinos. On the island of Negros, the Brownies decide to try native clothing in deference to the Philippines' "killing heat" (Cox 1904, 127). Although Cox's introductory description of "Native Costume" focuses somewhat titillatingly on its scantiness ("The native costume, as a rule, / Takes little cotton from the spool"), he makes it clear that such skimpy clothing is in accord with the

10. "Hail to the Chief" in *Brownies in the Philippines*.

island's climate ("what [the Brownies] lose by naked knees, / To say the least, they get in breeze"). But the Brownies do not simply borrow the basic native garments; they take on elaborate costumes, complete with turbans, jewelry, and native weapons. This episode is more about the Brownies' adventure as vicarious natives than it is about relieving their heat prostration. While the individual Brownies retain enough of their visual markers to make them recognizable once they are in native costume (for example, the Fisherman retains

So tunes that brought the tears in showers
From those who lived through lawless hours,
Were blown around that hut so high,
Nor brought the moisture to an eye;
In fact, the chief and people near
For Brownie music had no ear.

11. Rombloños' reception of the Brownies' serenade in *Brownies in the Philippines*.

his creel and rod, and the Uncle Sam Brownie's wraparound skirt is made of Stars-and-Stripes material), Cox's visual transformation of the Brownies focuses on racial stereotypes of Filipino natives, clearly signaling to his young readers Filipinos' uncivilized nature, their savagery, their outlandish other-ness. (The racial stereotyping Cox introduces in the illustrations moves even beyond clothing and ornaments; one newly bedecked Brownie has suddenly sprouted a wide Afro hair-do [129]). In addition to taking up native arms as part of their costumes, the Brownies visually remind readers of native Filipinos' supposed propensity for war and violence by taking on even more disturbing ornamentation. In addition to taking up a sword, the Uncle Sam Brownie dons a small, apparently human skull strung on a necklace. On the book's first page, Cox presented a sign warning "LOOK OUT FOR HEAD-HUNTERS." The Uncle Sam Brownie's skull necklace in the Negros episode reasserts the stereotype that Filipino natives are cannibals, those most barbarous of savages.

Completely outfitted in their new costumes, the Brownies continue their travels, only to run up against another encampment of natives. We first see the fence of the native camp, over which bristles an alarming display of spears and other weapons. Three skulls, impaled on pikes, rise above the fence, scalplike topknots of hair flying in the breeze in a travesty of the flag a "civilized" fort would fly. The natives soon show themselves above the top of their fence, revealing "faces, dark with sun and crime" (131). Cox's narrative description corroborates the illustration's portrayal of the natives' bloodthirstiness as their defining characteristic:

> . . . shining weapons drew each eye
> That plainly told of danger nigh,
> And by the nature of each blade
> They feared that murder was their trade.
> The executioners were there
> . . . [with] their knives—broad, bright, and bare,
> And always found with space allowed
> For them in every native crowd. (130)

Before the natives have even shown their faces, Cox characterizes them as "executioners" whose "trade" was "murder." The Brownies do not wait to discover if the natives mean them harm: the iconography of violence surrounding them precludes any meaningful encounter.

> . . . [E]ven were they best of men,
> The Brownies had no wishes then
> To give or take a friendly hand
> While bearing out their scheme as planned.
> [The] flourishing of weapons gave

Some hints about an early grave,
Which put, indeed, another face
At once upon the Brownies' case. (132)

The Brownies succumb to their fear of "an early grave" even though part of
Cox's Brownie mythology is the rule that Brownies can come to no serious
harm. The Brownies briefly entertain the idea that the natives might be the
"best of men," but their "faces, dark with sun and crime," and their "language
wild" cannot be trusted. The fact that the Brownies have heavily armed themselves in this episode apparently does not make the natives' weapons less
threatening; of course, the implication is that the Brownies' weapons are part
of their costumes—part of the episode's "fun"—whereas the natives' weapons
are for deadly use rather than for adornment. If the Brownies bear arms, it is
simply another aspect of their love of dressing up. If the Negros natives bran-
dish arms, it is a direct manifestation of their murderous natures. It is Cox's
and the Brownies' interpretation of the natives' appearance that literally and
figuratively "puts another face" on the Filipinos.

Like Cox's depiction of the Rombloños, the illustration on page 132
depicting the Negros natives emerging over the top of their fence portrays the
natives according to widely held Negro stereotypes. By constructing Filipino
natives as Negroid savages, Cox grafted preexisting racial stereotypes about
Africans/African Americans onto Filipinos to emphasize their purported inferiority and savagery. Cox's conflation of Filipinos with Africans, however, still put
him in the problematic position of having the Brownies encounter humans, a
violation of one of his basic Brownie rules. Thus Cox ran up against what Albert
Memmi calls imperialism's "intolerable contradiction": if the colony could be
emptied of its troublesome natives, it would be a paradise—until "the colonial-
ist realizes that without the colonized, the colony would no longer have any
meaning" (Memmi 1965, 66). Apart from the two episodes depicting brief
brushes with human natives, Cox solved the problem of the Brownies interacting with humans by allegorizing Filipinos as animals, which resolved Memmi's
colonial contradiction by simultaneously effacing and upholding American
colonialism in the Philippines. By removing most natives from his narrative,
Cox was able to obscure American colonization of the Philippines simply
because we see few Filipinos being subdued or ruled. At the same time, Cox
promoted American colonial rule of the Philippines by having the Brownies
subdue, control, or engage in battles with animal stand-ins for native Filipinos.

Cox's portrayal of Filipinos as animals aligned with racist stereotypes of
the time. As the nineteenth century gave way to the twentieth, American
politicians, military personnel, and writers often portrayed Filipinos as animals. American soldiers and commanders alike bestialized Filipinos during the
Philippine-American War. A private from Utah wrote home to his family,

"The old boys will say that no cruelty is too severe for these brainless monkeys. . . . With an enemy like this to fight, it is not surprising that the boys should soon adopt 'no quarter' as a motto, and fill the blacks full of lead before finding out whether or not they are friends or enemies" (Wexler 2000, 29; also Miller 1982, 189). Even a generation after the Philippine-American War, bestial metaphors for Filipinos persisted in narratives of the Philippine-American War. In 1931 George Durston, describing Gen. John Pershing's campaign during the war, depicted the Moros of Mindanao as "the little brown men whose tantrums have caused us so much trouble. . . . The Moros are an undersized race and seem easily able to live anywhere a snake can live . . . They slide under the dense tropical foliage of their forests, shadows among the shadows" (Netzorg 1985, 134).

Durston portrayed the "Igorrotes" of Central Mindanao as dogs, writing "They are the famous head hunters of whom you have read. They are untamed, relentless savages, living in low huts scarcely larger than good-sized dog kennels. . . . They are . . . like mongrel dogs that snap and bite and tear at the hand that tries to feed them" (quoted in Netzorg 1985, 134–35).[16] A war correspondent for the *Philadelphia Ledger* summed up such attitudes regarding Filipinos, reporting in November 1900 that American soldiers held "the Filipino, as such, . . . little better than a dog, a noisome reptile in some instances, whose best disposition was the rubbish heap" (Miller 1982, 211).

Cox's animal natives both drew from and fed racist stereotypes. Although in most books in the Brownies series Cox drew his animals as affable, silly, or placid-looking, in *Brownies in the Philippines* Cox gave them more sinister characteristics: an ant army, a monkey congress full of "rascals," etc. Cox's characterization of Philippine animals reproduced racist stereotypes of Filipinos of the time—stereotypes that rationalized American colonial control.

Simian metaphors for Filipinos were particularly significant at a time when Filipino "insurgents" continued to resist American pacification. For instance, Gen. Adna Chaffee's 1903 sneering reference to Filipinos as "gorillas" gave voice to his frustration over Filipinos' maddeningly effective campaign of guerilla warfare, one which stubbornly continued despite Roosevelt's 1902 declaration that the Philippine-American War was over (Drinnon 1980, 321).

In *Brownies in the Philippines'* fifth chapter, the Brownies interrupt a "strange convention" of monkeys on the island of Tawi Tawi:

A strange convention seemed to be
In session there, on rock and tree.
Perhaps they met to frame new laws,
Or mend the old, too full of flaws (Cox 1904, 30)

This "strange convention" is not merely a simple social gathering: it is a monkey congress or parliament, a legislative body attempting to reform a hopelessly flawed government. The monkey congress references the American imperialist belief that Filipinos, "monkeys without tails," according to a song popular among American soldiers during the war, were patently incapable of self-government (Patajo-Legasto 1993a, 2). Cox made this point clear by changing the episode from the serialized to the book version. The Tawi Tawi monkey episode also appeared in the comic strip version of *Brownies in the Philippines* (*New York Herald,* November 22, 1903), but without the element of Philippine political allegory. The *Herald* version simply depicts the Brownies discovering a group of monkeys sitting in trees and behind rocks. The cartoon's caption states that the Brownies, upon discovering the monkeys, decided that "while such a chance was nigh / To get some showman his supply." There is no mention of the monkeys framing laws, as there is in the book version. By changing the Tawi Tawi monkey episode from the *New York Herald*'s simple group of monkeys in the jungle to the book version's "strange convention," Cox deliberately emphasized the episode's political allegory: from the early American colonial view, a native Filipino congress attempting to frame a working legislature was an event as ludicrous as monkeys trying to act like men. Cox makes clear the allegory of bestial Filipinos "aping" their betters by emphasizing both the connections and crucial distinctions between the monkeys and men:

> Said one: "Those objects [monkeys] we survey,
> Those freaks of nature, let me say,
> From which they tell us lordly man
> Through evolution's stages ran,
> Would in the market bring a price
> That would be counted something nice.
> . . . . that old rascal hiding there,
> Who carries such a mop of hair,
> And crop of whiskers round his chin,
> And seems to man so near of kin,
> Would bring a showman lasting fame,
> In any country you could name." (Cox 1904, 30–31)

The monkeys' freakish but misleading similarity to men convinces the Brownies that the monkeys would bring a high price; what makes these monkeys so valuable is not just that they are exotic tropical animals, but that they are so uncannily reminiscent of real men. Cox's depiction of Filipino natives as monkeys, the evolutionary precursors of "real" men, appealed to a pseudoscientific facet of colonial ideology that argued that evolutionarily regressive savages were incapable of self-government and therefore required government by their more evolved, white brethren. W. J. McGee, one of the chief officers of the 1904 St. Louis World's Fair, articulated such assumptions in "National

Growth and National Character" (1904), arguing that "it is the duty of the strong man to subjugate lower nature" (Rydell 1984, 161). By identifying Filipino natives with an atavistic prehistory (that is, as simian precursors to "real" humans), Cox naturalizes Filipinos' subordination by positioning them at both the spatial and temporal periphery of modern (American) nation-building.

While posing the monkeys as evolutionary throwbacks, Cox simultaneously alluded to the Philippine-American War. Cox implicitly compares the monkeys to Filipino revolutionaries, calling the monkeys "fighting rogue[s]" whose "struggles might be seen / Through open space or foliage green" (Cox 1904, 34, 32). Cox also notes how "bitter was the pill. . . . [for those who] for a moment seemed to see / The open door to liberty," an oblique reference to Filipino revolutionaries' near successful completion of their overthrow of Spanish colonial rule—a revolution that would have found its completion had the Americans not intervened in 1898. Despite Cox's momentary sympathy for the "stubborn creatures [who] firmly stood / Against departure from the wood," the Brownies truss the monkeys securely, confining them in coffle lines, on leashes, or in cages. The Brownies meditate upon the monkeys' inherently intractable characters by pitying those who "tr[y] to plant within [the monkey's] breast / Some traits and feelings of the best" (35). This invocation of the white man's burden concludes that in the end, confinement is in the native creatures' best interest. The Brownies decide:

> . . . "We'll use some tact,
> As self-appointed agents act,
> Secure the best, then take them down
> And leave them at the nearest town,
> And in the interests of the trade
> Some well-deserving merchant aid;
> They'll lead a life unknown before,
> Have food and water at their door,
> And do much better, never fear,
> Than cracking nuts on branches here." (31–32)

Here Cox perfectly metaphorizes American colonialism's self-image: as "self-appointed agents" the Americans, by capture and colonial control, would give native Filipinos a better life than Filipinos had the capability to imagine, much less obtain on their own. That the project would also benefit "some well-deserving merchant," a stand-in for American commercial interests in the Philippines, was a seemingly accidental windfall.[17]

Cox rationalized the Brownies' seizure of the monkeys for profit by transforming their capture from a simple market transaction into a pseudoscientific project in zoological taxonomy, thus bolstering the implication that the Brownies' actions are a public service rather than simple opportunism. When

12. "Howling Kicker" in *Brownies in the Philippines.*

the Brownies capture their quarry, they taxonomically categorize them. Sorting the monkeys alphabetically, the Brownies label each "with its tag marked A B C, / To note its type or pedigree." At first the Brownies appear to be pursing their putatively scientific agenda by labeling the monkeys by simian type—for example, "ape," "baboon," "chimpanzee," "gorilla." But quasi-scientific categorization quickly devolves into commentary on the monkeys' characters rather than their genus: "howling kicker" (for *H*), "tough species" (for *T*), and "bald-headed rascal" (what letter that designates is unclear) (Cox 1904, 34–36). The breakdown of the Brownies' seemingly rational taxonomy into name-calling inadvertently replicates the tendency of scientific thought during this period to slide into explicit self-serving racism. Moreover, the monkeys' more colorful designations reveal that their forcible restraints and their labeling are intended to control their rebelliousness, not to represent an expedient packaging for scientific specimens.

The Brownies' taxonomic categorization of the monkey congress also allegorizes the American colonial project in another way; at the time that *Brownies in the Philippines* was published, the American government had just completed a census of Filipinos as a measure both to assure the public at home that the archipelago had been pacified and to distinguish between "wild" and

13. "Bald-Headed Rascal" in *Brownies in the Philippines.*

"civilized" Filipinos. In his analysis of the 1903 census of the Philippine Islands, Vicente Rafael has noted that, on one hand, the census "attempted to constitute a population by enumerating the totality of heterogeneous peoples and recording them onto a grid of reified categories. On the other hand, the census sought to affix to each member of the population an essentialized, regulated, and therefore retrievable identity" (Rafael 2000, 31). The Brownies' categorization of the Tawi Tawi monkeys enacts a comic version of the 1903 census. The monkey coffle line, with each monkey bound or caged and labeled, simultaneously identifies and erases the monkeys' heterogeneity: although the simian group began, like the Filipino people, as one group, they were quickly broken into "scientifically" determined samples. Cox's opening metaphoric comparison of the monkeys to inept legislators (the monkey congress) and then to Filipino insurgents (the "fighting rogues" who embody the guerilla/gorilla pun) set up the capture and taxonomic discipline of the monkeys as acts of allegorical colonial conquest.

Cox's construction of the Tawi Tawi monkeys as bestialized versions of Filipino insurgents was relatively subtle. However, he presents an overt representation of Filipino insurgency in the ant army of Sulu (chapter 14 of *Brownies in the Philippines*). Whereas in the Tawi Tawi/monkey congress episode Cox primarily focused on Filipinos' "freakish" attempt at self-government, and only secondarily on the Filipinos' military efforts to secure independence, the Sulu ant army episode focuses on military resistance. Cox makes a brief allusion to the literal conflict to which the ant battle refers. As the Brownies catch up an assortment of native arms, Cox notes, "Such weapons in the rebel lines / Would have been prized like diamond-mines" (Cox 1904, 102).

> The band on Sulu soon got sight
> Of ants so noted for their bite.
> They marched in rows and wheeled in line
> Like soldiers out for practice fine. . . .
> While in the rear, with even stride,
> Advanced the rest in columns wide. . . .
> The ants now seemed to nothing lack
> But Brownie blood, and made attack. (Cox 1904, 105, 100–101)

The ants' raison d'être is to make war on the Brownies, without provocation or rational cause. Although in the Tawi Tawi/monkey congress episode Cox made that brief, albeit condescending, sympathetic allusion to the Filipinos' desire to be simply left alone, even if only to pursue their own laughable attempts at self-government, he shows no such sympathy for the Filipinos fighting for their freedom. Rather, Cox's conclusion is that the ants attack out of their essential, violent nature.

Cox describes the Brownies' battle with the Sulu ants in surprisingly graphic terms.

> . . . [T]hough oft [the Brownies] cleared a space,
> Still other [ants] quickly took the place,
> So little profit came from stroke
> Or shooting thousands into smoke.
> It seemed, indeed, a waste of skill
> To string them on a spear, until
> They hung as trophies, red and raw,
> Like berries on a summer straw (102–3)

The Brownies' battle against the ant army violates another of Cox's governing rules of Browniedom: the injunction against their engaging in violence of any kind. It was a point about which Cox felt so strongly that he repeated it in an interview: "Harmless and helpful. . . . Harmless and helpful. That's what the Brownies are" (Senick 1991, 67).[18] Cox explicitly addressed the issue of violence and bloodshed in another interview, stating, "there must be no death and pain. The children will find pain and suffering enough as they go on through life. The Brownies, you know, never give pain, nor do they ever suffer real pain. . . . I would let the cat go hungry rather than have the mouse eaten. It is time enough for children when they get big to learn that a reckoning must be made with suffering and bloodshed" (Cummins 1973, 85, 114–15).[19] Cox's insistence on the Brownies' pacific nature, and his refusal to expose children to the distressing realities of violence and bloodshed, give particular significance to his descriptions of the Brownies "shooting thousands into smoke" and "string[ing the Sulu ants] on a spear, until / They hung as trophies, red and raw, / Like berries on a summer straw." The accompanying illustration shows two Brownies spitting as many as five and six ants at a time on their spears, while the ants, with mouths open, eyes staring, and legs waving, appear to be shrieking and writhing in pain.

The resolution of the Sulu ant army episode confirms its allegorization of the Philippine-American War. Despite the superior skills of the Brownies, the ants are simply too numerous to defeat, a dynamic that replicated the Americans' experience against Filipino insurgents, as demonstrated in one American soldier's complaint in 1899 that "there are so many [Filipinos] that, no matter how many we kill or capture, it doesn't seem to lessen their number" (Foner 1986, 317). Routed by the sheer size of the ant army, the Brownies flee, eventually taking refuge in a pond. Strengthened by reinforcements, the ants, unable to attack the Brownies in the water, surround the pond. Despite the fact that the Brownies are badly outnumbered—the episode's final illustration shows thirty-seven Brownies in the pond surrounded by thousands of ants, with thousands more swarming down the hillside—the ants finally realize that the Brownies have the resources to hold out indefinitely.

> At last this thought put [the ants] to rights:
> That they were up against some sprites
> Whose staying power would doubtless last
> When they themselves to dust had passed.
> So off they marched, with anger tossed,
> Because of time and patience lost. (Cox 1904, 106)

Two Brownies who figure prominently in the illustrations of the Sulu ant episode underscore its metaphoric meaning. The Uncle Sam and Rough Rider Brownies seldom appear together centrally in *Brownies in the Philippines,* but the first page of "Attacked by Ants" shows the Rough Rider and Uncle Sam together, in the central foreground of the illustration, facing an ant army

THE BROWNIES ON SULU.

So little profit came from stroke
Or shooting thousands into smoke.
It seemed, indeed, a waste of skill
To string them on a spear, until
They hung as trophies, red
    and raw,
Like berries on a summer
    straw,

14. Brownies battle the Sulu ants in *Brownies in the Philippines.*

thousands strong. In the episode's last illustration the Rough Rider and Uncle Sam appear again in the foreground. The Filipino insurgents, represented by the ant army, give up only when they reluctantly realize that the Brownies/ Americans, represented by the Rough Rider and Uncle Sam, can outlast any siege. The Brownies win, in the final analysis, simply because they are determined to stay. By 1903 and 1904, when Cox published the comic strip and book versions of *Brownies in the Philippines,* the United States had officially ended the war and was focusing its efforts on the more unobtrusive work of colonial government. However, hostilities by Philippine "rebels" were still ongoing and bloody. The conclusion of the ant battle suggests that, like the Brownies, Americans would prevail simply out of sheer determination, even in the face of bloodthirsty and innumerable native forces.

The American determination to stay the colonial course is also the theme of the Brownies' adventure in Sulu in the serial version of *Brownies in the Philippines,* but the scenario is different. On November 1, 1903 (the twenty-second installment in the *New York Herald* run), the Brownies travel to Sulu, where they find "a wild bird's egg." The band debates what to do with the egg; one wants to eat it, the Fisherman wants to use it as bait, etc. In the end they decide to use the egg for target practice, an opportunity to showcase the skills of the band's "sure shot," who is, of course, the Rough Rider. The Uncle Sam Brownie balances the egg on his top hat and it comes as little surprise that the Rough Rider Brownie hits his target. What is a surprise, however, is the outcome of the shot. Out of the fragments of the egg shell flies an eagle clutching an American flag in its talons. The Brownies stand agog at this asseveration of the U.S. colonial staying power:

> . . . much surprise the Brownies knew
> When from the shell an eagle flew
> That bore Old Glory streaming gay,
> A sign the flag had come to stay.

This is one of the few episodes that appears in the comic strip version of *Brownies in the Philippines* that does not appear also in the book version. By displacing the flag and eagle as relatively overt symbols of U.S. political might and instead creating the Sulu ants as covert symbols of Filipino insurgents, Cox paradoxically strengthened his political commentary even as he obscured it by allegorizing the Philippine-American War into the skirmish with the ant army.

TO "SET AT PEACE THE ANXIOUS MIND": THE PHILIPPINE-AMERICAN WAR

While the encounters between the Brownies and the savage natives/ vicious animals work to provide ideological justification for American control of the Philippines, *Brownies in the Philippines* also recognizes and reflects American anxiety about the ongoing Filipino resistance—that is, the fact that the war was not really over. These narrative impulses operate in ironic tension: on the one hand, the Americans are depicted as naturally, even evolutionarily, destined to rule and in fact as obligated to do so; on the other, however, the final outcome of the conflict is still undetermined and this uncertainty is manifested in the narrative as literal danger (for Brownies who supposedly can never really be in danger), and in moments of uneasiness at not really knowing what is out there or what is coming next.

In chapter 12, the Brownies travel to Manila Bay, where they equip themselves with diving bells to explore the sunken wrecks from Dewey's resounding defeat of the Spanish fleet on the morning of May 1, 1898. Dewey's fleet defeated the aging and decrepit Spanish naval forces so handily that, as Laura Wexler relates, Dewey's men were able to break "'for breakfast' and had largely finished before lunch" (Wexler 2000, 16). This brisk morning's work made Dewey an instant national hero; President McKinley gushed of Dewey's

They formed in line to watch the sport
And waited for the sharp report.

And much surprise the Brownies knew
When from the shell an eagle flew
That bore Old Glory streaming gay.
A sign the flag had come to stay.

(COPYRIGHT, 1903, BY THE NEW YORK HERALD CO.)

PALMER COX

15. The Sulu battle in the serial version of *Brownies in the Philippines* proclaims "the flag had come to stay," *New York Herald*, November 1, 1903.

achievement in Manila Bay that "the magnitude of this victory can hardly be measured by the ordinary standards of naval warfare" (17). Dewey himself modestly recalled the battle as "one of the most remarkable naval battles of the ages" (Karnow 1989, 103).

Dewey's triumph at Manila Bay was, however, principally significant for its ideological rather than military value. The American forces so outgunned the Spanish armada in Manila Bay that victory was a foregone conclusion. For the Americans, the real value of the Battle of Manila Bay was the boost it gave to the American morale, still smarting from the insult of the sinking of the *Maine* in Havana harbor, as well as the rationale it provided the Americans in claiming the Philippines from Spain by right of conquest.

Cox, however, portrays Manila Bay as a site of uncertainty, a place of a battle not quite concluded and of ships not quite sunk. Instead of reflecting on the Americans' splendid defeat of the Spaniards, the Brownies reveal an "anxious mind" when surveying waters that might harbor lurking danger. One Brownie declares,

"down we'll go and take a peep
At parts that lie below the deep.
A mystery will forever rest
About the sunken ship at best,
Until some diving-bells we find,
And set at peace the anxious mind,
And leave a hint or two, perchance,
That may the [U.S.] nation's cause advance." (Cox 1904, 85)

The Brownies' deceptively casual statement that their object in surveying the wreckage at Manila Bay was not only to "set at peace the anxious mind" but to "leave a hint or two . . . / That may the nation's cause advance" explicitly acknowledges Cox's agenda throughout the *Brownies in the Philippines* book and serial versions: to advance American nationalism through colonization. Cox later clarifies the source of the American "anxious mind": the supposedly sunken ships actually might still be "live":

> . . . piles of unexploded shell
> That long had kept their secret well,
> But still, though old, and surely wet,
> Might all be full of mischief yet. (92)

The trepidation with which the Brownies view the semi-sunken hulks left from a battle widely reported to be a resounding triumph for the American military suggests that the United States was very aware that the Philippines remained "full of mischief" from an American military perspective. The Manila Bay chapter is one of the book's key episodes in its acknowledgment of American anxiety over "the nation's cause" in the Philippines.

Cox's reference to the war and its ongoing dangers becomes more literal in the book's seventeenth chapter, in which the Brownies find themselves caught in the middle of a battle. In this chapter, Cox comes closest to recognizing the cost of the conflict to the Philippine people, but, in a significant displacement, he portrays the Brownies themselves as the innocent civilians caught in the crossfire. Landing on Masbate, the Brownies find themselves embroiled in the conflict. The Brownies reflect on the cost of war to the common people, who often pay the heaviest toll but stand to gain the least:

> Said one: " 'Tis thus the world around,
> Wherever ruthless war is found:
> Those knowing least about the mess,
> Who have no grievance to redress,
> No ax to edge, no purse to fill,
> No land to stake or race to kill,
> Are bounced about in ways unjust,
> And trampled in the very dust." (122)

On the surface this speech seems to be an unusually sympathetic observation about the cost of the Philippine-American War to the *tao,* which was appallingly high: as Mark Twain succinctly put it, "Thirty thousand [Americans] killed a million [Filipinos]" (Twain 1992, 61). However, the half-page illustration that accompanies this sympathetic speech visually implies that the ones unjustly trampled by war are not, in fact, the Filipinos but the Brownies themselves. The illustration shows a cannon ball blowing a palm tree in half,

THE BROWNIES ON MASBATE.

Until the branches, trunk, and all
Fell round the field in pieces small.
'T was strange so many shot and shell
From cannon that were sighted well
Should whizzing fly, to miss the foe,
And keep the Brownies on the go.
To prove what shield from harm it gave,
The Brownies sought a bomb-proof cave.

16. "No Civilization to Offer" in *Brownies in the Philippines.*

showering shrapnel amongst a group of fleeing Brownies. The illustration
implies that "those knowing least about the mess . . . [and] trampled in the
very dust" are the Brownies, not the natives to whom the Brownies obliquely
refer on the preceding page. Cox buttresses the implication that the Brownies
rather than the Filipino revolutionaries are the beleaguered noncombatants in
illustrations on the following pages, which show the Brownies taking refuge
in what they hope will prove a "bomb-proof cave," trying to protect themselves from attack by flying a "BROWNIE HOSPITAL" banner and waving a white
flag (Cox 1904, 123–24).

This episode contains a number of displacements that operate in tension
with each other. On one hand, by figuring the Brownies as innocents caught

THE BROWNIES ON MASBATE.

And soon the cave and ground entire
Was lying in the zone of fire,
And then explosions swelled the din,
And roofs began to tumble in.
Then out again they scattered wide,
To find a better place to hide.
With flags disclaiming any hand
In war then raging through the land,

17. "No Fighters" in *Brownies in the Philippines.*

in the battle, Cox seems to connect the Brownies with Philippine civilians and to recognize for the first and only time in the book both the humanity of the Filipinos and their suffering during the war. However, even this covert recognition of humanity is undercut later in the scene. When the Brownies attempt the ruse of flying a "BROWNIES HOSPITAL" sign, they also display a sign proclaiming "NO CIVILIZATION TO OFFER," a reference to the putative justification for American colonial incursions. This disavowal of America's civilizing intentions has the ironic effect of reinforcing the colonial enterprise because the unseen aggressors presumably are Filipino insurgents. Cox therefore preempts any possible sympathy for the Filipinos because they are the ultimate source of the Brownies' unwarranted suffering. Moreover, on page 124, when the Brownies are fleeing the Brownie Hospital, the Rough Rider carries a "BROWNIES DON'T SHOOT" banner in one hand, while carrying his pistol in the other. (The Rough Rider's pistol is not just a prop or visual tag, like the Fisherman's creel, to identify the character. Despite the Brownie rule forbidding violence or bloodshed, the Rough Rider uses deadly force upon occasion, as on Palawan when he uses his pistol to shoot his way out of a gigantic serpent that has swallowed him whole.) The irony of the Rough Rider claiming noncombatant status while carrying a gun is a clear example of Cox's displacement of American imperialist aggression, substituting instead the American representatives as innocent victims, noncombatants at the mercy of merciless savages. The Masbate episode thus recapitulates the expansionist fantasy of the U.S. defensive wars—reinvoking the myth variously promulgated by Theodore Roosevelt, Buffalo Bill's Wild West, and other champions of U.S. frontier ideology. The fact that the Rough Rider invokes putative American victimhood while bearing arms once again demonstrates the U.S. deployment of the defensive-war strategy to cloak a war of colonial aggression.

By implying that the unseen Filipino insurgents are the aggressors in the Masbate episode, Cox projects American colonial aggression onto the actual victims of American colonial aggression. At the beginning of the American colonial period, both *Brownies in the Philippines* and the St. Louis World's Fair justified colonial appropriation by imposing closure on the ongoing military hostilities in the Philippines, thereby converting contemporary events in the Philippines into history. At the end of the Commonwealth period, a popular war film, *Back to Bataan,* carried out a similar ideological campaign through a similar ideological sleight of hand, projecting colonial culpability onto a Japanese foe and transforming the United States into the Philippines' liberator rather than its colonial master. While *Brownies in the Philippines* covertly imposed closure on ongoing military hostilities in the Philippines, however, *Back to Bataan* made the lack of closure—the undecided balance of power in World War II's Pacific theater—the overt focus of the film. Where *Brownies in the Philippines* attempted to assure American readers that the war in the Philippines was over, *Back to Bataan* attempted to assure American audiences that the war would end victoriously for Americans and Filipinos, now converted from the Philippine-American War's foes to World War II's allies. As with the Wild West, the St. Louis World's Fair, and *Brownies in the Philippines, Back to Bataan* again sought to impose closure by treating as history events that were still under way. In this case, however, the Philippine government joined in the effort, thereby initiating a new phase in the Filipino-American entanglement.

CHAPTER 3

Back to Bataan *Once More*

PAX AMERICANA AND THE PACIFIC THEATER

BROWNIES IN THE PHILIPPINES illustrates American anxieties regarding the "overness" of the supposedly—and, more important, *successfully*—concluded Philippine-American War. The book supported the U.S. government's political agenda to create closure on military hostilities that were still ongoing in order to facilitate the transition from military to civil government at the beginning of the American colonial era. The popular 1945 war film *Back to Bataan* pursued a similar agenda: a film made while events in the Pacific theater were still undecided, *Back to Bataan* invoked and revised Philippine revolutionary history in order to predict military victory when one could not yet be assured. While explicitly addressing American insecurity over the outcome of World War II, *Back to Bataan's* real concern is relieving American anxieties about the granting of Philippine independence. Whereas *Brownies in the Philippines* demonstrates the various ways in which American expansion rationalized the pacification of Filipino "insurgents" and necessitated colonial beliefs regarding the inherent impossibility in Filipino self-rule, *Back to Bataan*, produced and released one year before the U.S. conferral of official Philippine independence, covertly works to reinforce Filipino dependence even as plans continued to establish official political sovereignty.

In its manipulation of Philippine revolutionary hero Andres Bonifacio, *Back to Bataan* once again demonstrates the U.S. manipulation of the identity axis of Filipino nationalism through the (re)construction of national heroes. By creating a specious grandson of Katipunan Supremo Andres Bonifacio—a grandson who shares his grandfather's name and thus is heir to his grandfather's patriotic heroic status—*Back to Bataan* rewrites Philippine revolutionary and nationalist history in service of the film's ideological goal: the interpellation of Filipinos as neocolonial subjects once the United States has conferred official Philippine sovereignty. As with the case of José Rizal, the U.S. government, an active participant in the film's making, deliberately invoked and manipulated Philippine heroes in order to overtly foster Filipino nationalism while it covertly pursued U.S. national interests. In the early years of the

American colonial regime, colonial officials chose José Rizal as a Filipino national hero because Rizal's life and work conveniently fit the U.S. colonial agenda. At that time, U.S. colonial officials rejected Andres Bonifacio, figurehead of the 1896 Philippine Revolution, as "too radical." The facts of Andres Bonifacio's life did not immediately serve the U.S. agenda in 1945, so *Back to Bataan* reconstructs Bonifacio's revolutionary activity as well as his life by casting him as a veteran of the Philippine-American War and producing a grandson named Andres Bonifacio. This revised Bonifacio served as the focal point for the film's neocolonial subordination of Filipinos to American leadership. In its reconstruction of Andres Bonifacio, *Back to Bataan* defines Filipino identity on both an individual and national level to underwrite both the American war effort and, covertly but just as importantly, to establish the terms of Philippine-American relations after the U.S. official conferral of Philippine independence.

The ideological core of the film is its manipulation of the identity axis of nationalism. The film eases anxieties over the forthcoming moment of rupture between America and the Philippines by constituting Americans as ideal Filipinos. One of the film's culminating moments comes when Andres Bonifacio, the film's Filipino nationalist symbol, tells John Wayne, that quintessential American, "you're a better Filipino than I am." The film rewrites the history of the Philippines as the history of America in the Philippines—written by Americans who are better Filipinos than the Filipinos themselves. Thus this chapter draws together two threads from the two previous chapters: the co-optation of Philippine revolutionary history to underwrite the American military campaign, and the American invocation of Filipino heroes and, consequently, ostensible support of Filipino nationalism, as a way of subordinating Filipino political sovereignty to American (neo)colonial control. In its invocation of Philippine aspirations to political independence as embodied in both Andres Bonifacio Sr. and in the contemporary Filipinos' desire to overthrow Japanese imperial domination, *Back to Bataan* appears to support the cause of Filipino political sovereignty. But the film's manipulation of Philippine revolutionary history to reinstate American political domination on the eve of official Philippine independence demonstrates this study's fundamental thesis: that U.S. and Philippine nationalisms overtly seek to create and maintain their respective political sovereignties through a covert dependence on the other. While the United States appears to support Filipino aspirations to political independence in *Back to Bataan*, the film covertly constructs U.S. nationalism (Pax Americana) through the co-optation of the very Filipino political independence it ostensibly champions.

The year 1945 was crucial for America as a world power: while war still raged in the Pacific, America was preparing to release control of its overseas colony by granting independence to what was then the Philippine Commonwealth. In 1945, the loss of the Philippines threatened the United States' position as a world power on two levels. The Japanese Occupation of the Philippines represented an external threat, an untenable foreign theft of an American territory. On an internal level, the granting of Philippine independence, set for July 4, 1946, would be the first time the United States relinquished ownership of an American possession. Whether by foreign invasion or voluntary cession, the loss of the Philippines posed a challenge to America's self-assurance as the world's superpower. Although *Back to Bataan*'s dramatic action was set in the Philippines, its true stage was the home front. In this film, the military theater and the cinematic theater converged to wage an intertwined campaign to salve American anxieties about the U.S. loss of world status. This is the Pacific theater, indeed, for the film collapses military campaigns with ideological campaigns. The film purports to fight the good fight in movie theaters as well as military theaters—for in the end they were virtually interchangeable.

Although *Back to Bataan* was made and consumed as popular culture, it, like the ethnological exhibits of exotic peoples at the 1904 St. Louis World's Fair, enjoyed government support and in turn supported the interests of the U.S. government. The film makes this point explicitly in the film's opening frames, noting in an on-screen acknowledgment "the cooperation of the U.S. Army, Navy, Marine Corps, Coast Guard, and the Government of the Commonwealth of the Philippines" in its making. Col. George S. Clarke, who had served in the Philippines, served as the film's technical adviser to ensure military accuracy, and real-life veterans of World War II's Philippine campaigns appear in the film as well. Presumably, the film's acknowledgment of the involvement of various governmental agencies are there to bolster the film's military and historical accuracy, but they also reveal the film as a production of U.S. state interests at the time—interests the American government was negotiating with the Philippine government during the Philippines' last year as a U.S. Commonwealth possession. Although the primary nationalist axis in *Back to Bataan* is the identity axis, this film reveals the interplay between the identity and state axes of nationalism. Like José Rizal at an earlier moment, here Andres Bonifacio serves as a Filipino hero, mediating between individuals and the state through nationalist identification. *Back to Bataan* functions as a site of memory on two levels: at level of form, by promoting itself as mimetically reflecting real history as it occurred moment by moment, and at the level of its dramatic content, which presses Philippine revolutionary history into service for the construction of the Philippines' neocolonial dependence on the United States once formal independence was granted, creating the past best suited to secure a future political relationship between the two state governments.

Back to Bataan promotes an image of liberatory global Americanism through the fruition of colonial tutelage in the Philippines. In its portrayal of the fight for Philippine independence from the Japanese Occupation during

World War II, *Back to Bataan* pursues two objectives. While the film purports to narrate the American war against the Japanese in the Pacific, its latent agenda is to show that the Philippines, having absorbed the American patriotic values of freedom, independence, and resistance to military despotism—and, just as importantly, having learned its rightfully subordinate position relative to the United States—has finally earned the right to self-government. The film's central fantasy posits Americans and Filipinos fighting side by side against Japanese colonialism, an active denial of the United States' history of colonialism in the Philippines that the Japanese Occupation interrupted. The film's fantasized coalition of Filipinos and Americans joining forces against colonialism, however, is not to be an equal partnership. The era of colonial tutelage has not run its course, and *Back to Bataan* shows Filipinos readying themselves for independence only by reinforcing their subordination to the Americans.

Freedom as the largesse of American benevolence is *Back to Bataan*'s not-so-covert theme. While the film is framed by scenes celebrating the march of Pax Americana celebrated in a liberation parade, freedom is not given gratuitously. The Filipino characters in *Back to Bataan* all must demonstrate, in various ways, their subordination to American guidance. Ironically, in order to prove their worthiness for independence, Filipinos must reaffirm their dependence on American leadership, thus fulfilling the lessons of colonial tutelage. Tutelage functions in *Back to Bataan* on two levels. On a manifest level, the film portrays the American educational system teaching a second generation of Filipino pupils lessons in the American ideals of independence and national pride. On a latent level, American teaching reaches beyond the schoolhouse: it is just as important that the film's main Filipino character, Andres Bonifacio, learns that the only way to recuperate his Filipino identity is through dependence on American military leadership as it is that the Balintawak schoolchildren learn that freedom was America's gift to the Philippines. All Filipinos, from child to school principal to the leader of the Philippine Scouts, can gain "Liburty" only insofar as they have internalized an American construction of their own history.

REEL WAR

Released in early April 1945, Edward Dmytryk's *Back to Bataan* (RKO Radio Pictures) was lauded by film critics for its historical accuracy as well as its bracing patriotism. Purporting to be a factual film showing the real thing about the ongoing war in the Pacific theater, *Back to Bataan* premiered only six months after General MacArthur gloriously fulfilled his famous promise to return to the Philippines—an important moment of military recuperation following the wrenching American defeats in Bataan and Corregidor.

Although from the beginning Dmytryk positions the film as a factual rather than fictional narrative, *Back to Bataan*'s much-lauded historical realism derives from a careful mixing of history and fiction. Employing a newsreel tone, a voice-over narrator opens the film with the informative declaration, "This story was not invented. The events you are about to see are based on actual incidents. The characters are based on real people." Although real people were used in the film, others, such as the film's main Filipino character, the ostensible grandson of Philippine revolutionary hero Andres Bonifacio, were fictitious. The assertion that the film's "characters are based on real people," plus the fact that Andres Bonifacio (Sr.) was a "real person," confers a specious realism upon the junior Bonifacio character. The film's ostensible insistence on historical authenticity applied only to the ongoing military events in the Pacific theater. When it came to Filipino-American history, *Back to Bataan* threw historical veracity to the winds. The film's (mis)use of "real people" functioned in much the same way as did the Wild West's putative historical authenticity: by blurring the borders between fact and fiction, real people and dramatic characters, actual events and staged narratives, *Back to Bataan*, like the Wild West, obscured the fabrication of history and their narratives' ideological agenda behind ostensible historical reportage.

Historical reportage played a significant role in *Back to Bataan*. The film was made while the military events in the Philippines it depicts were ongoing, and the film's narrative was reconstructed constantly in response to continuing developments. Although the film claimed it simply chronicled history in the making and was lauded for its historical authenticity, *Back to Bataan* is a case study in constructing history rather than simply reporting it. As Richard Slotkin notes in *Gunfighter Nation*, war films presented Americans with cinematic war reportage for the first time. The journalistic development of the newsreel introduced audiences to visual depictions of current events. War films such as *Back to Bataan*, which employed actual veterans of various campaigns as well as newsreelesque narrators and musical soundtracks, blurred the distinction between war reportage and fictional drama, collapsing reel war and real war. Partly because, as Slotkin points out, World War II films led the audience to believe it was " 'see[ing] for itself' the reality of war without the polemical distortions of the written word," films in this developing genre were in fact highly polemical (Slotkin 1992, 314). *Back to Bataan* is an example of this genre, introducing a war film that purported to be an unmediated representation of history in the making to an audience steeped in newsreel conventions and inattentive to the ways in which real/reel images could be manipulated.

PAX AMERICANA: "SOON THE WHOLE WORLD WOULD BE FREE"

In 1945, as the fate of World War II in the Pacific theater remained undecided, *Back to Bataan* celebrated the fulfillment of Manifest Destiny across the

Pacific and, at the same time, embodied an important renegotiation of America's self-concept as a world power. The film projects American colonial guilt onto the Japanese and then celebrates American liberation from these imperial oppressors as proof of the inherent goodness and inevitability of American freedom. *Back to Bataan* thus promotes the globalization of American domination as the march of Pax Americana, renegotiating Manifest Destiny as the advancement of freedom rather than of possession, of liberation rather than domination.

The film's narrative opens with a reenactment of the liberation of the American prisoners at the Japanese prison camp at Cabanatuan, Luzon, on January 30, 1945. The next scene presents a victory parade with a military rendition of "California Here I Come" playing on the soundtrack. As men march by, with their names, military affiliations, and home origins listed below them (for example, Manson, Navy, Worthington, Minnesota; Baumgardner, Navy, Yonkers, New York; Rainwater, Marine Corps, Paris, Arkansas; etc.), the narrator explains, "The men you are about to see are actual survivors of three terrible years in the Jap prison camp at Cabanatuan." While the song continues in the soundtrack, the narrator globalizes the impact of the veterans' march. The victory parade does not merely celebrate the liberation of one contingent of American troops; it manifests Pax Americana on the march, as the narrator predicts, "Americans had been freed—hundreds of them. This was a promise of what was to come. Soon the whole world would be free."

The victory parade is not, however, just a celebration and globalization of Manifest Destiny. It also recuperates the crushing American defeats at Bataan and Corregidor. The Japanese attack on Pearl Harbor and the Japanese Occupation of the Philippines had already eroded Americans' sense of the United States' unassailable supremacy as a world power. Stanley Karnow identifies Maj. Gen. Edward King's surrender of 76,000 Filipino and American troops at Bataan on April 9, 1942, as the largest military capitulation in U.S. history (Karnow 1989, 301).[1] Some 70,000 American and Filipino survivors of the Fall of Bataan then faced the grueling Bataan Death March, in the course of which roughly 10 percent of the captives died and the Japanese committed infamous atrocities (Zich 1977, 100). The roughly 13,000 Americans and Filipinos remaining at Corregidor held out another month, enduring an almost constant bombardment by the Japanese and suffering the ravages of disease and starvation before surrendering. The Japanese paraded them through the streets of Manila as trophies before shipping them to the prison camp at Cabanatuan (100). The Japanese Occupation of the Philippines and their taking of the supposedly impregnable Bataan and Corregidor were galling to Americans. The humiliations to American national pride Bataan and Corregidor represented were even more bitter for the military debacles they entailed. Sam Grashio, veteran of the Fall of Bataan, described the battle as a military nightmare: "Sick, starved, dazed, terrified men abandoned arms and equipment, and milled about aimlessly, many so tired that they fell asleep as soon as they sat down. Communications broke down, and nobody knew what anyone else was doing. Some Filipino detachments had to be driven to their positions at gunpoint. . . . It was confusion beyond my wildest imagination" (Karnow 1989, 300). As Richard Slotkin points out, "That a non-White people who had been stereotyped as racial and technological inferiors should be capable of inflicting such defeats" made the Japanese victories at Pearl Harbor, Manila, Bataan, and Corregidor doubly offensive (Slotkin 1992, 318–19).

Back to Bataan's manifest purpose is to recuperate these military defeats and their concomitant blows to American national pride. Late in the film there is a short scene set during the Bataan Death March with fleeting glimpses of its attendant cruelties, but that scene is simply a shorthand reminder of why Bataan needed to be gone back to. The film's emphasis is on the liberation of the American POWs from the Cabanatuan camp and on the victory parade that follows. The film's depiction of the actual survivors of the Cabanatuan camp is critical more for the purposes of recuperating American national pride than for bolstering the film's much-vaunted historical realism. The American survivors of the Japanese POW camp had been weakened by starvation and disease to fragile, skeletal men, many of whom were barely alive. The American veterans featured in the Cabanatuan victory parade appear hale and strong, even apple-cheeked, providing a visual recuperation of the images of the frail, starved scarecrows who survived the infamous Bataan Death March and the grueling hardships of the Japanese prison camps.[2] The celebratory military parades that frame the film's dramatic narrative, showcasing smiling veterans marching in orderly rows, identified by name, rank, and geographical origin, supplant the humiliating confusion and impotence of the battle of Bataan described by veterans such as Sam Grashio.

The Fall of Bataan and Corregidor signaled not only a breach of the United States' presumptive national impregnability; it also entailed the United States' inability to keep its responsibility to the Philippines as a colonial protectorate. Douglas MacArthur, appointed field marshal of the Philippine army by President Manuel Quezon, abandoned the field to assume command of the Allied Pacific Fleet, promising, "I shall return." The declaration became one of the catchphrases of the war, but it signaled the U.S. abdication of its responsibility as a colonial master. The important point, from the Philippine perspective, was not that MacArthur would return, but that he left in the first place, particularly as he abandoned Quezon, the Philippine first family, and thousands of Filipino and American soldiers beleaguered on Corregidor. When MacArthur left the Philippines on March 11, 1942, it was a critical symbolic defection for Filipinos who for two generations had been brought up to depend on American economic, governmental, and military support.

Back to Bataan explicitly addresses the point of the American defection of the Philippines: during a key scene, Andres Bonifacio upbraids Col. John Madden for the United States' failure to provide military support. "You know that alone we're helpless. Where are all those American warships that were promised? All those American guns and planes? Why didn't they come to Bataan and Corregidor?" Bonifacio asks Madden in anguish. Madden can only answer heavily, "I don't know." The film's title alludes to the fulfillment of MacArthur's promise to return. *Back to Bataan's* ideological campaign is not just to rescue the Americans from the Japanese POW camp; it is also to recuperate the U.S. betrayal of its military and political responsibilities to the Philippines.

The film recuperates MacArthur's desertion of the Philippines by substituting John Wayne, America's movie hero, for Douglas MacArthur. In the film, Wayne, playing Col. John Madden, takes MacArthur's place in the Philippine-American military hierarchy when MacArthur leaves the Philippines. General Wainwright explicitly gives Madden his orders to take MacArthur's command position in a scene about two-thirds of the way through the film. *Back to Bataan* then subsumes Madden's character into MacArthur, a point Dmytryk makes explicit by having Madden return to the Philippines by landing at Leyte, the site of MacArthur's landing in October 1944.

The film's contemporary audiences accepted the substitution wholeheartedly; they read Madden as MacArthur. Kate Cameron makes this point clear in her September 13, 1945, review of the film for the *New York Daily Times*. Cameron summarizes the film as the chronicle of Madden/Wayne's "organiz[ation of] the handful of American soldiers and Philippine guerrillas who've fled to the hills, into an effective military machine . . . until General MacArthur's victorious return to the Islands." Similarly, Louella Parsons's July 19, 1945, review of *Back to Bataan* summarizes the film as a narrative "starting with the fall of Bataan and Corregidor up to the moment when MacArthur triumphantly landed his troops on Leyte and made the way safe to take back the stolen Philippines," and Larry Sloan's July 17, 1945, review calls *Back to Bataan* a "now-it-can-be-told story of the heroic Philippine resistance which paved the way for General MacArthur's return."[3]

These contemporary reviews show that, as Edward Dmytryk intended, *Back to Bataan's* audiences took Wayne's Madden to *be* MacArthur. The Madden-as-MacArthur substitution assuages American and Philippine anxiety about America's failure to carry through with its promised military support to the Philippines by presenting his return in the figure of Wayne/Madden. That this distortion involved the conflation of MacArthur with John Wayne, that quintessential frontier hero, suggests the depth of America's anxiety over its failure in the Philippines. The film figures MacArthur's promise to return as the healing of the breach of American promises of military support to the Philippines. Clearly, American anxieties over the Pacific theater in the military sense needed bolstering by reassurance via Pacific theater in the cinematic sense. A Freudian slip in Kate Cameron's review reveals the effectiveness of *Back to Bataan*'s ideological strategy: Dmytryk's film, Cameron wrote, "makes the blood tingle in the beholder as he relieves [*sic*] that segment of the war with the survivors of the Philippine campaign" (Cameron 1945). Despite *Back to Bataan*'s universally acclaimed military accuracy, Dmytryk's film is not about *reliving* the military campaign; it is about *relieving* the anxiety aroused by America's past, present, and future in the Pacific.

BACK TO BATAAN'S RECONTAINMENT OF EARLY COLONIAL FILIPINO NATIONALIST DRAMA

While *Back to Bataan*'s main story line follows the film's manifest military plot, the film's secondary plot follows the symbolic romance of the film's gendered archetypes of Filipino nationalism. Anthony Quinn plays Andres Bonifacio, captain of the Philippine Scouts, who has lost his taste for the war and his faith in American support for the Philippines. Bonifacio's lack of faith is not a merely personal crisis; it endangers the Filipino war effort, as Bonifacio holds tremendous symbolic power as the grandson of the great Filipino revolutionary hero Andres Bonifacio. (There was no grandson of the Katipunan Supremo alive during World War II, much less involved in the campaigns on Bataan or Corregidor—a glaring example of the film's betrayal of the historical verisimilitude for which it nevertheless received kudos by American critics.) Bonifacio's main task in the film is less to lead his group of Philippine Scouts—for the most part Madden does that—than to regain his faith in America, and therefore in the war effort, and to take his hereditary place as a revolutionary leader, albeit in subordination to American leadership. In addition to his disillusionment over the war effort and his anxiety over his grandfather's revolutionary legacy, Bonifacio is further tormented by the apparent defection of his sweetheart, Dalisay Delgado (played by Fely Franquelli), a beautiful Filipina who appears to have become a Japanese collaborator and is doing considerable damage to Filipino and American morale by broadcasting impassioned pleas to Filipinos to join their Asian brothers and throw off the yoke of American imperialism. Unbeknownst to Bonifacio, however, Delgado is a double agent, transmitting crucial information to the American headquarters and setting up the Japanese for an ambush at Balintawak, "the birthplace of Filipino freedom." The film figures Dalisay Delgado and Andres Bonifacio as gendered archetypes of Filipino nationalism who have both deviated from their legitimate gender roles (Delgado is treacherous and dangerously sexual, Bonifacio is vacillating and emasculated) and the film's secondary plot line focuses on the recuperation of Bonifacio and Delgado into their proper roles in the Filipino nation (he as soldier, she as teacher) and their reunion as lovers. With the long-awaited grant of Philippine independence only one year hence, *Back to Bataan*'s romantic subplot performs the important symbolic function of reuniting the male and female archetypes of the Filipino nation and setting them up as the symbolic patriarch and matriarch of the nation to come.

Bonifacio and Delgado hearken back to stock allegorical figures in nineteenth-century nationalist dramas performed by Filipinos as acts of resistance to early American colonization. *Back to Bataan*'s construction of Dalisay Delgado and Andres Bonifacio's romantic-nationalist relationship conforms in remarkable detail to the conventions of the turn-of-the-century Tagalog dramas described by Vicente Rafael.[4] In these dramas, staged as popular, vernacular protests against the American colonial regime,

> plots usually revolved around the relationship between a female beloved and her male lover-protector. . . . One personified the nation and freedom, while the other stood for the patriot and the people. Their relationship is invariably threatened by a male foreign intruder harboring designs on the woman-nation. . . . Although the endings of the plays may vary in their details, they all envision in one form or another the spectacular reunification of the beloved nation . . . with her lover-patriot returning from imprisonment or death itself to lead the people to victory. (Rafael 1993, 207–8)

The similarities between the conventions of early colonial anti-American vernacular dramas and *Back to Bataan*'s construction of the Bonifacio-Delgado pair are remarkable, especially because the film recontains Filipino anticolonial nationalism, harnessing it in the service of the colonial American power these nationalist cultural productions originally protested. In the film, Delgado plays the role of the beloved but endangered woman-nation and Bonifacio plays the hero-patriot unable to come to the woman-nation's rescue without her encouragement and guidance. *Back to Bataan* does figure Delgado as the feminized personification of the beleaguered Philippines; in her broadcasts Delgado implicitly speaks to all Filipinos as the voice of the country.[5] Delgado's double-agent activities have estranged her from her lover-patriot and incapacitated him to fulfill the role of hero-patriot, and in his absence the Japanese military commander Kuroki steps in to symbolically abduct Delgado by politically and sexually compromising her. It is not until Bonifacio's emotional and political faith in Delgado are restored—restored not only because he finds out that she has been a double agent all along, but also because she urges him to join the fight—that he can assume his role as the symbolic leader of Philippine resistance. Bonifacio and Delgado's romantic reunion at the film's close represents "the spectacular reunification" of the male and female counterparts of the "beloved nation" following the "victory against foreigners and collaborators alike," thus closely following the standard plotline of the nineteenth century resistance plays Rafael describes (Rafael 1993, 208). *Back to Bataan* recontains Filipino resistance to American imperial domination by appropriating the founding allegory of such resistance into the service of that which these plays were produced to resist: American colonialism.

INVENTING A HERO: IDENTITY POLITICS AND THE (RE)CONSTRUCTION OF ANDRES BONIFACIO

American historian Glenn May prompted a storm of Filipino historiographical debate with the publication of his *Inventing a Hero: The Posthumous Re-creation of Andres Bonifacio* (1997). In this controversial book, May deconstructed Bonifacio as he is commonly figured in Filipino historical texts and the collective Filipino national memory. Analyzing the extant primary documents purportedly written by or about Andres Bonifacio, May debunks not only large pieces of the Bonifacio legend but also asserts that most of the writings attributed to Bonifacio were either written by someone else or deliberately forged, and, more shockingly, that several of the Philippines' most well-respected historians, those who have written the authoritative historical studies of Bonifacio, "often adopted questionable methods . . . consciously dissembled . . . [or] altered evidence." In "Nationalism and Myth," the book's concluding chapter, May concludes that Andres Bonifacio as most Filipinos know him "turns out to be a historian's imaginative construction. . . . In the end, the Bonifacio we have before us is mostly an illusion, the product of undocumented statements, unreliable, doctored, or otherwise spurious sources, and the collective imagination of several historians" (May 1997, 1, 163).

In *Inventing a Hero,* May asserts that historians are both the product and the producers of their political climate and that they transfer the ideological agendas of their political climate into the histories they write. Rather than simply violating the conventions of historical research, May argues that historians' (re)creations of Andres Bonifacio fulfill the need for national heroes as a critical component of Filipino nationalism. "On one level, the story I have told here can be read as merely a cautionary tale about the perils of doing historical research," writes May. "On another level, however, it is a tale about nationalism and the function of history in emerging nation-states. . . . [T]o understand the invention of Andres Bonifacio, we must recognize that the process of posthumous re-creation was as much concerned with the promotion of Philippine nationalism as it was with historical reconstruction." Thus, May interprets Manuel Artigas's, Epifanio de los Santos's, and José P. Santos's biographies of Bonifacio as motivated by the desire to "promote nationalist feeling in a colonial environment" by focusing on Bonifacio's relevance to "independence and national unity," nationalist concerns that were paramount during the U.S. colonial era. Writing after the U.S. official grant of independence in 1946, however, Teodoro Agoncillo's version of Andres Bonifacio focused on "nation-building," reflecting the needs of the newly independent Philippine nation. Reynaldo Ileto's Bonifacio addressed the next generation's nationalist concerns. May argues that by the 1979 publication of *Pasyon and Revolution,* Ileto "moved the locus of nationalism from the dominant elites to the common people" because of his generation's view that although "the Philippine state had been independent for more than thirty years[,] . . . true nation building had not taken place because a majority of the people were excluded or exploited" (May 1997, 164, 165). Like José Rizal, Andres Bonifacio has been fashioned by both Filipinos and Americans to serve the political ends of each country's nationalist agenda.

May's study of Bonifacio provoked a storm of historiographical rebuttals, several of which were collected in *Determining the Truth: The Story of Andres Bonifacio* (1997), jointly published by the Manila Studies Association, the National Commission for Culture and the Arts Committee on Historical Research, and the Philippine National Historical Society. The ire with which many Filipinos responded to May's publication of *Inventing a Hero* indicates the depth of feeling Filipinos have, even today, for Bonifacio as a nationalist icon. At least one factor in many Filipinos' umbrage in response to May's analysis of the "Bonifacio myth" is identity politics: when a Filipino and native Tagalog speaker such as Ambeth Ocampo debunks Filipino history, often with a satiric touch, the essays become well-selling books; when an "outsider" such as May casts aspersions on Filipino history and historians, Malcolm Churchill chalks it up to May as a representative of "a certain breed of American academic that brings to the study of the Philippines an unshakable sense of superiority" (Churchill 1997, 52). It is interesting, therefore, that *Back to Bataan* still is aired on Philippine television and is fondly remembered by many Filipinos, including academics. If May's hypotheses questioning the provenance of many aspects of Bonifacio as Philippine hero ignite such storms of rebuttal, it is curious that *Back to Bataan*'s egregious misrepresentations of both the specious Andres Bonifacio Jr. character and the fabricated history of Andres Bonifacio Sr.'s ostensible participation in the Philippine-American War raise few eyebrows. Perhaps this lack of response to the film's (re)construction of Andres Bonifacio (Jr. and Sr.) stems from the fact that people perceive the film as popular culture, as not serious and thus as relatively inconsequential. But the ideology of the film's manipulation of the Andres Bonifacio character and the resulting promulgation of American neocolonialism is not inconsequential. Through the invocation and manipulation of both the Andres Bonifacio Jr. character and his ostensible (off-screen) grandfather, the film appeals to the identity axis of nationalism to define real Filipinos as subordinated to the American cause. Considering the profound negative reaction with which

Filipinos have responded to both American manipulations of José Rizal and to May's deconstruction of the Bonifacio myth, it is surprising that the egregious misrepresentations of Andres Bonifacio (Sr. and Jr.) in *Back to Bataan* have not produced a similar reaction—or, at least, that the film has not disappeared into the dusty archive of embarrassingly bad popular films.

"YOU'RE A BETTER FILIPINO THAN I AM": ANDRES BONIFACIO AND THE RECONSTRUCTION OF PHILIPPINE NATIONALISM

At the beginning of the colonial period, the United States promoted José Rizal as a Philippine national hero to buttress the U.S. colonial agenda at the time: from the American perspective, Rizal was a safe hero because of his explicit opposition to revolution. At the end of the colonial period, *Back to Bataan* offers another example of American invocation, manipulation, and promotion of Philippine national heroic iconography to buttress the United States' new political agenda: the solidification of Filipino neocolonial dependency before official independence was actually granted. The film's portrayal of Andres Bonifacio demonstrates the interplay between the state and identity axes of nationalism. As noted in the earlier chapters of this book, the identity axis focuses on the individual: it is the point through which the individual privately, but significantly, determines his or her inclusion in and allegiance to the nation. As Glenn May noted in this analysis of Filipino historians' (re)construction of Andres Bonifacio as Philippine national hero, the figure of Andres Bonifacio has changed to reflect the political needs of the era. This nationalist-historical plasticity is just as true of American nationalist histories as it is of its Philippine counterparts—and this holds true regarding not only American histories of American heroes but also American histories of Philippine heroes. In the early 1900s, the United States needed a Filipino hero who opposed revolution and promoted José Rizal accordingly. In 1945, the United States resurrected the Filipino hero perhaps most identified with the Philippine Revolution, and, through considerable revision of the Philippine historical record, produced an Andres Bonifacio whose revolutionary iconography was simultaneously pitted against a new colonial enemy (the Japanese) and interpellated into colonial dependency on the United States. Andres Bonifacio (Jr.)'s true task in the film is less to become a Filipino freedom fighter per se than to assume a subordinate position in the American military hierarchy, for the film predicates the one upon the other. Bonifacio is a man confused about both his familial and national identity, and the film presents colonial tutelage as the solution to this identity crisis.

Back to Bataan's Bonifacio is a man laboring under the burden of his grandpaternal legacy. The film presents Bonifacio as valued more for his symbolic leadership value than for his military expertise. In other words, Bonifacio is valued in the film more for what he *is* (the Katipunan Supremo's grandson) than what he *does* (lead the Philippine Scouts). Although he is aware that, for other Filipinos, he is a figurehead of tremendous symbolic power, he is distrustful of promises of American military support and all too well aware of the tremendous casualties the historically under-armed Filipinos have endured fighting their colonial rulers, whether Spanish, American, or Japanese ("Bolos . . . against machine guns?" one Filipino Scout doubtfully ponders). Bonifacio begins the film under Madden/Wayne's command but later is captured by the Japanese and takes part in the infamous Bataan Death March. Madden, telling his Scouts about the odds against successfully completing their mission to destroy a Japanese airfield outside Balintawak, asks the Scouts if they would follow Andres Bonifacio, and they answer a grim affirmation. Madden's group rescues Bonifacio from the Death March, and Bonifacio is aware that he was rescued because of his symbolic value. But he is reluctant to let the Americans use him as a figurehead to lead Filipinos into almost inevitable slaughter.

After listening to the radio news of Japanese victories across the islands, Madden and Bonifacio play a key scene in an American bunker. Bonifacio has sunk into despair because of the heavy casualties Filipinos are suffering, and he is frustrated over the Americans' failure to live up to their promises of military support. Bonifacio criticizes Madden for choosing him, of all the Death March participants, to rescue, insisting, "You picked the wrong guy, Joe." Madden responds levelly, "I picked Andres Bonifacio." "I know you did," retorts Bonifacio. "Now you expect him to spread the word that Bonifacio's back to arm Filipinos." Bonifacio refers to himself in the third person in this exchange to underscore the fact that Madden is exploiting him for his symbolic capital as his grandfather's namesake rather than for his own military abilities or leadership. He refuses to "spread the word that Bonifacio's back to arm Filipinos" in memory of the Katipunan, telling Madden that he, Bonifacio, will not lead Filipinos into certain defeat. In his despair, Bonifacio abruptly transfers Filipino identity from himself to Madden. He expostulates, "you want me to lead them to more slaughter? It's easy for you, they're not your people!" but immediately retracts his harsh accusation, saying, "I don't mean that, Joe. You're a better Filipino than I am. . . . It's just that we've taken too much in these last few months."

Madden sends Bonifacio to Manila to reunite him with his supposedly traitorous sweetheart, Dalisay Delgado. In Manila, Delgado urges Bonifacio to return to the fight for Filipino freedom, which she explicitly posits as independent of American assistance: "We're not waiting for anyone [that is, the Americans] to come back. We don't want freedom as a gift. We want it as a right, as something we've fought and died for. . . . We must fight, Andres." This is the film's one moment in which anyone, Filipino or American, asserts that Filipinos not only deserve independence but also are capable of and obliged to earn it through their own efforts, not through subordination to the Americans or to the Japanese.

In a manner that corresponds to the film's thematic harnessing of Filipino independence to American paternalism, Delgado's exhortation not to depend on American assistance sends Bonifacio back to the campaign headed by Madden. Bonifacio and Madden meet again upon Madden's MacArthurian return at Leyte. To Madden's surprise, Bonifacio is among the Filipinos camped on the beach desperately awaiting American support. Bonifacio informs Madden that he has decided to rejoin the war effort. "I belong here," he tells Madden. So Madden's stratagem to get Bonifacio to rejoin the Philippine-American campaign in the bunker scene succeeds. By sending Bonifacio to Manila with the comment "You don't belong here," Madden maneuvers Bonifacio into just assuming his subordinate position at the conjunction of the colonial, revolutionary, military, and historical tensions the film seeks to resolve by manipulating Bonifacio into admitting that where he belongs is not, as Dalisay Delgado urged, fighting for Filipino independence as an a priori right but rather on the beach awaiting salvation by the Americans. In teaching Bonifacio that where he belongs is as a subordinate to the Americans, *Back to Bataan* constructs the true Filipino as the little brown brother, still dependent upon American direction. Earlier in the Leyte scene, Bonifacio voiced his doubts about American promises of relief to one of the Filipino refugees awaiting American help. "Why are you troubled [that is, doubting American promises of support]?" asks the other man. "Aren't you a Filipino?" The film thus constructs Filipino nationalism as American nationalism: Bonifacio and the other Filipinos at Leyte beach are Filipinos *only through* their unswerving faith in American might and benevolence. Similarly, Bonifacio's admission that Madden is "a better Filipino than [he]" cedes to Madden the authority to define who is or is not Filipino.

The film thus enacts neocolonial interpellation. While ostensibly focusing on the course of the ongoing war in the Pacific, the film's real campaign looks to the future, to the U.S. conferral of formal Philippine independence. Bonifacio's capitulation to Madden of true Filipino identity reveals the film's agenda to reinforce colonial tutelage on the eve of the assumption of Filipino independence. Bonifacio's crisis in his Filipino identity comes not because he has lost faith in the Philippines but because he has lost faith in America. Instead of repudiating America because even Madden cannot ensure that the Americans will carry through on their promises of military support, Bonifacio obediently follows Madden's order to go to Manila. Once there, Bonifacio responds to Delgado's assertion that Filipino independence can and should only come through independent Filipino action by returning to Leyte to prove his Filipino identity by joining the masses awaiting salvation by the Americans. Bonifacio's realization that his place is with his people, that where he belongs is with the other Filipinos awaiting American rescue, puts him in the proper position of Filipino colonial subject. With formal Philippine independence only one year away, the film emphasizes that Filipino independence can only be earned through Filipino subordination. The film rationalizes Filipino subordination to American leadership as a necessary step in Filipino self-liberation and simultaneously identifies independence with continuing dependence upon the Americans as arbiters of legitimate Filipino identity. In this film, one is not free, nor even Filipino, unless so designated by representatives of the American state.

Balintawak, the site of Andres Bonifacio (Sr.) and the Katipuneros' declaration of the beginning of the Philippine Revolution, provides the setting for the recuperation of Dalisay Delgado as woman-nation and, even more importantly, provides the scene for Filipinos' and Americans' wresting of Filipino independence from oppressive Japanese imperialism. To mislead Filipinos into thinking that the Japanese are colonial liberators rather than yet another colonial ruler, the Japanese plan a ceremony purportedly granting Philippine independence. Delgado, in her role as apparent Japanese collaborator, suggests that Balintawak is the birthplace of Philippine independence and therefore a symbolically appropriate site for the independence ceremony. Balintawak is indeed a symbolic site for Filipino nationalism, but what Delgado does not tell the Japanese officers is that her erstwhile sweetheart's grandfather, Andres Bonifacio (Sr.), had symbolically declared Philippine independence at Balintawak in August 1896 by leading Katipuneros in tearing their *cedulas*, documents symbolizing Spanish colonial oppression. Bonifacio's tearing of the cedula became known as the "Cry of Balintawak" and is one of the icons of Filipino history. Acting as a double agent, Delgado sets up the Japanese for a surprise attack from the Americans at Balintawak during the independence ceremony.

Delgado's suggestion to the Japanese that the independence ceremony should be held at Balintawak is meant to be ironic: the film, in its unrelenting anti-Japanese bias, clearly implies that the Japanese promise of independence for Filipinos is spurious, a sop they dangle before Filipinos to ensure their cooperation. The film implies that the Japanese independence ceremony will actually inaugurate the Philippines into a new stage of political dependence. The American ambush of the Japanese at Balintawak implicitly portrays the Americans as conferring true Filipino independence. The historical irony of the Balintawak scene is that in 1946 it would be the Americans, not the Japanese, who would stage an independence ceremony that formally liberated the Philippines from colonial rule, only to place the Philippines in a state of neocolonial subordination. Dmytryk underscores the significance of the American liberation of Balintawak by choosing that scene as the moment for Delgado to declare her heretofore hidden anti-Japanese nationalism. By revealing her status as an American double agent rather than a Japanese collaborator, Delgado's declaration publicly establishes her political legitimacy, thereby facilitating her reunion with her troubled beloved. The Balintawak scene reveals that Delgado has been true (politically and sexually) all along. Recuperated as woman-nation, Delgado is ready to be reunited with Bonifacio as lover-patriot.

Bonifacio and Delgado are reunited symbolically at Balad in the film's penultimate scene. Here Dmytryk once again deploys Andres Bonifacio (Sr.)'s fictitious anti-American insurgency. *Back to Bataan* does not end with Wayne/ Madden/MacArthur's landing at Leyte, although given the symbolic resonance of MacArthur's declared intention to return, one might expect the Leyte landing to function as the film's climax. Instead, Madden receives orders from American headquarters to hold the road at Balad to prevent the Japanese from sending reinforcements. Giving Madden his mission, Gen. Johnathan Wainwright warns Madden that he and his men will face tremendous odds at Balad: somehow they have to launch a surprise attack against a village set in open country. Madden assures Wainwright that he will accomplish the mission by using "trickery. . . . Sheer trickery. As a matter of fact an old Filipino trick that I learned the hard way—from Captain Bonifacio's grandfather."

The "old Filipino trick" Madden uses to surprise the Japanese at Balad involves moving his men close to the village under the cover of night and hiding them underwater in rice paddies until the time for the attack. Madden and his men breathe through small hollow reeds, staying submerged throughout the night. The next day, Madden leads his men out of the water, seemingly coming from nowhere to launch the surprise attack Wainwright had warned them was necessary to gain their objective. The "old Filipino trick" works. Madden, Bonifacio, and their men surprise the Japanese and take the village without the help of the American tanks sent in to finish the job. Madden's singular victory at Balad achieves a recuperation of the defeat he supposedly suffered at the hands of Andres Bonifacio's grandfather two generations before. Madden's use of Filipino trickery at Balad turns his fictitious former defeat at Bonifacio Sr.'s hands into a crucial victory against the Japanese.

The film's allusion to Bonifacio's and Madden's previous interaction, presumably during the Philippine-American War, is historical revisionism indeed: the American forces of the Philippine-American War never fought against Andres Bonifacio (Sr.) because Bonifacio died the year before the Americans came to the Philippines. Bonifacio was a Philippine revolutionary leader, and he had been the hero of Balintawak and Pugad Lawin. But Andres Bonifacio never fought against the Americans. A schism developed within the Katipunan as Emilio Aguinaldo challenged Bonifacio for its leadership. Bonifacio lost the leadership of the Katipunan at the Tejeros Assembly of March 1897, and the Aguinaldo faction engineered Bonifacio's execution on grounds of sedition. Bonifacio was executed on May 10, 1897—almost a year before

America declared war on Spain and Dewey arrived in Manila. In *Back to Bataan*'s bunker scene, Madden refers to Bonifacio's grandfather, Katipunan *Supremo* Andres Bonifacio (Sr.), as a participant in the Philippine-American War. "Military textbooks say a war is over when the objectives are taken," Madden declaims. "The United States fought your grandfather. We found the textbooks were wrong." Madden's statement to Bonifacio that his grandfather taught Americans during the Philippine-American War that military textbooks were wrong appears to be a brief overturning of colonial tutelage. But by speciously re-creating Andres Bonifacio as a combatant in the Philippine-American War, and by having his supposed grandson assume his nationalistic legacy only in learning that true Filipinos are subordinate to American direction, *Back to Bataan* yokes Philippine revolutionary history to American colonial tutelage.

The Balintawak and Balad scenes both appropriate Filipino anti-American nationalism through specious constructions of Filipino revolutionary history in the service of the film's promotion of U.S. nationalism, one that both underwrites an ostensibly beneficent U.S. expansionism (in the form of Pax Americana, "soon the whole world would be free"), and one that preserves U.S. control of the Philippines in a neocolonial twilight once formal Philippine independence is granted. In its crafty manipulation of Philippine history—the invention of an Andres Bonifacio Jr. who is not only alive during World War II but also active in the Bataan campaign, the reconstruction of the original Andres Bonifacio's life history so that he was not only alive during the Philippine-American War but also teaching the Americans old Filipino tricks like the one Madden used at Balad, and the stretching of John Madden's age within the filmic narrative so that he could have fought Bonifacio in the Philippine-American War and still have been a vigorous middle-aged colonel half a century later—*Back to Bataan*, while scrupulously committing itself to historical accuracy in regard to some contemporary military events, was not at all scrupulous about its depictions of Philippine history.[6] *Back to Bataan* forges an ideologically necessary link of military partnership and anti-imperial brotherhood between the American and Filipino forces, but this link is forged in both senses of the word. *Back to Bataan* plays an active role in the construction of a Filipino-American brotherhood forged in the crucible of the Pacific theater—a phrase invoked by both Filipino and American leaders even today—but it does so by creating its own forgery of Filipino revolutionary history.[7] Even while *Back to Bataan* portrays the Filipino-American military alliance of 1945 in admiring terms, the film falsifies the history of the Philippine Revolution and the Filipino-American enmity of 1898 in order to reconstitute earlier conflict as a shared history bonding Filipinos and Americans in a national identity in which Filipinos remain the junior partner.

LEARNING "LIBURTY": *BACK TO*
BATAAN'S COLONIAL TUTELAGE

For a war film, *Back to Bataan* has surprisingly few battle scenes. That is because the film is more concerned with ideological battles than military ones. The schoolhouse at Balintawak is the film's real battleground. *Back to Bataan* reflects the inseparability of American militarism and American education in the colonial Philippines. The film's educational subplot assured Americans, in that last year of colonial apprenticeship, that the native pupils had learned their lessons well. The schoolhouse provides the setting for four key nonmilitary characters' enlistment in the American military/pedagogical campaign: Miss Barnes, the spinster schoolmarm who stands firm in her duty to her charges; Señor Bello, her former pupil now grown into the school's native principal; Maximo, the spunky schoolboy who learns the true meaning of "liburty"; and Dalisay Delgado, who joins Miss Barnes in taking the Balad schoolhouse back from the Japanese while the men wage the (victorious) battle to take the village.

Military conquest and pedagogy always have been intertwined threads in the American imperialist project. The resolve to "teach the natives a lesson" was an objective repeated throughout the Philippine-American War; politicians, soldiers, and the press all used the figure of the teacher-student relationship to rationalize America's colonial possession of the Philippines.[8] Almost as soon as the Philippine-American War was declared over, America began a massive educational campaign in its new territory. The educational campaign followed on the heels of the military campaign, and the earliest teachers were American soldiers not yet sent home from the war.[9] In August 1901, five hundred young Americans arrived on the former cattle ship *Thomas* to begin the new program of universal primary education through which English replaced Spanish as the country's official language. E. San Juan Jr. points out American education's subjugating effect, stating, "U.S. colonialism harnessed the educational system as the chief vehicle of 'benevolent assimilation'" (San Juan 1991, 96). The American educational campaign was effective, as T. H. Pardo de Tavera (a member of one of the two Philippine commissions charged with evaluating the Philippines' readiness for self-government) revealed when he declared, "After peace is established, all our efforts will be directed to Americanizing ourselves; to cause a knowledge of the English language to be extended and generalized in the Philippines, in order that through its agency, the American spirit may take possession of us, and that we may so adopt its principles, its political customs, and its peculiar civilization that our redemption may be complete and radical" (97). Although the American educational campaign brought, in certain respects, undeniable benefits—unlike the Spaniards, Americans did not reserve education for the chosen elite—

American teachers, from the Thomasites to *Back to Bataan*'s redoubtable Miss Barnes, taught Filipinos their place: as colonial subordinates. Certainly it was a less bloody way of "teaching the natives a lesson" than the lethal military "educational" initiative that preceded it, but it is important to note that only a fine line divided the American educational and military campaigns.

In *Back to Bataan*, when we first see the schoolhouse at Balintawak, schoolmarm Miss Barnes is leading the class in primary lessons on Philippine history. Barnes begins the schoolroom scene by noting that the "American period of occupation . . . will be terminated by a grant of independence [on] July 4, 1946." While Barnes concedes some benefit from Spanish colonization in the Philippines ("the Spaniards brought us Christianity"), she teaches her students that America "gave" the Philippines something even more important than religion: a belief in the innate right to freedom. When the Balintawak children identify American consumer goods and popular culture ("Soda pop! Hot dogs! Radio! Movies!") as "what America gave the Philippines," Señor Bello, Barnes's "first . . . pupil" stands and recites like the schoolboy he once was, "Americans taught us that men are free, or they are nothing. Since then we have walked with high heads among all men." Miss Barnes replies, "Thank you, Señor Bello. But at first the Philippines did not feel that way. They resisted the American occupation," and notes that the resistance was resolved only when the insurgent Filipinos "were beaten." As a representative of the American colonial order, Miss Barnes is teaching her second generation of Filipino pupils that Filipinos, through their allegiance to the United States, have an unalienable right to be "free." The irony of this lesson—that while freedom is both an inalienable right and that which, a priori, defines a people, the Filipinos who learned the lesson at such great cost have yet to receive their freedom—seems lost on Barnes, but Maximo, one of the students, rebelliously asserts that Filipinos continue to fight for the freedom still being withheld by the Americans. When a female student states that Filipinos who did not appreciate the lessons of American freedom "were beaten" by the Americans, Maximo allegorizes his brother's boxing career as a continuation of the Philippine-American War. Jumping to his feet, Maximo shouts, "We were not [beaten]! Americans cannot beat Filipinos. My brother Ramon licked every American in the U.S.A. At a hundred and eighteen pounds." When Barnes reminds Maximo that his brother Ramon, like the Filipinos of 1898, "lost his fight," Maximo voices the paradigmatic anticolonial protest, "We was robbed!"

Although Miss Barnes admonishes Maximo to stick to the facts of Filipino history, she does not hold herself to the same exactitude in teaching history to her students. Pointing out that the revolutionaries of 1898, like Maximo's brother Ramon, lost their fight for Filipino freedom, Barnes summarily reconstructs Filipino revolutionary history to stress the need for Filipino-American solidarity in the face of Japanese aggression. Barnes holds up

Gregorio del Pilar, the boy-hero of the Philippine-American War, as an example of "a Filipino who was not beaten." When Maximo cannot remember "the
last words of General del Pilar for those who left him behind," Señor Bello
solemnly recites, "I am surrounded by fearful odds that will overcome me and
my gallant men. But I am well pleased with the thought that I died fighting
for my beloved country. Go you into the hills, and defend it to the death." The
students are still cheering Señor Bello's recitation as the Japanese invade the
school.

It is characteristic of the colonial irony that permeates *Back to Bataan* that
Bello quotes General del Pilar as exemplifying the ideals of prideful independence in the face of overwhelming odds as an implicit tribute to Filipinos'
absorption of the American lessons "that men are free, or they are nothing."
What Bello and Barnes neglect to mention is that Gregorio del Pilar was one
of those misguided Filipinos who "resisted the American occupation." General del Pilar was killed in December 1899 defending Emilio Aguinaldo's
retreat across central Luzon. Aguinaldo sent sixty men to defend the Tirad Pass
against the American Thirty-Third Volunteer Infantry; all but seven of those
Filipinos died in that battle. When the Americans surveyed the wreckage of
the fight, they found del Pilar's nearly naked body. Richard Henry, one of the
American soldiers, described the scene to the *Chicago Tribune:*

> "That's old Pilar," [a soldier] said, "we got the old rascal. I guess he's sorry
> he ever went up against the Thirty-Third."
>
> "There ain't no doubt about its being Pilar," rattled on the young sol-
> dier. "We got his diary and letters and all his papers, and Sullivan of our
> company's got his pants, and Snider's got his shoes, but he can't wear
> them because they're too small, and a sergeant in G Company got one of
> his silver spurs, and a lieutenant got the other, and somebody swiped the
> cuff buttons before I got here or I would have swiped them, and all I got
> was a stud button and his collar with blood on it."
>
> So this was the end of Gregorio del Pilar. Only twenty-two years old,
> he managed to make himself a leader of men when he was hardly more
> than a boy. (de la Costa 1965, 217)

Not taking the time to bury del Pilar or even throw a blanket over the body,
Henry reflected, "we left him alone in his glory. . . . And when Private Sulli-
van went by in [Pilar's] trousers, and Snider with his shoes, and the other man
who had the cuff buttons. . . . it suddenly occurred to me that his glory was
about all we had left him" (217).

Señor Bello's solemn recitation of del Pilar's swan song is a testament to
Filipino pride and independence. The irony of the del Pilar quote is that Miss
Barnes introduces del Pilar as an example of a Filipino who refused to be
"beaten" and thus, implicitly, as a case study in the American lesson that "men

are free, or they are nothing." What Barnes's history lesson obscures is that fact that del Pilar died fighting for Filipino freedom from American rule. Here, as with the putative biography of Katipunan Supremo Andres Bonifacio, *Back to Bataan* manipulates and misrepresents Filipino revolutionary history to reinforce Filipino subordination in the name of American-defined—and controlled—freedom.

In Señor Bello, Miss Barnes's oldest pupil, we see the gratifying fulfillment of American colonial tutelage. Barnes recalls that when Bello was a child, he "hated Americans because his father fought with Aguinaldo. . . . I gave him an apple, the first he'd ever seen, [and] then we became friends." The fruit wooed the young Bello over to the American colonial cause despite the fact that his father, along with Emilio Aguinaldo and Gregorio del Pilar, had fought against the Americans for Philippine independence. Bello learned Miss Barnes's lessons so well that he grew up to join the American educational system. Although Bello, as principal, officially has a higher position than Barnes, he adopts a subordinate manner around his former teacher, displaying studious, childlike body language and tone of voice in obediently answering Barnes's questions. Bello serves as a role model for the young native children who still exhibit flashes of obstinate ingratitude for the gifts of American colonialism. In the figure of Bello, we can see most clearly *Back to Bataan*'s ideological transition from colonial to neocolonial tutelage: even when Filipinos, through literal American tutelage (education in the American-sponsored public school system), attain high positions within the Filipino system, they never graduate from being figurative pupils to their former teachers.

Señor Bello functions as the ideal American colonial pupil outside the schoolroom as well as inside it. The Japanese invade Balintawak just as Bello finishes quoting del Pilar. The Japanese have come, as commander Major Hasko (played by Richard Loo) explains, to "put an end to [Filipino] domination by an exploiting and arrogant American race. [The hand of His Imperial Majesty] will next put an end to a system of education designed to impress upon you a sense of inferiority." The film thus here, as elsewhere, expiates American colonial guilt by having America's wrongs articulated as propaganda spread by the villainized "Japs." Hasko commands Señor Bello to take down the American flag that flies above the Balintawak schoolhouse alongside the Philippine flag, threatening to hang him in its place if he refuses. Alarmed, Barnes implores the principal to lower the flag: "Haul down the flag. I speak to you in the name of every man, woman, and child in the United States." But Bello, a pupil who has learned his lessons of colonial subjugation too well, shakes his head and puts his hands behind him with the air of a child submitting to parental discipline. Hasko carries out his threat, and next we see Bello's body hanging from the flagpole, partially covered by the folds of the American flag he refused to lower. By representing the American flag as Bello's winding sheet, the film emphasizes his adherence to the American ideals of freedom and resistance to imperial despotism and gives Bello a tacit soldier's burial. Bello later gets a formal burial by Madden's men. Amidst sentimental background music, Miss Barnes recites, "The place matters not: Cyprus, or laurel, or lily white; scaffold, or open plain, combat or martyrdom's plight." She identifies the quotation as the final statement of Rizal, "the Philippines' greatest hero, on the night before he was executed by the Spaniards. Remember those words. Carry them in your heart so that wherever men fight for freedom there it may be said 'here lies Bueneventura Bello, schoolteacher of Balintawak.'" Señor Bello's quotation of General del Pilar preserved Pilar's position as a Philippine revolutionary leader but ignored both the fact that the revolution for which del Pilar fought was against Americans and that the conquering Americans left him with little but his glory. With Señor Bello's symbolic soldier's burial, Dmytryk makes reparations of a sort: the martyred schoolteacher gets the hero's burial that the hero he quoted did not, and Barnes, by reciting José Rizal's epitaph for Bello, once again marshals Philippine revolutionary history in the service of the American agenda, rewarding the faithful Filipino who maintains his loyalty to the United States with the words of the Philippines' preeminent hero.

Señor Bello's martyrdom at the hands of the sadistic Japanese reveals the film's construction of the Balintawak schoolhouse as a central battleground between the "bad" colonialism represented by the Japanese and the "good" colonialism represented by the Americans (although, as the previous analysis has shown, the film presents colonial interpellation as a series of lessons in freedom rather than colonial subjugation). The film achieves the camouflaging of American tutelage/subordination as tutelage/freedom partly, as I have just shown, through a careful manipulation of Philippine revolutionary history. The film's denunciation of the Japanese completes its recuperation of colonial tutelage. By presenting the Japanese as cruelly and violently paternalistic, *Back to Bataan* implicitly highlights American (colonial) benevolence.

The film figures the Japanese as evil imperialists avariciously seeking to pull the Philippines back into the East Asia family. The leader of the Japanese Imperial Army, Gen. Masaharu Homma (whose name as pronounced in *Back to Bataan* sounds suspiciously like General "Homo," a misnomer buttressed by Homma's effeminate portrayal) tells Dalisay Delgado, "We Japanese look upon you Filipinos as our nephews and nieces. You have been out of our East Asia family for too long. We are waiting to embrace you, to welcome you to the fold—providing you behave yourselves." The film's Japanese imperialism is riddled with not-so-subtle hints of paternal discipline. Homma cautions, "remember, we are kindly, but not indulgent. We shall not hesitate to spank the unruly ones." And, indeed, the Japanese officers deliver the ultimate paternal punishment by killing Bello for not lowering the American flag when the

Japanese take over the Balintawak schoolhouse—a point the film implicitly underscores through Bello's juvenile body language when refusing Major Hasko's command to lower the American flag. Hasko also delivers a figurative spanking when he strikes Maximo, who attempts to defend Bello. *Back to Bataan*'s portrayal of "bad" Japanese colonialism as opposed to America's "good" colonialism is clear in the Balintawak schoolhouse scene: while the Japanese invade the schoolhouse and kill Bello, the Americans, as represented by Miss Barnes, teach lessons in (ostensible) Filipino freedom. The cruelty of the Japanese spankings is contrasted with the wholesome beneficence of Barnes's educational apple.

Señor Bello's heroic and pseudomilitary death serves to pass the patriotic torch to the next generation. Maximo, the Filipino boy who had protested America's subjugation of the Philippines, tries to come to Bello's defense in the schoolyard during the flag-lowering incident. It is Maximo's first act in support of the American cause. By the film's end, Maximo, like Señor Bello, dies a martyr's death that sentimentally melds colonial pedagogy and a symbolic enlistment in the American war effort.

Maximo, like Bello, undergoes a symbolic initiation into the American military agenda through the agency of the American-dominated educational system.[10] The Philippine-American War is long over by Maximo's time, but the symbolic struggle is going on still, emblematized in the boxing matches Maximo's brother Ramon fought—and lost—against "every American in the USA." Maximo's family is still wrestling with America's possession of the Philippines, as is made clear by Maximo's reading of his brother's match against the Americans as a continuation of the Philippine fight for independence.

Maximo's allegiance to the anti-American fight dies, however, with Señor Bello. After Bello's death, Maximo follows Miss Barnes into the bush and becomes a clandestine member of the Philippine Scouts under Madden's command. Dmytryk makes it clear that Maximo joins the war as an American rather than a Filipino recruit: it is Madden who gives Maximo his orders, not Bonifacio, even after Bonifacio has taken up the cause. Madden sends Maximo to spy on the Japanese preparations for the independence ceremony at Balintawak, and proposes that "Private" Maximo should get a Red Star for accomplishing his "mission." Miss Barnes snorts at this proposal, noting that Maximo wrote "liburty" in his last composition. Miss Barnes scoffs at Maximo's military pretensions: in her eyes, one cannot be a good soldier without first being a good pupil. It is not surprising that Miss Barnes sees Filipino soldiering and scholarship as interdependent; at this point in the film Miss Barnes visually embodies the symbiotic relationship between American militarism and education when she exchanges her starched white schoolmarm's blouse for a green army shirt (to which she still pins her lapel watch, a reminder of colonial discipline and orderliness).

Barnes wants Maximo to keep the other Filipino children up with their studies and hygiene lessons—in other words, to become another Señor Bello. But Maximo wants to be a soldier, not a teacher; he has graduated from the American pedagogical campaign to the military campaign. Madden tells Maximo that he cannot go into active combat because, in essence, he is the civilian reserve: "You're much too important to risk. You're the guy we're fighting this war for. [After the war is over] you're going to have to be the one to build and plan. You're going to be the one to make the Philippines a great nation." Madden orders Maximo to obey Miss Barnes. Since a Red Star is out of the question for a recruit barred from active military duty, Madden gives his own colonel's insignia to Maximo as a symbolic military appointment. This insignia, however, is Maximo's undoing when the Japanese find it after the American ambush of the Japanese independence ceremony at Balintawak. The Japanese rightly interpret the colonel's insignia as a sign of Maximo's collaboration with the Americans. They torture Maximo, forcing him to take them to the Americans. Maximo saves Madden's troop by causing the Japanese troop's truck to crash just as the Japanese are about to destroy Madden and his company. Madden and Miss Barnes pull a mortally wounded Maximo from the wreck and witness his death. Having proven his worth as a soldier by saving the American unit and destroying the Japanese, Maximo reverts to a schoolboy at his death. With his last breath, Maximo apologizes to Miss Barnes for having misspelled *liberty,* but Miss Barnes eulogizes him as the colonial pupil par excellence, declaring, as melodramatic music swells in the background, "Dear God—who ever learned it so well!" Once again, in Maximo's death, *Back to Bataan*'s ideological focus on tutelage supersedes the war plot: it is less important that Maximo die as a soldier than that he, by dying, prove how well he learned the lessons of American-sponsored liberty. In Maximo, as in Señor Bello, we see that it is less important to graduate Filipinos to positions of either military or educational professionalism than to reinforce their subordination to American leadership.

Although in the figures of both Señor Bello and Maximo we see the Pyrrhic victory of American colonial tutelage, the film's conflation of military and educational campaigns has not yet been completed. Wainwright had given Madden orders to take Balad as a military objective, but the American-Filipino victory at Balad does not end when the military battle is won. Because in *Back to Bataan* the military and educational campaigns are indivisible, the battle at Balad is not truly over until the schoolhouse, which evidently was being used as a Japanese command post, is reclaimed. The final battle scene that comes at Balad accomplishes two important ideological goals: first, Madden, Bonifacio, and the Filipino scouts trounce the Japanese without the help of the American tank force; second, Miss Barnes and Dalisay Delgado, dressed in army shirts, reclaim the village schoolhouse. By assuming military uniforms, the tenacious spinster-schoolteacher and the formerly untrustworthy native sweetheart take on their own roles in the war effort. As Miss Barnes and Dalisay Delgado tear down the large Japanese flag that had been hung across the schoolroom's blackboard, Miss Barnes notes triumphantly, "Our boys are landing now." In *Back to Bataan,* the schoolhouse is an ideological reflection of the battlefield; as the men take their military objective, the women secure the pedagogical objective. Throughout the film, the schoolhouse and the battlefield are the sites of the American campaign, and both campaigns must be won to bring the film to its resolution.

The retaking of the schoolhouse at Balad does more than simply recuperate the loss of the schoolhouse at Balintawak: it also recuperates the film's dangerous woman, the one native Filipino/a who not only is powerful but also apparently used that power in the service of the enemy. Delgado signals her transformation from a treacherous, sexualized collaborator into a uniformed military recruit by trading the attractive *saya* she has worn through most of the film for military greens. Having reclaimed her true Filipino (that is, pro-American) identity, Delgado replaces Señor Bello as a teacher to continue American-sponsored education beyond the Commonwealth era and is thus an appropriate consort for Bonifacio. The Balad scene reunites Delgado and Bonifacio as recuperated and triumphant embodiments of the beloved nation and the hero-patriot, respectively, and ready to function as the symbolic matriarch and patriarch of the reconstituted nation to come.

At the end of the Balad scene, Bonifacio and Delgado embrace. "I brought you something: free Filipino soil," Bonifacio tells an enraptured Delgado. Madden joins the couple and admonishes Bonifacio to have his wounded arm tended to, noting the work ahead and, nodding approvingly at the handful of soil Delgado and Bonifacio hold, generously declares, "There's plenty more where that came from." Although for the briefest of moments it appears that Filipinos have assumed agency in the attainment of Filipino independence (that is, Bonifacio's first-person declaration that he is the bearer of "free Filipino soil"), the film hastens to reaffirm American control of the Philippines: it is Madden, not Bonifacio, that assures freedom for the archipelago as a whole. The film's central narrative ends with Madden literally having the last word, leaving the last scene with the image of the Filipino and American flags flying side-by-side in triumph from the Balad schoolhouse.

The film's major conflicts resolved—Madden/MacArthur having triumphantly returned, Bonifacio having accepted his place in the Filipino cause, Delgado having been recuperated into her proper political and romantic position, Miss Barnes having regained her schoolhouse—*Back to Bataan* concludes with a reprise of the celebratory parade of Bataan veterans, marching again to the tune of "California Here I Come." "The blood, sweat, and tears have not been in vain. Freedom is on the march again," intones the film's newsreel narrator. As in the film's opening parade, the concluding parade begins with a file of real American veterans listed by their names, military ranks, and places of origin. But then the screen splits: the parade of actual Bataan veterans continues on one side while the film's characters occupy the other side of the screen. One of Madden's Filipino scouts is the first to appear, smiling and marching in time with the American veteran on the opposite side of the screen. Quinn as Bonifacio appears as the parade's penultimate character, smiling and with a more relaxed mien than he ever exhibited in the body of the film. Finally, Wayne as Madden joins the march, bringing the film to a jaunty conclusion.

Using "California Here I Come" as the soundtrack for *Back to Bataan's* victory parades to frame the film's main narrative implicitly reassures American audiences that while the war in the Pacific was still ongoing, the ultimate outcome was not really in question. As the film's narrator affirms, "freedom is on the march," and the veterans' parade for which "California Here I Come" serves as the soundtrack reassured Americans that their boys would come home again. But salving American anxieties about the outcome of the war while the war was still ongoing necessarily compromises *Back to Bataan's* much vaunted commitment to historical reality. Although *Back to Bataan* linked filmic theater to the martial (Pacific) theater, these two theaters could not conjoin and maintain the historical integrity both the film's makers and critics claimed for it. The ultimate power balance in the Pacific was still undecided when *Back to Bataan* was released.[11] A minor exchange between one of Madden's American soldiers and Madden himself in the middle of the film reveals the film's suppressed anxiety about the war's outcome. Jackson, one of the Americans in Madden's troop, laments "that's the worst part about war. . . . You see something but you never know how it ends. It'd be nice to know right now how all this is going to end, wouldn't it?" Madden replies with an air of resignation: "[It] certainly would." The film's framing parades, with their comforting audio and visual attestation that American soldiers could recover from the debilitating defeats at Bataan and Corregidor and the accompanying assurance that "freedom is on the march," give an implicit answer to what the film explicitly poses as an unanswerable question: the outcome of the war in the Pacific.

Critics of the time emphasized the currency of Dmytryk's film as well as its supposed historical accuracy; thus the film would seem to be limited by military events not yet decided. In her February 16, 1945, review for the *Los Angeles Daily News*, Virginia Wright discussed the narrative complications imposed by the ever-changing course of events in the Pacific theater. "Originally, the plan was to end the film on the rescue of the prisoners," Wright wrote, presumably referring to the liberation of the American prisoners at Cabanatuan that eventually served as the film's beginning, not its end. "Producer Robert Fellows had the okeh [*sic*] of the War Department [for a certain scene]," Wright related, "although when and how it would happen no one knew. That plan was abandoned in the interests of authenticity, and the ending left up in the air until history could take its course" (Wright 1945). Wright notes that Ben Barzman, who wrote the script for the film, "was brought onto the picture a week before it went into production. Because of incomplete reports from the Philippines, the original script . . . had to be revised constantly in accordance with new data. . . . The film was nearing completion when the Americans landed on Leyte, an event which provided a logical conclusion. To avoid leaving the spectator, however, with the comfortable feeling of the happy ending, Barzman wrote a final scene between a wounded guerrilla leader and a girl which reminds us of the terrible cost in blood" (Wright 1945). The final scene to which Wright refers is presumably the taking of Balad. But contrary to Barzman's stated intentions, the Balad scene does provide exactly "the comfortable feeling of [a] happy ending" through the retaking of the schoolhouse and through Bonifacio and Delgado's ecstatic reunion. Indeed, Bonifacio and Delgado's joyful embrace, as well as the exhibition of "free Filipino soil," downplays rather than acknowledges war's "terrible cost in blood" (Bonifacio's wound is minor). The scene's closing display of the Philippine and American flags manifests precisely the happy ending Barzman repudiated in the interest of realism.

Moreover, the film's final scene is not the one at Balad. Instead, the film's final scene is the "California Here I Come" parade that joins the film's narrative characters and the healthy, recovered veterans of the debilitating Philippine campaign. *Back to Bataan* leaves its viewer not with a reminder of war's "terrible cost," but an image celebrating the almost divinely foredestined triumph of Pax Americana. Despite its own explicit anxiety about not knowing how the war will end, *Back to Bataan* predicts an eventual American victory, a victory of Truth and Freedom through a comfortingly circular ending—an ending that promises to bring American soldiers back, hale, hearty, and triumphant, while simultaneously reconstituting Americans' national "home" as straddling both sides of the Pacific. An anonymous review of *Back to Bataan* bears out this point, calling the film "a tense, exciting drama of guerrilla warfare in our own backyard, the Philippines" (unidentified review 1945).[12] *Back to Bataan*'s careful manipulation of America's colonial history in the Philippines reveals Edward Dmytryk's film as a piece of wartime propaganda carefully constructed to persuade its viewers at home that, despite the vicissitudes of war, victory lay ahead and America's position as a global power—both in the military theater and its colonial possession of the Philippines—was assured.

The renegotiation of American expansionism on the march from acquisition to liberation had particular cogency for the Philippines, poised as it was to receive its own long-awaited freedom on July 4, 1946. *Back to Bataan* is no mere piece of war propaganda. Although part of the film's ideological agenda is to reassure its viewers that American freedom was destined to win the war in the Pacific, it was not just a successful military outcome that the film celebrated. *Back to Bataan* shows the United States at a particular ideological crossroads, and the film's real ideological campaign is not the overt military one but the renegotiation of political relations between the United States and the Philippines on the eve of the U.S. restoration of Philippine political sovereignty. In *Back to Bataan,* Filipinos must prove themselves worthy of independence not by asserting their ability to manage their affairs without American help, but rather by reinforcing their dependence on American leadership. The final lesson of American colonial tutelage is that Americans such as John Wayne are "better Filipinos" than the Filipinos themselves, and that, as Maximo and Señor Bello show, to correctly learn "Liburty," Filipinos had to figuratively enlist in the American campaign. While exorcising American colonial guilt via projection onto the Japanese, *Back to Bataan* also constructs Filipino independence as possible only through renewed subordination to the (soon-to-be) former colonial master. While faulty in its depictions of the Filipino-American past, *Back to Bataan* was all too prophetic in its predictions concerning the future of Filipino-American relations. Through its careful reconstructions of the Filipino-American past, *Back to Bataan* helped to construct a neocolonial Filipino-American future.

CHAPTER 4

The Star-Entangled Banner

COMMEMORATING ONE HUNDRED YEARS OF PHILIPPINE (IN)DEPENDENCE AND PHILIPPINE-AMERICAN RELATIONS

BACK TO BATAAN proleptically constructed the dynamic between the United States and the Philippines the year before the United States' official recognition of Philippine independence, scheduled for July 4, 1946. July 4, the U.S. Independence Day, already had been utilized to ironically mark the relationship between the two countries when on July 4, 1902, Theodore Roosevelt declared the Philippine "insurrection" officially over. July 4, 1902, then, functioned as a kind of Independence Day in the Philippines, but not one for Filipinos. Declaring the Philippine-American War officially over marked the U.S. official emancipation from a war that had lost considerable popular support at home and had been highly controversial from the start. By declaring the Philippine insurrection over, the United States moved on to the job of colonial administration, thus definitively signifying Filipinos' lack of independence. July 4, 1902, therefore signified a kind of freedom for Americans and a concomitant and conclusive lack of freedom for Filipinos. The July 4, 1946, conferral of Philippine independence ostensibly would, from the Filipino perspective, right that wrong: though long deferred, the Philippines would at last obtain official independence and become a sovereign state. But full political equality has been elusive for the Philippines; instead, it has assumed toward the United States the neocolonial dependency prefigured in *Back to Bataan*.

Filipinos are keenly aware of the multiple layers of irony inherent in both their nation's relationship to its former colonial master and how these ironies manifest themselves in attempts to historically locate the best date on which to commemorate Philippine independence. These tensions gathered in 1996 as commemorative attention focused around both the centenary of the 1896 Philippine Revolution and the half centenary of the United States' 1946 conferral of Philippine independence. Controversy intensified over the meaning of July 4, formerly officially marking Philippine Independence Day and now celebrated as Philippine-American Friendship Day, and climaxed in the state-sponsored celebration of Phil-Am Friendship Day, held at Manila's Luneta Park, during which the July 4, 1946, Philippine independence ceremony was reenacted. Through an examination of government-sponsored public commemorations—speeches by both Philippine and American politicians and diplomats, social events hosted by the U.S. embassy in Manila, as well as the July 4 event at the Luneta—this chapter focuses on the state axis of nationalism. An analysis of individuals' private views on Philippine-American relations, carried out in debates in the major Philippine newspapers, however, reveals the active and sometimes contentious interplay between the state and individual citizens by demonstrating individuals' contestation of official representations of national history. July 4 has become a site of memory for both Philippine and American nationalism, and the controversy that surrounded and refracted through the public commemorations of July 4, 1996, as Philippine-American Friendship Day reveals the continuing contestation of Philippine-American history as well as current Philippine-American relations. Whereas the previous chapters have explored the ways in which the state constructs and manipulates nationalism through the identity axis as embodied in national heroes such as José Rizal and Andres Bonifacio, this chapter examines the state's symbolization of national history through the calendar of public holidays. National holidays are state-sponsored events encapsulating and giving the state imprimatur on national history, a perennial rehearsal of the national narrative. However, the state imprimatur does not guarantee acceptance throughout the national polity; individual citizens, motivated by their identification with the nation, can be moved to challenge the state in defense of their own sense of national values, championing their interpretation of the national good when they perceive a divergence between the state's interest and the nation's. This chapter examines the plasticity of the nationalist dynamic through the interplay between the state and the people, the official national narrative as handed down by state representatives at state venues, and challenges to that narrative raised by individuals and played out through the press, which, during the controversial summer of 1996, served as a forum for heated debates about the myths versus the reality of Philippine-American relations.

COMMEMORATING THE PHILIPPINE CENTENNIAL(S)

Like the United States, the Philippines arose out of a revolution against a colonial master. But due to the U.S. preemption of the Philippine Revolution, the Philippines, unlike the United States, did not decisively win its revolution. By the time the United States entered the Philippine scene in 1898, Filipino revolutionaries had largely won their revolution. Under Emilio Aguinaldo's leadership, the Katipuneros had nearly succeeded in overthrowing colonial rule in the Philippines. Aguinaldo's forces laid siege to Manila in the early summer of 1898. When American Admiral Dewey confronted the Spanish government officials and military personnel barricaded inside Intramuros (the walled city that was the Spanish capital of the Philippines) in August 1898, Aguinaldo's forces had been laying siege to the city for over a month and the Spaniards' surrender was only a matter of time. Even American historians such as Stanley Karnow, who is regarded often as an apologist for American imperialism in the Philippines, admits that Filipino revolutionaries had brought the Spanish colonial capital to its knees after three months under siege. "It was only a matter of time before the city fell," concedes Karnow (1989, 123). By the time the Treaty of Paris was concluded on December 10, 1898, "Spain actually controlled only a few isolated outposts in the country. The Filipino people had won their war of liberation," asserts Renato Constantino (1994, 219). If not for the American intervention, presumably, all would have been well for the First Philippine Republic—or at least, the new nation would have embarked as does any other, shaky at first, then flourishing or failing as time progressed.[1]

The United States' forcible annexation of the Philippines, its eventual recognition of Philippine sovereignty, and its continuing neocolonial influence render the meaning, much less the dating, of Philippine independence complex, elusive, and politically charged. The U.S. preemption of the Philippine Revolution has greatly problematized Filipino national history, for historians, politicians, academicians, and the *masa* alike continue, even today, to debate the originary point of Philippine nationhood. Anthony D. Smith (1996, 177) declares that "the nation dates from the moment of nationalist success." If "the moment of nationalist success" is, as I assume, the establishment of a sovereign state, the "dating" of the Philippine nation remains a difficult task. For Americans, the issue is simple, because they won their revolution. Most Americans would define 1776 as the United States' originary date. Although the United States was not yet a sovereign state, it did become one, and American historians subsequently antedated national history to the Revolution and the Declaration of Independence. Americans celebrate their national independence on July 4 because the Declaration of Independence marks the declaration of the *aspiration* to political sovereignty, not its formal achievement (in which case, the United States might identify 1787 as the year of the U.S. advent as a nation because of the ratification of the Constitution). Americans do not date national independence from September 3, 1783, the date on which England recognized U.S. independence, yet that is the situation the Philippines faced in observing July 4 as Philippine Independence Day.[2] In the U.S. case, it is the declaration of nationalist determination, not formal recognition by the international community, that determines the originating point of our national narrative: it was Americans' declaration of themselves as a nation, not recognition by outsiders, that mattered. If that standard applies to

the Philippines, then June 12, 1898, the date on which Emilio Aguinaldo proclaimed the Philippine Declaration of Independence from the balcony of his
house in Kawit, Cavite, is the logical originary point for the Philippine
Republic. Diosdado Macapagal established June 12 as the Philippines' official
Independence Day in 1962 by presidential proclamation—thus it was valid
only as long as he was president. In order for it to become permanent, congressional action was necessary (Ancheta 1998, 85). In 1964, Republic Act
4166 officially made June 12 Philippine Independence Day. July 4 officially
became Republic Day—somewhat awkwardly, since Teddy Roosevelt's July 4,
1902, declaration officially ending the Philippine-American War heralded the
death of the First Philippine Republic inaugurated by Aguinaldo on June 12,
1898. July 4 as Republic Day proved too problematic, and eventually July 4
was redesignated Philippine-American Friendship Day to honor the two
countries' long and close ties. But the nationalist and historiographical debates
focusing on June 12 versus July 4 as Philippine Independence Day continued
to simmer.[3]

The summer of 1996 was a period of intense historical and historiographical controversy in the Philippines. The Philippines commemorates two
national centennials, the first of which occurred in August 1996: the one hundredth anniversary of the beginning of the Philippine Revolution against
Spain. The second centennial, seen by many as "the" centennial or "the major"
centennial, occurred on June 12, 1998: the one hundredth anniversary of the
Philippine Declaration of Independence.[4] Ironically, the centennial commemorations of 1996 focused much greater attention on two noncentennial historical events, both of which pertained to the relationship between the
Philippines and the United States: the fiftieth anniversary of the United States'
formal grant of independence to its former colony on July 4, 1946, and the
ninety-eighth anniversary of June 12, 1898.

The efforts to fix the date of the "real" centennial of Philippine independence and the seemingly disproportionate attention paid to the "wrong"
dates is revealing about both the historical relationship between the United
States and the Philippines as well as the process of making history. The ubiq-
uity of the United States in a centennial year ostensibly dealing with the
Philippines' colonial relationship to Spain, as well as the highly ambivalent
attitudes of Filipinos toward the United States, demonstrate the fact that the
vexed relationship between the United States and the Philippines continues
today and that the reality of the Philippines' continued economic dependence
on the United States shades any attempt to understand the historical roots of
that relationship. The pressure that the present exerts on the past emerges from
the arguments over which dates mark the most meaningful anniversary, which
dates constitute "real" history. In the struggle over whether to commemorate
liberation from Spain (1896), an unsuccessful claim of independence from the

18. The Philippines five-peso bill features an illustration of Emilio Aguinaldo's declaration of Philippine independence, June 12, 1898.

United States (1898), or the granting of independence by the United States (1946), we see the process of constructing nationalist history. The palpable tensions between competing ideologies throw into relief the contested and entangled process of creating a meaningful national past.

Despite fifty years of putative Filipino independence, the United States continues to exert a dominating influence on the Philippines. Hence, the diversion of centennial attention away from Spanish postcolonialism to American neocolonialism eclipsed the centennial of 1996, transforming the centennial of 1996 into a prequel for 1998. The Philippine Centennial Commission attempted to solve this conundrum by designating the Philippine centennial a five-year event, with highlights in 1996 and 1998; but the commission subsequently undermined its own attempt at nationalist diplomacy by noting (only) the dates "1898–1998" on its official logo (see figure 20). Thus the 1896 Philippine Revolution against Spain—predating America's involvement in the Philippines—was overshadowed by attention to America's *arrival* in the Philippines in 1898, as well as America's putative *departure* from the Philippines in 1946. The nationalist historiographical preemption of the 1996 centennial, enacted in the Philippines largely by Filipinos, ironically mirrors the American preemption of the Philippine Revolution ninety-eight years ago. The preemption of the 1996 centennial represents a national response to a collective

19. A spoof of Aguinaldo's declaration of Philippine independence in the *Philippine Star*, June 12, 1996. The artist's insertion of the Katipunan flag is a reminder of the schism within Philippine revolutionary/nationalist leadership as well as the Philippine-American War.

history that largely has been effaced not only within the United States but within the Philippines as well.

The upstaging of the August 1996 centennial arose from the continuing antinomies of Philippine–American relations. The fact that the United States has been and continues to be the largest source of foreign investment in the Philippines and the fact that the Philippines is also one of the largest recipients of United States Aid for International Development (USAID) both problematize Philippine independence. These two facts encapsulate the United States' continuing domination of Philippine economic and political (especially foreign) policy, a domination so pronounced it makes the concept of Philippine independence itself a problematic issue. Ultimately, the Philippines and the

20. The official logo of the Philippine centennial. The interior features the colors of the Philippine flag: gold, red, blue, and white. The three gold stars signify the archipelago's geographical division: the North (main island, Luzon), the Visayas (the middle group of islands), and the South (main island, Mindanao). The eight-rayed sun, also depicted in the Philippine flag, symbolizes the eight provinces that originally participated in the 1896 revolution. The motto "Kalayaan Kayamanan ng Bayan" means "Freedom/Independence is the wealth/treasure of the nation."

United States are enmeshed in a postcolonial entanglement in which both countries skirt political realities they are deeply unwilling to acknowledge: that the United States still enjoys the economic and cultural privileges of neocolonial domination, and that the Philippine Republic, despite vociferously anti-American nationalism, continues to be economically dependent on American interests. So both countries continue diplomatic relations locked in a multifaceted but covert *danse colonial*.

July 4, 1996: Commemorating Philippine (In)Dependence

Despite fifty years of formal Philippine independence, the United States continues to be a dominant influence on Filipino politics and the Philippine economy. The love-hate dynamic of Philippine-American relations is fueled by the continuing neocolonial economic and diplomatic relationship between the two countries. Discussing the impact of the United States on the Philippines, Renato Constantino (1997, 116) observes, "The United States is the biggest reality in our lives." Because 1996 marked the centennial of the Philippine Revolution against Spain, it would seem to afford the rare opportunity for a nationalist celebration free of the persistent conundrum of Philippine-American relations. The fact that in 1996 the fiftieth anniversary of the

U.S. formal grant of independence on July 4, 1946, overshadowed the one-hundredth anniversary of the Philippine Revolution (August 1996) demonstrated the inescapable pervasiveness of the American influence on Philippine politics.

The fiftieth anniversary of Philippine-American Friendship Day became a lightning rod for both the pro- and anti-American schools of Philippine nationalism. The two opposing schools of Philippine nationalism reflect a fundamental ambivalence on the part of the Philippine state: while national sovereignty demands political and economic independence from the United States, American investment and foreign aid are irresistible. At a symposium on "Fifty Years of Philippine-American Relations" hosted by the Philippine Department of Foreign Affairs on July 3, 1996, in honor of the fiftieth anniversary of Philippine-American Friendship Day, Alex Magno gave a cogent overview of Filipino ambivalence toward American dominance in Philippine politics, culture, and education. "The Philippine-American entanglement, now nearly a century old," stated Magno, "has always been problematic. It has always been a relationship constantly trapped in the cross-currents of each nation's concept of its destiny and each people's understanding of their fate." On one hand, Magno stated, "it became standard for all aspiring Filipino political leaders of whatever ideological stripe to blame America for all our miseries," but on the other hand Filipinos "became a clinging-vine partner in the [Filipino-American] relationship" (Magno 1996).

The Philippines' clinging-vine dependence on the United States stems in large part from the Philippines' developing economy, one which on one hand actively courts foreign multinational corporations to supply jobs and on the other is the grateful recipient of USAID. The Philippines' continuing dependence on American economic aid formed a counterpoint in the nationalistic public discourse surrounding the 1996 July Fourth celebrations. The Philippines' dependence on foreign largesse was particularly noticeable at this time because the General Santos airport in Mindanao had just been completed using USAID funds. In a 1993 meeting to discuss APEC (Asian-Pacific Economic Cooperation) and Manila's hosting of the APEC summit in 1996, Philippine President Fidel V. Ramos told American President Bill Clinton that "it was [Ramos's] intention to concentrate on 'trade not aid' with the United States" (Ramos 1996). Ramos repeated this statement in his July 3, 1996, speech at a Malacañang Palace celebration of the July 4 festivities. That Ramos should need to make this statement during the commemoration of America's recognition of Philippine independence, at the same time that the Philippines celebrated another major development completed through U.S. economic aid, underscores the profound ambivalences and ironies that pervade Philippine independence.

The incongruity between the Philippines' continuing reliance on American economic support even as the country celebrated its official independence from the United States can be seen clearly in President Fidel Ramos's celebratory July 3 speech. Entitled "Our Common Future in the Asia-Pacific," Ramos's speech emphasized not only that "American investors have consistently been the largest group of investors in the Philippines since the turn of the century" but also that "American security and development assistance has contributed in no small measure to our efforts to alleviate poverty and empower ordinary Filipinos with better job opportunities and higher family incomes." Astonishingly, Ramos also noted with approbation that "Mobil Oil . . . set up offices in Manila way back in 1898," during the first year of the Philippine-American War (Ramos 1996). In noting the coincidence between the Filipino-American political and economic relationships, Ramos makes relatively explicit a reality that is largely suppressed in both American and Filipino nationalist histories: the marketplace motivated the battlefield. During the early stages of the Philippine-American War, there was considerable debate in the United States about both the practical as well as the ethical issues involved in forcibly annexing the Philippines. On June 6, 1899, the *New York Times* declared, "The Philippines are pretty costly real estate" (Miller 1982, 113). As Steward Creighton Miller relates, "Senator Carter assured the swelling ranks of doubters that 'the Republican Party will return the Philippines as a matter of profit. This is a practical age. We are going to deal with the question on the basis of dollars and cents. Neither religion nor sentiment will have much influence in determining the verdict. The great question is 'will it pay?'" (113).[5]

The marketplace motive has been conjoined from the beginning in Philippine-American relations, a fact manifested clearly in parity rights as a condition for formal Philippine independence. That Ramos would cite with approbation such a history is anathema to the anti-American nationalists, who see nothing celebratory in a century of American battening on the Philippines. While Ramos's statement was intended to remind Filipinos as well as Americans of the Philippine-American history of economic cooperation, by mentioning 1898 Ramos unintentionally reminded Filipinos of the indivisible connection between American economic imperialism and the forcible acquisition of the Philippines, thereby revealing one of the repressed, and most sensitive, elements of colonialism: the profit motive. Countries ostensibly fight wars for lofty causes: freedom, repelling evil, protecting the American way of life, etc. Although nations will enthusiastically espouse shared prosperity, few readily will admit that they undertake armed conflict in the interest of the national economy or openly discuss exploitative economic relations they hold with less (or more) powerful or prosperous nations. Filipinos, as much as

Americans, hold it a matter of national pride to disavow the economic disparity between the two countries—a disparity founded in their colonial history and sustained during the half century of ostensible Philippine independence.

PHILIPPINE-AMERICAN FRIENDSHIP DAY?

While Fidel Ramos's speech was heard only by a small diplomatic audience, he made his pro-American position clear to the Filipino public by designating July 4, 1996, a "non-working public holiday." July 4 is normally a working holiday, but in 1996, just two weeks in advance of the date, Ramos changed the day's official status ("For a Meaningful Fourth of July" 1996). Although one might expect the gift of an unexpected national holiday to be enthusiastically received, Ramos's sudden move to make July 4 a nonworking holiday aroused a great deal of controversy. An editorial in the July 4 *Manila Chronicle* noted, "The celebration promises to be simple and subdued, perhaps because the Ramos administration is aware of the controversial nature of his declaration" ("For a Meaningful Fourth of July" 1996). However, neither the July 4 commemoration nor the editorials that accompanied it were simple or subdued. The commemorations of July 4, 1996, as Phil-Am Friendship Day prompted vigorous debates in the Philippines' main newspapers contesting the diplomatic facade of Philippine-American relations. These debates centered on the galling political and economic disparity between the two countries, thence leading to even more sensitive national issues: the reality vs. the myth of Philippine political sovereignty and the United States' continuing neocolonial influence over its ostensible political equal. By giving the state imprimatur to Phil-Am Friendship Day, Ramos supplied the spark to anti-American sentiments that had already been smoldering.

In the weeks leading up to July 4, 1996, the Philippine press roiled with debates over the meaning of Phil-Am friendship. Herman Tiu Laurel was acerbic in his reaction to the revival of Phil-Am Friendship Day, tartly asserting, "I will not yet use the term *friendship*." "The revival of the celebration" of Phil-Am Friendship Day, Laurel wrote, "particularly by making it an official holiday, diverts from the truth [about Philippine-American relations] and more urgent tasks in the evolution of a stronger nation. . . . [T]he history of the [Philippine-American] relationship speaks more of condescension and exploitation" than friendship (Laurel 1996). Delfo Cortina Canceran and Rose Yaya's letter to the editors of the *Manila Times* was printed in the July 4, 1996, opinion section under the ironic title "We the People":

Today, we don't have classes because July 4 has been declared an official holiday. It is RP [Republic of the Philippines]-US friendship day!

But what is there to celebrate? In the first place, was [sic] there really friendly relations between the Philippines and the United States? Wasn't the relationship one of colonial dependency?

Let us deconstruct this [sic] so-called friendly ties. (Canceran and Yaya 1996, 7)

Although both the United States and the Philippines would be celebrating July 4, in his editorial for the *Philippine Daily Inquirer* Adrian Cristobal noted the postcolonial irony inherent in the asymmetry of the two countries' Fourth of July celebrations:

As Americans celebrate their day of independence, will they also find it significant that it is also the Friendship Day for our two nations? It's questionable that our American friends will be toasting Philippine-American Friendship Day as they watch the fireworks of July 4.

So if our Friendship Day practically means next to nothing to Americans—it's after all the triumph of their revolution against the British Empire—what can it possibly mean to us? (Cristobal 1996)

Instead of "friendship," Cristobal asserted that the Philippines' continuing neo-colonial relationship with the United States was what was really being celebrated: "It's [the special relationship] that our leaders want to preserve on the centennial of our Revolution and the eve of our national day. The bitter taste of that relationship is not salved by the slogan of 'equal partnership'" (Cristobal 1996).

In his statement on the meaning of July 4 and why the Filipino people should celebrate it, Ramos had glorified the lofty ideals Filipinos and Americans shared: "When we celebrate PAFD [Philippine-American Friendship Day], we honor once more the heroism and vision of Filipino leaders who fought to build an independent nation based on the universal ideals of representative democracy, their rule of law, and respect for human rights" (Ramos 1996). But Ramos's lofty ideals were undercut in a statement made by American Ambassador to the Philippines John Negroponte. "The fiftieth Anniversary of 'Philippine-American Friendship Day' provides the perfect opportunity for us to reflect on nearly a century of shared history and friendship between Filipinos and Americans," said Negroponte, affirming the continuing relevance of the term *unique relationship* to describe contemporary Philippine-American relations (Negroponte 1996). Negroponte's use of the telling political phrase "unique relationship" supports Laurel and Cristobal's anti-Americanist analysis, as "unique relationship" or "special relationship" have been traditional euphemisms for the U.S. (post)colonial relationship with the Philippines.[6] Negroponte's praise of the "special relationship" between the United States and the Philippines obliquely reveals the continuing power of the colonial relationship.

"AN INDEPENDENT REPUBLIC LIKE OUR
VERY OWN": REENACTING THE JULY 4, 1946,
INDEPENDENCE CEREMONY

The fiftieth anniversary of Philippine-American Friendship Day was
commemorated by a reenactment of the U.S. independence ceremony that
symbolized the inauguration of an independent Philippine Republic held at
the Luneta on July 4, 1946.[7] Army Maj. Gen. Joseph DeFrancisco read the
speech of Douglas MacArthur. Benjamin Cayetano, a Filipino-American and
governor of Hawaii, read the speech of Sen. Millard Tydings (of the Tydings-
McDuffie Act, which set the date for Philippine independence). The speech
of the first Philippine Republic president, Manuel L. Roxas, was read by his
grandson, Manuel A. Roxas, a Philippine congressman. U.S. Ambassador to
the Philippines John Negroponte read the part of U.S. high (colonial) commissioner to the Philippines, Paul V. McNutt, who read Harry S. Truman's
independence decree on July 4, 1946:

> I [McNutt] am authorized and directed by the President of the United
> States to proclaim the independence of the Philippines as a separate and
> self-governing nation.
>
> Seldom in the history of the world has one nation proclaimed the
> independence of another. . . .
>
> Yet, it cannot be said that this independence was earned by the Filipino
> people without struggle or strife: The people of the Philippines have
> striven well, have fought courageously, and have sought tirelessly their
> national freedom. By petition and persuasion the Filipino people have
> pursued their independence, even while the American Flag was being
> firmly planted here. The people of these Islands have shown by word and
> deed their deep desire for national sovereignty. That desire was under-
> stood and appreciated by the American people . . . and the American
> Congress, which had already, in 1916, pledged freedom to the Philip-
> pines, [and] set a definite date, July 4, 1946, for that unprecedented grant
> of sovereignty.
>
> This is the result. Today is the climax of that gathering of hopes and
> aspirations and convictions. In a few moments this will be an independent
> republic, like our very own, conceived in liberty, with a government like
> our own, of the people, by the people and for the people.
>
> We have taken the unparalleled action of transferring sovereignty over
> this land to the Philippine Republic because we recognize the inalienable
> right of all peoples to be the masters of their own fate . . . .
>
> This is the first democratic Republic of western mold to be established
> in the Orient. (Negroponte 1996)

Truman's specifying that for a few last minutes the Philippines remained under U.S. control, as his statement that "in a few moments this will be an independent republic" delimits, emphasized the U.S. retention of colonial control to the very end. At the same time that Truman highlighted Filipinos' "inalienable right . . . to be the masters of their own fate," he also highlighted the United States' continuing control of the Philippines, thus admitting the fact that the United States, even at that precise moment, continued to violate the very inalienable right Truman acknowledged.

Truman's invocation of U.S. nationalist rhetoric, of government "of the people, by the people and for the people" and the "inalienable right" phrase, as well as his acknowledgement of Filipinos' "deep desire for national sovereignty" and their determination to gain "their national freedom" recapitulate the fundamental irony of the United States' forcible annexation of the Philippines: that the United States, a nation born of revolution to overthrow colonial domination and explicitly holding as a key national value government by the consent of the governed, preempted Filipinos' similar revolution to overthrow colonial domination, then imposed a government that ignored the consent of the governed. The Philippine-American War is the repressed primal scene in Truman's speech. He alludes to Filipinos' "hav[ing] striven well, [and] . . . fought courageously," but he fails to mention that these Filipinos had fought courageously *against America*. Insurgency, the "deed" by which Filipinos "show[ed] . . . their deep desire for national sovereignty," is elided in favor of the more pacific "petition and persuasion," and colonial occupation is glossed over with the euphemism of the "firm plant[ing] of the American flag."

Truman also occluded any reference to Emilio Aguinaldo, leader of the Filipinos who "fought courageously" during the American flag's firm planting. Although aging veterans of the Philippine-American War, wearing the *rayadillo* that was their uniform during the revolution, were present at the July 4, 1946, celebration, Aguinaldo was not included in the independence ceremony. The Philippine Declaration of Independence is traditionally iconized by the image of Aguinaldo's waving of the Philippine flag from the balcony of his house at Cavite, just after he proclaimed the Declaration of Independence on June 12, 1898 (as illustrated on the five-peso bill). In spite of—or perhaps because of—Aguinaldo's centrality to the iconography of Philippine independence, he was conspicuously absent at the July 4, 1946, ceremony. It was Aguinaldo who in 1898 had studied America's revolutionary foundations to interrogate America's motivation for aiding Filipino revolutionaries. Aguinaldo questioned the United States' intention to establish in the Philippines "an independent republic . . . conceived in liberty, with a government like our own, of the people, by the people and for the people," but was manipulated by American officials who were determined that the Philippines would *not* be "a separate and self-governing nation." Aguinaldo gambled the Philippines' sovereignty on his faith in America's anticolonial foundation—and lost.

In his July 4, 1946, statement, Harry Truman was chary to preserve the superiority of the American democratic original over the Oriental copy (the Philippines was "the first democratic Republic *of western mold* to be established in the Orient"). This point was emphasized visually on the cover of the official program of the 1946 independence ceremony, which was reproduced for the 1996 commemoration. On the 1946 program cover the Statue of Liberty figures prominently, vertically centered on the right side of the cover. Filipinas, the feminine nationalistic icon who is Columbia's Filipina counterpart, is roughly one-half the size of the Statue of Liberty. While the Statue of Liberty is clearly foregrounded, Filipinas is in the background. Positioned in the lower left corner of the cover, Filipinas is dwarfed by the Statue of Liberty. The Statue of Liberty triumphantly and assertively lifts her lamp beside the golden door, but Filipinas is portrayed as an uncertain figure. While Liberty's muscular upraised arm and angular face give her a strong, sturdy air, Filipinas's diminutive femininity is emphasized in her rounded face and the faintly defensive air with which she clutches the Philippine flag to her body. The subtly upward angle of Liberty's portrayal draws the viewer's eye upward; the angle of the folds of her drapery and the proportion of the bottom of the figure (knees to feet) to the top of the figure (her face) visually position the viewer as being below Lady Liberty. This is the view one might have of her when looking up from the ground. While the graininess of the program cover's illustration somewhat blurs the details of Filipinas's face, she too appears to be literally looking up to Liberty. Although the ceremony recognized the occasion of Philippine independence, the visual imagery of the program cover emphasized American primacy and implicitly forecast continuing Philippine dependence on American might and the light provided by Liberty's torch.

The flag Filipinas holds makes her blend into the procession of flags she heads, foremost of which is the American flag (which is almost as big as she is!). While the Statue of Liberty proudly stands alone, Filipinas appears to be heading a parade of nations. The imagery is ambiguous, but clearly while the American nationalist icon stands apart and continues to light the way for the world's tired, poor, and provincial peoples, the Filipino nationalist icon is but one of many—for this moment at the head of the parade but perhaps soon to fall in with the endless line of other flags, to dwindle into obscurity in the background. Thus the cover illustration of the independence ceremony program, like the text of Truman's speech, ambivalently presents Philippine "independence" by focusing not on Philippine sovereignty but on neocolonial subordination to the former colonial master.

21. The program cover illustration for the July 4, 1996, commemorative program originally appeared as the cover for the July 4, 1946, independence ceremony.

THE STAR ENTANGLED BANNER

The reproduction of the 1946 Filipinas/Statue of Liberty illustration served as one cover for the 1996 program. On the other side of the 1996 program was a picture of the Philippine and American flags, taken at the 1946 ceremony. The so-called flag ceremony has been conventionalized as the icon for the granting of Philippine independence; the ceremonial lowering of the American flag symbolized the decline of American rule, while the raising of the Philippine flag denoted the ascendancy of Philippine sovereignty.[8] At the 1996 reenactment, however, the symbolism of the two flags iconized in the 1946 photo was spontaneously and aptly reconstituted. Following the rereading of the decree of formal independence in a ceremony accented by parades of schoolchildren and confetti dropped by helicopter, the Philippine national anthem was played as the American flag was ceremonially lowered and the Philippine flag was simultaneously raised. At approximately the halfway point, however, the flag ropes snagged and the two flags became entangled, jerking as the actors below tugged in an effort to bring the ropes in line. After several seconds of the half-sympathetic silence with which audiences greet an obvious glitch in a live performance, individual spectators, who had been sweltering under the hot morning sun, began to comment on the aptness of the symbolism being played out before them while fanning themselves vigorously with the commemorative fans given out earlier that morning in which, ironically, the Philippine and American flags were blended in a yin-yang symbol of friendship.

The flags were eventually untangled, of course, but few had missed the symbolism of the snag. In the picture taken at the original 1946 ceremony, the American and Philippine flags are shown approximately at midpoint; the Philippine flag, while slightly ascendant, nonetheless appears slightly smaller than the Stars and Stripes below it, which is visually centered in the photograph and is larger than the Philippine flag—a photographic reminder that although the Philippines had ascended to ostensible independence, the United States remained the center of attention. At the 1996 commemoration, the flags snarled at roughly the same point: the Philippine flag appeared to be struggling to rise, while the American flag, draped slightly above it, appeared to be reluctant to yield. The *Manila Times* captured the moment for its front page the next day. The headline—"Flags Get Entangled, a Mirror of Love-Hate Ties?"—was accompanied by a picture of the flag ceremony, under which appeared the caption "Star-Entangled Banner. Uncannily reflecting Philippine-U.S. relations, the flags of both countries fly separately but nevertheless get in a bind in yesterday's celebration of the fiftieth anniversary of Philippine independence from American colonial rule."

Journalistic representations of the ceremonial blooper varied. However, one interesting commonality was the recurrence of the verb *refuse*, which

50TH ANNIVERSARY
OF THE
PHILIPPINE REPUBLIC
AND
PHILIPPINE-AMERICAN
FRIENDSHIP DAY

JULY 4, 1996

22. This flag ceremony photograph from the July 4, 1946, independence ceremony is often reprinted in Philippine history textbooks. A colorized version appeared on the back cover of the July 4, 1996, commemorative program.

23. The official logo of Philippine-American Friendship Day, July 4, 1996. The imagery of the entwined Philippine and American flags was ironically manifested in the "Star-Entangled Banner" during the reenactment of the turnover ceremony.

journalists used to describe the American flag's position in the entanglement. Despite the article's title, the *Manila Chronicle*'s "Tale of Two Snagged Flags at July 4 Rites" did not show the two flags entangled; the photo showed the Philippine flag ascendant over the Stars and Stripes, yet the caption commented, "The U.S. flag refused to come down from its mast in yesterday's first official celebration of Filipino-American Friendship Day, sending people [in]to laughter in an otherwise solemn re-enactment of the granting of Philippine Independence on July 4, 1946" (Parungao and Porcalla 1996). Manila's *Today* ran a front-page picture of the July 4 ceremony with the caption "the American flag, which was supposed to go down, gets entangled with the Philippine flag and 'refuses' to budge." The *Philippine Daily Star* ran an article entitled "The Star-Entangled Banner" with the comment that "yesterday's

24. The front-page photo accompanying the "Star-Entangled Banner" article in the *Manila Times*, July 5, 1996. The caption reads, "Uncannily reflecting Philippine-US relations, the flags of both countries fly separately but nevertheless get in a bind in yesterday's celebration of the fiftieth anniversary of Philippine independence from American colonial rule at the Quirino Grandstand in Manila." Photo courtesy of the *Manila Times*.

symbolism was hard to avoid—as the U.S. flag was being lowered, it wrapped itself around the ascending RP flag and refused to let go" (Villanueva 1996).

In every journalistic treatment of the ceremonial glitch, the symbolism of the flags universally was interpreted as indicating the U.S. refusal to let its colonial possession go. For example, the *Philippine Daily Inquirer's* front-page article by Stella O. Gonzales and Rocky Nazareno said of the entangled flags, "As the American flag was lowered, it draped itself with the Philippine flag and was pulling it down. It took several seconds before the two flags were untangled. The audience cheered when the Philippine flag was finally set free and hoisted up the flagpole" (Gonzales and Nazareno 1996). (To underscore the triumph of Philippine independence, the *Philippine Daily Inquirer* front-page photos of the ceremony featured a large picture of the July 4 ceremony's climax, showing a dense group of cheering Filipinos, doves flying, and a phalanx of Filipino flags, along with a smaller picture of the Philippine flag ascendant over the American flag.) The *Manila Times,* which coined the "Star-Entangled Banner" phrase, reported that "when the two flags were finally disengaged, the crowd broke into cheers. The incident prompted a presidential guard to remark: "*Mukha talagang ayaw umalis ng mga Kano sa atin*" [It really looks like the Americans have no plans to leave our country] (Rufio 1996).

Not one newspaper suggested that the imagery could have emblematized the Philippine flag's reluctance to ascend rather than the American flag's refusal to descend—that the Philippines might be reluctant to take on the onus of independence. It is a point worth noting, given the repeated editorials excoriating continuing Philippine dependence on U.S. aid and trade, as well as efforts by Philippine leaders such as Presidents Manuel Quezon and Manuel Roxas to delay official independence during the Commonwealth period. Marichu Villanueva briefly alluded to this idea when she commented on the "unintended symbolism" of the entangled flags by suggesting that "the transition to independence has not been easy for the Philippines" (Villanueva 1996). It is true that the transition to independence has not always been easy for the Philippines. During the colonial period, a—if not *the*—major consideration in Philippine independence movements was the Philippine economy, which depended almost wholly on trade relations with the United States.[9] During the Commonwealth period (1933–46), when the date for full Philippine independence was being negotiated, the Philippine economy was geared toward export agriculture for American markets—so much so, Teodoro Agoncillo (1990, 362) tells us, that "the Philippines, potentially one of the great food-surplus-producing areas in Asia, became one of the major food deficit areas." After fifty years of independence, the Philippines continues to labor under a rice deficit. While the contemporary rice deficit may not be directly attributable to the Philippine economy's dependence on the American market, the Philippines' economic relationship with the United States continues to be a major factor in Philippine politics. The role of the Philippines' continuing economic dependence on the United States was on many Filipino minds during the debates over Phil-Am Friendship. Reynaldo Ronairo, a World War II veteran who attended the July 4, 1996, independence ceremony, said, "I don't think we [Filipinos/the Philippines] are completely independent. . . . Politically, maybe, but not economically" (Gonzales and Nazareno 1996, 13).

On the same day that Philippine newspapers covered the entangled flags, the *Manila Bulletin* reflected the continuing dissonance between Philippine sovereignty and the country's continuing dependence on American economic aid by dividing the July 4 front page between pictures of the July 4 festivities and the opening ceremony for the new General Santos airport in Mindanao, the latest fruit of U.S. aid.[10] The airport's opening festivities were presided over by USAID administrator Brian Atwood, U.S. ambassador to the Philippines John Negroponte, and Philippine president Fidel Ramos. The connection between putative Filipino independence and the Republic's continuing dependence on American aid was not lost on Filipinos. In the front-page article on "The Star-Entangled Banner," Marichu Villanueva wrote in the *Philippine Star*, "After granting Philippine independence in 1946, heavy American aid continued to prop up the economy. As if to underscore that history, the top American official attending Thursday's fiftieth anniversary ceremony was J. Brian Atwood, head of the U.S. Agency for International Development" (Villanueva 1996). At the July 4 ceremony at the Luneta, Atwood, acting as the "Personal Representative of H. E. William Clinton," read a message just before the independence ceremony reenactment. In his message, Atwood, speaking for the American presidency, tried to recuperate the United States' colonizing mission in the Philippines. "Fifty years before [1946—that is, 1898] an American President moved by missionary zeal spoke the words 'manifest destiny,'" Atwood intoned. "But America was never comfortable with the role of colonial power. Its manifest destiny was not to control, but to liberate" (Atwood 1996). That in 1996 the American president would feel the need to insist that America's motivation in forcibly assimilating the Philippines was motivated by a divinely ordained destiny "to liberate" rather than "to control" reveals more about the United States' continuing discomfort "with the role of colonial power" than anything else. That the United States needed to focus on Manifest Destiny rather than "benevolent assimilation" as the point on which the historical record needed to be righted reveals the United States' continuing need to rationalize its role in Philippine history. By invoking and trying to recuperate the U.S. "manifest destiny" in the Philippines, Clinton, like Truman before him, ironically reasserts the very expansionist ideology that he explicitly appears to be disavowing: obscuring American imperialism as liberation lamentably misunderstood by the ungrateful colonized. In fact, Clinton's speech invokes exactly the same construction of Manifest Destiny as worldwide liberation that *Back to Bataan* employed.

Atwood read a message from Bill Clinton to those assembled at the Luneta:

> "On behalf of the American people, I extend best wishes to all the Filipino people on the special occasion of the fiftieth anniversary of the independence of the Philippines.
>
> Fifty years ago, the United States and the Filipino people took an unprecedented step: Together, we created a free and democratic country. Through legislation rather than revolution, agreement rather than bloodshed, the independence sought for centuries by the Filipino people became a reality. On July 4, 1946, as the American flag was lowered and the Philippine flag raised, a half-century of American governance came to an end and the Republic of the Philippines took its rightful place in the community of nations." (Clinton 1996)

Fifty years after Harry Truman's carefully worded independence speech, Clinton's message similarly navigates dangerous shoals in Philippine-American history. Clinton's assertion that the United States liberated the Philippines "through legislation rather than revolution" elides the fact that the United States acquired the Philippines by squelching the Philippines' own revolution to overthrow Spanish colonial rule. Clinton's comment that with the 1946 U.S. grant of Philippine independence "the Republic of the Philippines took its rightful place in the community of nations" obscures the fact that the U.S. colonization denied "the Republic of the Philippines . . . its rightful place in the community of nations" for a half century. Fifty years after recognizing Philippine sovereignty, the United States's official position remains exactly the same, focusing on the goal of Filipino independence as (finally) achieved through American generosity. This point was underscored by the fact that the U.S. diplomatic greetings came not through the American ambassador, as might be expected, but through Atwood, the representative of American largesse. In 1996 we see the same rationalization of American expansionism that *Back to Bataan* deployed in 1945. It is worth noting again that *Back to Bataan* was made with the active participation of the U.S. government, and while the extent to which the film promulgated the American government's political agenda cannot be determined, the film's central focus on ideological rather than military campaigns suggests the film's commitment to political propaganda at that critical moment, not just in terms of World War II's Pacific theater but also in terms of Philippine-American relations during the last year of the Commonwealth. That the U.S. government in 1946 and 1996 deployed precisely the same rationalization of American colonization-as-liberation and

Philippine sovereignty as an American gift—whether in *Back to Bataan's* Andres Bonifacio, in Harry Truman's July 4, 1946, speech or in Bill Clinton's July 4, 1996, speech—reveals the United States' entrenched dedication to colonial dominance of the Philippines before, at the moment of, and even fifty years after its official recognition of Philippine independence.

JUAN DE LA CRUZ AND UNCLE SAM: TWO FACES OF PHILIPPINE-AMERICAN FRIENDSHIP

Although the U.S. state position focused on American beneficence (and thus, implicitly, on American superiority) in granting Philippine independence in 1946, the United States also partnered with pro-American Filipino media to promote the July 4, 1996, celebration of Philippine-American friendship as symbolizing a relationship expressing Philippine-American political equality. On July 4, three days ahead of its appearance with the rest of the Sunday paper on July 7, the *Philippine Panorama* (Sunday magazine of the *Manila Bulletin*) was distributed at the U.S. embassy's official July 4 diplomatic reception at which President Ramos was the honored guest. The *Panorama* cover illustration shows the two masculine nationalist icons, Uncle Sam and Juan de la Cruz, shaking hands against the background of their respective flags and under the caption "Philippine-American Friendship Day 50th Anniversary." The visual layout of the cover illustration meticulously positions the two nationalist icons equally; smiling affably, the two representatives literally meet in the middle to shake hands. The *Panorama's* smiling, meet-in-the-middle depiction of Philippine-American Friendship Day is clearly a pro-American image for Filipino bourgeois nationalism.

In this illustration Juan de la Cruz, wearing a native straw hat and a *barong tagalog*, is pictured as considerably shorter than Uncle Sam. Although Juan de la Cruz's shorter height may reflect the fact that the average Filipino is shorter than the average American, the disparity between the two figures' height implies that Filipinos' stature is inferior when compared to that of Americans.[11] Because of the height disparity, the two figures meet in the middle but do not look each other in the eye. While Juan de la Cruz appears to be looking slightly upwards at Uncle Sam, the latter stares straight ahead, at the top of de la Cruz's hat. The symbolism of the political gaze here perpetuates the Philippines' neocolonial relationship with the United States: while the representative Filipino looks up to America, the representative American appears to meet the Filipino as an equal, but keeps his colonial counterpart out of his line of sight. Direct communication would necessitate Uncle Sam's looking down at Juan de la Cruz. Rather than acknowledge the reality of political superiority over his former colonial subordinate, Uncle Sam maintains an affable but vacuous blindness. The symbolic implications of Uncle Sam and Juan de la Cruz's stature and line of sight recapitulate those of the Statue of Liberty and

**Philippine-American Friendship Day
50th Anniversary**

25. Uncle Sam and Juan de la Cruz in an officially sanctioned image of Philippine-American Friendship Day. Copies of this issue of the *Philippine Panorama* magazine were given to guests at the U.S. embassy's formal reception on July 4, 1996, three days in advance of the magazine's distribution with the regular Sunday newspaper. Image courtesy of Norman Isaac.

Filipinas on the cover of the July 4, 1946, independence ceremony program. After fifty years of independence, iconizations of Philippine-American relations have changed little.

While the *Philippine Panorama* magazine gave the U.S. state-sanctioned depiction of Filipino-American friendship and (relative) equality, an anti-American view of Philippine-American Friendship Day appeared on the same day in the *Manila Times*. This political cartoon, which appeared in the opinion section, again shows Uncle Sam and Juan de la Cruz meeting in the middle to

Figure 26. Uncle Sam and Juan de la Cruz in a critical view of Phil-Am Friendship Day. From the *Manila Times*, July 4, 1996. Image courtesy of Leonilo Doloricon/ *Manila Times*.

embrace in friendship. Rather than meeting in front of the two national flags, as in the *Philippine Panorama*, the *Manila Times* cartoon shows Juan de la Cruz and Uncle Sam against a tropical horizon. The two figures have evidently paused from looking over this vista to gaze at each other, each with one arm slung affectionately over the other's shoulder. This depiction of Phil-Am Friendship Day, however, highlights America's underhandedness in dealing with Filipinos under the guise of friendship. While Juan de la Cruz gazes with a neutral expression at the (still taller) Uncle Sam, the avuncular American gazes back with a slight smile while his other hand reaches behind him to plunder the pockets of the barefoot Pinoy.[12] Unlike the *Panorama* cartoon, in the *Manila Times* cartoon the representative American makes clear, direct eye contact. But here, the gaze deliberately misleads: Uncle Sam makes eye contact with Juan de la Cruz to prevent the latter from realizing that he is being robbed. While in the *Panorama* cartoon the representative American denies his neocolonial superiority, in the *Manila Times* cartoon he directly acknowledges his relationship with his former colonial subject only in order to exploit him, looking the representative Filipino straight in the eye to rob him in the embrace of friendship.

Together the *Philippine Panorama* and *Manila Times* illustrations of Philippine-American Friendship Day portray the Janus-faces of Philippine-American relations: each country reaping the benefit inherent in the continuing neocolonial dynamic while at the same time denying the unpalatable ramifi-cations of that dynamic. The *Philippine Panorama* cartoon symbolizes the ben-efit of Philippine-American neocolonialism: for the U.S. a profitable and favorable market in the densely populated Philippines, in addition to an eco-nomic base for the burgeoning Asian-Pacific market, and for the Philippines, continuing economic aid. Simultaneously, however, both states repudiate the downside of the continuing "special relationship" between the two countries in the unmasking of national myths both countries cherish: for the United States, the myth of American exceptionalism both past and present, and for the Philippines, the myth of true independence. The return of the colonial repressed was manifested in the entangled flags on July 4, 1996, aptly symbol-izing the endurance of the Philippine-American entanglement at precisely the moment that ostensibly symbolized the two nations' long-awaited separation.

CHAPTER 5

Canto del Viajero

F. SIONIL JOSÉ'S RESTORATIVE
HISTORICAL PASSAGE

> The Filipinos in the U.S. today, about a million strong, are
> trying to define their collective "identity" by analyzing the
> historical causes of their exile, their uprooting from a U.S.
> colony (now a neo-colony), and their prospects of returning
> to a liberated homeland.
> —E. San Juan Jr., *Writing and National Liberation*

THE ONGOING ENTANGLEMENT of Philippine-American
economic, social, and cultural interests exerts an effect even on Filipinos' most
earnest efforts to envision a Philippine nationalism free from American neocolonial influence. F. Sionil José's *Viajero: A Filipino Novel* (1993) appears to
present the fulfillment of a Filipino emergent-nationalism, one which is free
of the complicated imbrication with America that each of the earlier chapters
here has examined. The emergence of the novel's protagonist, Salvador dela
Raza ("Savior of the Race") as a nationalist hero apparently models a Filipino
nationalism that is truly independent of the pervasive American colonial influence. Sionil José casts dela Raza as a Filipino "wanderer" *(viajero)* born in the
Philippines. He is adopted, raised, and educated by a wealthy African American and rejects the economic and cultural privilege of his bourgeois American
upbringing to return to the Philippines and devote himself to healing the historic inequalities of the Filipino nation.[1] *Viajero* recuperates the Filipino diaspora, which many Filipino and Filipino American critics have identified as the
fundamental disjunction in the Filipino national identity, for the Philippine
diaspora runs so deep in the Filipino psyche that the (arch)typical Filipino is
in exile even when ostensibly at home in the Philippines. Thus *Viajero* appears
to resolve two critical and interrelated problems in Filipino nationhood: the
lingering neocolonial influence and a cultural malaise so fundamental to the
national identity that it has become a definitive national characteristic.

On closer examination, however, *Viajero* reinforces the very ideological
interdependence it appears to reject. Throughout the novel, Sionil José por-

trays the United States' lingering colonial influence as significantly undermining Filipino nationalism, and thus *Viajero*'s portrayal of Salvador dela Raza's
emergence as a model Filipino nationalist entails his rejection of his American
identity, political affiliation, and economic privilege. However, although *Viajero* focuses on Salvador dela Raza's long journey toward fulfilling Sionil José's
nationalist ethos, the novel's conclusion explicitly posits this seeming fulfillment of a successful (anti-American) Filipino nationalism as combined with
two key American factors. First, the novel ends with dela Raza explicitly
attributing his nationalist vision to the neocolonial tutelage of his adopted
American father, James Wack. The irony of Sionil José's "Filipino Novel"
about the long-awaited successful emergence of an effective Filipino nationalism is that the Filipino "Savior of the Race" could not have fulfilled the
promise of his name without nurturance from the United States. Ultimately,
despite the novel's subtitle, *Viajero* is as much a novel of America as it is a Filipino novel. Second, dela Raza can only finalize his commitment to the
Filipino *masa*—which Sionil José defines as a critical, definitive element of
Filipino emergent-nationalism—when his adopted sister Jessica makes a similar commitment to an American version of the *tao*.[2] The long-awaited fruition
of Filipino nationalism, which Sionil José conceptualizes as devotion to the
national betterment of the poor, can only occur in conjunction with a similar
move in the United States. Sionil José posits the apotheosis of Filipino nationalism, one which is in part definitively anti-American, as simultaneously
underwritten by and conjoined with the very American influences it overtly
rejects. Thus, a detailed examination of *Viajero* demonstrates the continuing
entanglement of Filipino and American nationalisms at precisely the moments
at which they appear at last to have achieved separation.

NATION AND NARRATION IN FILIPINO/
FILIPINO AMERICAN LITERATURE

Oscar Campomanes (1992, 54) states that "the obsessive search for identity . . . marks Philippine literature in the colonial language." He has argued
that the central characteristic in Filipino American literature is a diasporic
consciousness in which

> motifs of departure, nostalgia, incompletion, rootlessness, leave taking,
> and dispossession recur with force . . . , with the Philippines as either the
> original or terminal reference point. Rather than the United States as . . .
> "the promised land" . . . the Filipino case represents a reverse telos, an
> opposite movement. It is on this basis that I argue for a literature of exile
> and emergence rather than a literature of immigration and settlement
> whereby life in the United States serves as the space for displacement, sus-

pension, and perspective. Exile becomes a necessary, if inescapable, state for Filipinos in the United States. (1992, 51)

Although Campomanes's influential article "Filipinos in the United States and Their Literature of Exile" focuses, as the title indicates, on Filipino American literature, the exilic sensibility is just as fundamental in Filipino literature. In his analysis of twenty volumes of the academic journal *Philippine Studies,* Joseph Galdon writes that he was "struck by the common denominator that occurs time and again in critics' evaluation of Philippine writers of fiction in English. Almost every critic underlines the theme that the Filipino is a stranger in his own house. Over and over again, the Filipino is pictured as an outsider . . . searching for his identity, struggling with alienation of one form or another." As a result, Galdon claims, "the search and the journey are pervasive symbols" in Philippine literature (1972, xi, xii). In effect, the Filipino is an exile whether at home or abroad, and the exilic consciousness is central to Philippine literature in English regardless of the side of the Pacific on which it is published or written, or in which country such literature's characters reside.

Gerald Burns has claimed that repatriation is another fundamental theme in Philippine literature. In Burns's formulation, the most basic element of what he calls the repatriate genre is "a protagonist returning to the homeland in search of a whole personal and cultural identity and intent on bettering in some ways the lives of his or her countrymen." However, Burns observes that the repatriate theme is marked by failure. "None of the protagonists [in Burns's study] achieve the vision or project or desire with which they return to their homeland." He goes even further, claiming that whereas "in other national traditions the hero is customarily allowed a measure of personal triumph, . . . the Filipino hero is 'doomed to suffer and die' " (Burns, 206, 210, 212). The sense of individual as well as collective dislocation is so pervasive in Filipino literature that even Filipinos in the Philippines need to be repatriated.

These central thematic categories of Filipino/Filipino American literature are manifest in *Viajero,* which works through the problematic dynamic of exile and repatriation. Born in the Philippines, Salvador dela Raza is adopted and naturalized as an American citizen, and the novel's central project is his politicized reclamation of the natal identity from which he was alienated as a child. Salvador dela Raza is a diasporic Filipino haunted by the sense of a lost family, people, and homeland. He travels back to the Philippines only to find that there, too, he is a stranger. But through his historical research—in traveling back to the collective national past as well as his own familial origins—dela Raza figuratively finds himself and thereby repatriates himself to the Philippines. Dela Raza's repatriation occurs both on the level of subject and object.

His return to his patria signals his inclusion in the national patriarchal order, as he becomes a figurative patriarch for the Filipino emergent-nationalist (from the Philippine government's perspective, insurgent) cause. Thus the long journey of exile and repatriation Sionil José portrays in *Viajero* demonstrates the successful recuperation of both individual and collective exile.

While *Viajero* engages fundamental themes of identity, dislocation, exile, and repatriation central to both Philippine and Filipino-American literature, Sionil José's novel is equally concerned with the issue of nationalism. Through its engagement with the issues of nationalist development, (post/neo) colonialism, and the struggle for socioeconomic hegemony, *Viajero* is an example of what has been labeled variously as "emergent literature," "literature from the margins," "protest literature," "people's literature," "combat literature," and "resistance literature."[3] Emergent literature has at its heart colonized peoples' quest for national liberation from colonialism. As Frantz Fanon wrote in *The Wretched of the Earth*, "To fight for national culture means in the first place to fight for the liberation of the nation. . . . There is no other fight for culture which can develop apart from the popular struggle" (233). Fanon identifies the last phase of nationalist evolution as the stage at which the colonized native "turns himself into an awakener of the people; hence comes a fighting literature, a revolutionary literature, and a national literature. . . . which calls on the whole people to fight for their existence as a nation" (223, 240). Sionil José, like Fanon, locates the loss of culture in history—the history of colonialism—and both Fanon and Sionil José identify nationalism of the right sort as prerequisite to overthrowing the colonial influence.

Benedict Anderson has written that national histories are always a combination of remembering and forgetting; in the case of a colonized country, the precolonial national consciousness is lost along with the political structure, both erased by the imposition of the colonizer's version of history and culture (Anderson 1986, 659). Thus the crucial work of nationalism is not done by politicians; it is done by writers. As Fanon observes, "While politicians situate their action in actual present-day events, men of culture take their stand in the field of history," for "the truth of the nation turns paradoxically toward the past and away from actual events" (Fanon 1963, 209, 225). Fanon's theory of decolonization is an active and explicit influence in *Viajero;* Colonel Verdad, the novel's frame narrator, cites Fanon in the novel's foreword, comparing Salvador dela Raza's work on the Philippine Revolution to Fanon's *The Wretched of the Earth* and claiming that dela Raza's "seminal work on revolutionary nationalism has been a must reading [*sic*] for those who want to understand the motive force of nationalism in emerging countries" (Sionil José 1993, 3). *Viajero*'s Salvador dela Raza is, as his name suggests, the man of history who becomes a man of resistance, who not only documents the history of colonial oppression of the Philippines' indios but, by becoming a teacher, revitalizes the insurgency of the masa in the name of socioeconomic justice for all Filipinos. Thus in *Viajero* Sionil José portrays the genesis of Fanon's decolonized native, a man of both the written word and of combat, a "man of history" and an "awakener of the people."

For Sionil José, history, decolonization, and nationalism are inextricably conjoined, and the reclamation of the national history is indivisible from its decolonization. Dela Raza's mission is one of historical revisionism. He becomes determined to "create the document as it must have been" before historical hegemonic selectivity was imposed by the colonial conquerors (Sionil José 1993, 36). Scattered throughout *Viajero* are eight historical vignettes, dela Raza's reconstructed, imaginative histories recuperating the stories of Filipinos marginalized by Establishment history: precolonial natives, indios during Spanish colonization, Filipino nationalists and rebels (which, in Sionil José's formulation, are the same thing), a female member of the Hukbalahap. Struggling with the identity he lost by being torn from his parents and his homeland at such a young age, dela Raza hopes to recover his own lost life story by recovering the stories of other lost lives—lives lost not because they were insignificant or unworthy, but because they were marginalized by the imperialist historical record. Searching for his own historical past, Salvador dela Raza recovers the Philippines' past, a history similarly lost through colonial oppression. Thus for dela Raza his own life literally as well as figuratively becomes a site of memory, a microcosm of the national collective; he elects to "tak[e his] stand in the field of history" to struggle for national identity against historical hegemony.

Sionil José's Search for Filipino Nationalism: *Viajero* and the Rosales Novels

Salvador dela Raza is F. Sionil José's depiction of the true Filipino nationalist, a fulfillment of the quest for the nationalist engagement Sionil José sought throughout his best-known work, a quintet known as the Rosales novels. The Rosales novels trace five generations of two families, the Samsons, who are poor farmers, and the wealthy mestizo Asperris, through the Spanish and American colonial regimes into the postindependence era.[4] The first book, *Po-on*, focuses on the Samson family, encompasses the Philippine-American War, and endorses Filipino revolutionary nationalism. The second novel, *Tree*, follows the heir of the Asperri clan. *Tree*'s unnamed narrator witnesses the hardships of the Filipino peasants under the Spanish colonial *encomienda* system and the peasant uprisings that result but is unable to break free of his own position of cultural and economic privilege. The remaining three books in the Rosales cycle reinforce the tension between the Philippines' colonial legacy and an authentic nationalism. Luis Asperri, the illegitimate son of Don Vicente Asperri, is the protagonist of the third Rosales novel, *My Brother, My Executioner.* Set in the 1950s, this novel takes place against the backdrop of the Hukbalahap uprising. Lacking a legitimate son, Don Vicente claims Luis as his heir. Rejecting his ties to the peasantry through his mother, Luis embraces his role as a wealthy landlord. At the end of the novel Luis's revolutionary half brother, Victor, warns Luis that unless the peasants receive some economic justice, the Huks will decimate the local elite. Refusing to yield, Luis awaits death at the hands of the Huks at the end of the novel. *The Pretenders,* the fourth novel in the Rosales quintet, features Antonio (Tony) Samson, the son of *My Brother, My Executioner's* Victor, who is imprisoned for the murder of Luis Asperri. Tony gets a Ph.D. from Harvard, marries a wealthy Filipina, and joins the ilustrado elite by going to work for his father-in-law. However, Tony's true love is his peasant cousin, Emy, with whom he has an illegitimate son, Pepe. Tony's rejection of his peasant origins to gain ilustrado privilege poisons his life. At the end of the novel Tony commits suicide because he realizes that he is unworthy of Emy and his son, "the boy [who] would be rooted in the land, unlike [Tony] who had severed his roots" (Sionil José 1962, 169). Pepe, Tony's son, is the narrator of the last Rosales novel, *Mass.* Set in the pre–martial law and martial law years (the 1970s), Pepe travels to Manila for college and becomes a member of the Brotherhood, a revolutionary organization. *Mass* ends with Pepe leaving Manila to join the guerrillas in the mountains. As Elizabeth Yoder observes, "It is significant that the Rosales cycle ends with Pepe as a young revolutionary, leaving for the countryside to begin organizing in his own village on the eve of the declaration of martial law. It seems that this is Sionil José's hopeful answer to the conundrum of Filipino history. . . . [T]he hope for the future of the Philippines, is the conscientized masses, in people like Pepe Samson, who refuse to be bought off by the elite, who remember who they are and where they come from" (Yoder 1989, 70).

However, it is important to note that the Rosales cycle ends only with Pepe's journey to join the insurgent cause, not with his active engagement on behalf of nationalist liberation. The reappearance in *Viajero* of Pepe Samson and other Rosales characters is significant because it is only in *Viajero* that we learn that Samson did indeed go on to become an active insurgent, but that critical transformation happens offstage, in the interstices between *Mass* and *Viajero.* The fact that Samson's active commitment to Filipino nationalist activism happens offstage is a significant gap. In *Viajero* we see the step-by-step genesis of the emergent-nationalist commitment and, through the novel's frame narrator, Simplicio Verdad, the impact dela Raza achieved in the emergent-nationalist movement. Moreover, by portraying dela Raza as a representative of the Filipino diaspora, Sionil José connects to the exilic and repatriate themes that are fundamental to Filipino literature. Salvador dela Raza fulfills the promise of his name by resolving two fundamental—and interconnected—Filipino disjunctions: that between the ilustrado and the masa and that between the Filipino expatriate and the Filipino at home. It is in resolving these two intractable tensions that dela Raza succeeds where the various Rosales protagonists failed, and, by so doing, dela Raza becomes the nationalist protagonist the Rosales novels sought.

Sionil José predicates his conception of Filipino nationalism on the individual's deliberate choice to ally him- or herself with the masa to redress the Philippines' historic socioeconomic imbalance. In the Rosales novels, the wealth, power, and cultural status of the ilustrados present an almost irresistible temptation to those from the lower classes. Dudley de Souza writes, "Stated simply, the [Rosales novels'] dilemma is this: in order to rise from poverty to power, wealth and all the trappings of success[,] a brilliant or talented individual would have no other avenue except to cut his moorings with his people and join the exploitative class: the elite who have always been in power. He would, in other words[,] have to accept social injustice and join the oppressors" (de Souza 1998, 155).

For Sionil José, the nationalistic/ethical imperative is not simply a choice between present alternatives (ilustrado wealth vs. poverty with the masa); it is inextricably tied to the nation's past, its colonial and postcolonial history. In the Rosales quintet, this struggle to connect the past and the present—individually through the family and collectively through the nation—repeatedly takes the form of intellectualism and academic research (Fanon's "man of culture"). Several of the Rosales protagonists are intellectuals. *The Pretenders'* Tony Samson holds a history degree from Harvard, and his historical research is personally as well as academically motivated. Tony's academic research represents a quest into the deeper forces that influenced the past generations of Filipinos who collectively wrote the nation's history. Tony fails, however, to realize his own participation in these historical dynamics, which exert an influence on the present as well as representing the past. Consequently, Tony becomes one of what Thelma Kintanar calls "José's portrait gallery of failed intellectuals" (Kintanar 1989, 24).

Sionil José's intellectuals travel not just to libraries and archives but also to their regional origins. For Sionil José, Filipino nationalism is, indivisibly, both ideological and regional, as Miguel Bernad notes: "Being a historian, [*The Pretenders'* Tony] Samson never forgets his Ilocano ancestry and is intrigued by the story of . . . Ilocano migrations. He feels somehow that his own present life would have more meaning if he could better understand its obscure origins" (Bernad 1989, 4). Samson figuratively returns to his ancestry through his doctoral thesis and literally returns to his ancestral origins via automobile trips to Cabugaw and Rosales. *Mass* ends with Pepe Samson going back to his roots, literally as well as figuratively, to join the insurgent movement.

The central themes of the Rosales cycle—the nationalistic ethical imperative to ally oneself with the masa rather than the ilustrados, the link between academic research and the return to one's roots, and the conjoining of the past and the present—culminate in *Viajero*. *Viajero* is the story of the emblematic Filipino wanderer attempting to reunite his internal, familial, and national schisms—a process that leads him on an extended journey across time and space, reconstructing his own familial history as he reconstructs his country's national history.

In the novel's opening lines, dela Raza establishes the novel's major theme of the search for identity, which is both uniquely his own and representative of thousands of other diasporic Filipinos:

> I have travelled, but in another sense I have never really left the place where I was born.
>
> All over the world, in airports and bus stations, in shopping malls and under the garish lights of entertainment marquees, I have seen the faces of my countrymen—solemn, sullen, steadfast, stricken with pathos—men and women who have come from the sulky recesses of the provinces, from the slums of Manila and the smug comfort of middle-class neighborhoods. They are everywhere, I am now sure, even in the glacial isolation of the arctic. . . . Ah, my countrymen, dislodged from the warmth of their homes, to make a living no matter how perilous and demeaning, to strike out in alien geographies and eke from there with their own sweat and their cunning what they can. I have seen them lambasted in foreign newspapers, ridiculed and debased by those who do not know how it is to be Filipino, how it is to travel everywhere and yet hold ever precious and lasting this memory, stretching across mountains and oceans, of my unhappy country.
>
> This is my story, it is also theirs—and, maybe, yours.
>
> Memory, help me! (Sionil José 1993, 7–8)

Dela Raza's exhortation, however, catapults him back not to memory, but to its loss. Salvador's earliest memories are of loss: the loss of his parents, and even the memory of his parents, during World War II; the loss of his surrogate father and mother, Apo Tale and Inay ("Mother") Mayang, who take him in after he is separated from his biological parents in the chaos of a battle with the Japanese; the loss of his name and language through his subsequent rescue by American soldiers; and ultimately the loss of his homeland itself when he his adopted by James Wack, one of the American soldiers who rescued him after the Japanese kill Apo Tale and Inay Mayang. After World War II, James Wack becomes a well-known anthropologist, and, partly to follow in Wack's academic footsteps, Salvador grows up to become a historian. Salvador's choice of academic fields also is motivated by his diasporic dislocation, a dislocation he comes to find is not only individual but representative of Filipinos as a people. In a paradigmatic statement on a diasporic identity, Salvador muses, "*WHO AM I?* I look at my reflection . . . and I see a brown man with an inquiring face, eager to know. . . . I am alone, yet I know there are likenesses of me, with the same bone and muscle, and hungers that cannot be assuaged" (Sionil José 1993, 22). Traveling to the Philippines to research his thesis, Salvador begins the quest for identity, the intellectual project that will lead him to his roots and the decisive choice between allegiance with the tao or the elite.

Viajero's protagonist goes through nearly as many changes in his name as he does in parental figures. As a young child, Salvador goes by the Filipino nickname "Badong." The American soldiers rename him "Buddy" because "Badong is not easy for us to say," and the new nickname symbolizes the friendship the African Americans offer (Sionil José 1993, 20). James Wack, his adoptive father, explains the logic in Buddy's legal name, telling the young boy, "I did ask what your real name would be if, as you said, everyone called you Badong, and they told me, the Filipinos I asked, that most likely it would be Salvador. And the family name—you came from the village of Raza—that is why [your name] is Salvador of Raza" (20). Wack's explanation of his adopted son's name, however, provides a speciously convenient provenance for the name. Although formally adopted by James Wack, Buddy's legal name remains Salvador dela Raza. Buddy's task throughout the novel is to recognize that his life's work is to devote himself to the Filipino nation and thus become, in deed as well as name, Savior of the Race.

SIMPLICIÓ VERDAD: THE SIMPLE TRUTH AS NARRATIVE FRAME

Although Sionil José constructs *Viajero* as Salvador dela Raza's autobiographical narrative, the novel's narrative frame is provided by Col. Simplicio Verdad, the "intelligence chief for the Central Sector" and a paradigmatic example of colonial pathology (Sionil José 1993, 1). Verdad is indirectly responsible for Salvador dela Raza's death, and in searching the ruins of dela Raza's hut Verdad finds a box of computer disks on which dela Raza wrote his life story. The frame story provided by Verdad serves as a foil for Salvador dela Raza's narrative. While Sionil José offers in the figure of Salvador dela Raza a model of successful Filipino nationalism, he frames *Viajero* through Verdad as a negative alter ego, a reminder of Sionil José's other failed nationalists.

Simplicio Verdad has many similarities to Salvador dela Raza and feels both respect and sympathy for him. Both men had their graduate training in the United States. Verdad wished to stay in America, where he had been offered a faculty position at a California university, but his father pleaded with him to return home to carry on the family tradition of military service (Sionil

José 1993, 2). Thus Verdad, like dela Raza, returns to the Philippines from the States because of a paternal influence. Both Verdad and dela Raza follow in their fathers' professional footsteps, which in both cases leads them to an active engagement with the Philippine nation-state—Verdad on the side of the state, dela Raza in opposition to it.

In addition to the similarities of their paternal legacies, Verdad feels a deep sense of respect and admiration for dela Raza's academic work on Philippine revolutionary movements. Like dela Raza, Verdad did academic research on the Colorum and Sakdal insurgent movements, and also like dela Raza, Verdad's sympathies are with the rural oppressed: "I . . . agree completely with the conclusions of Reynaldo Ileto in his classic work, *Pasyon and Revolution,* about how nationalism and the aspiration for social justice have gone hand in hand in galvanizing our rural oppressed. But how does one utilize these sentiments for political action at a time when the movement seems to have already been emasculated by revolutionary fatigue?. . . . This is the fundamental dilemma Salvador dela Raza had addressed" (Sionil José 1993, 3).

Verdad's descriptions of dela Raza's work present dela Raza as a patriarch of Filipino nationalist insurgency. Verdad describes dela Raza's book on Philippine revolutionary movements as "seminal" and says that dela Raza's teachings revived the "emasculated" insurgent movement. Verdad identifies an unwavering commitment to economic justice for the rural oppressed as the key to dela Raza's nationalistic potency. Verdad reports that when dela Raza began his teachings from the mountain, the rebel movement

> had spent its energies and was beginning to alienate the very people—the rural and urban poor—which it had regarded as its "sea"; its doctrinaire approach to the national reality had caused many cadres to leave. But it seemed that [dela Raza's] arrival breathed new life into the moribund movement. With his guidance he was soon rejuvenating the cadres, attracting bright new recruits from the intelligentsia as well as from the lower classes . . . .
>
> From the mountain came this clear voice, infusing new strength to those who flagged, calling for a union with God who was also in the soil, in the nation and with those who worked the land. . . . [I]t was a unique approach to a revolutionary situation that continues to exist . . . because the poor are still poor, even poorer, while the rich get oppressive and richer. (1–2, 4–5)

Verdad's affirmation of sympathy for Ileto's pro-masa (and, in this context, anti-state) sentiment is self-deceiving. Verdad avers that he agrees with Ileto's theory of "nationalism . . . and social justice" in the interest of the "rural oppressed," but Verdad travels to the mountains in search of Salvador dela

Raza precisely because dela Raza has become a leader of the rural oppressed and is doing too good a job of galvanizing them.

Verdad's admiration for dela Raza sits ill with his official duty, which is to bring dela Raza in for questioning. Verdad opens the novel with the protest,

> First let me make this clear—we had never intended to kill Salvador dela Raza or even imprison him. . . . Alive he was very important to me personally—a man of such prodigious knowledge is a gift not just to the rebels but to the nation. I had merely wanted to question him in the most comfortable circumstances if that were at all possible and since he did not want to deal with us in any manner, and by his very actions revealed his hostility to the military, then his capture was my most important project. . . . From the beginning, the plan was to capture dela Raza and simply question him cordially. (1, 4)

Verdad's abstract approval of the impact of dela Raza's academic publication are Verdad's private thoughts; Verdad's actions, on behalf of the state dela Raza undermined, cause dela Raza's death. When intelligence agents finally determine the location of dela Raza's mountain home, Verdad's troops surround the hut just before dawn and send up flares as a signal to the backup troops below. Two of the flares fall on the nipa thatching of dela Raza's roof, and the hut becomes an instant pyre. Verdad "had expected whoever was within to rush out and escape that pyre. I had really hoped he would run out and give himself up." But dela Raza does not emerge, and when Verdad inspects the wreckage of the hut, he finds a human body reduced to "a lump of charcoal with a human shape, compact but recognizable." Next to dela Raza's body, Verdad finds a fireproof box, the only object to survive the fire. Inside Verdad finds five computer disks, dela Raza's life story. *Viajero* is the transcription of those disks, *"one man's account of his labyrinthian passage . . . [Verdad] purposely retained the title Salvador dela Raza himself gave his memoir, VIAJERO"* (5, 6).

Verdad's protestations of innocence in dela Raza's immolation ring hollow. Verdad, with his many similarities to and respect for dela Raza, chose the opposite path from dela Raza's. Instead of committing himself to the cause of the people—a cause whose justice Verdad indirectly acknowledges—Verdad is an agent of the military establishment that has historically and brutally repressed insurgent movements promoting the tao's cause, and which does so again in the murder of Salvador dela Raza. Sionil José presents Salvador dela Raza and Simplicio Verdad not merely as alter egos and representatives of emergent vs. bourgeois Filipino nationalism, but shows these two fundamental schools of Filipino nationalism as being fatally inimical to each other. Simplicio Verdad is ironically named, for Colonel Verdad does not represent the "Simple Truth" at all. That Simplicio Verdad should be the source of Salvador

dela Raza's destruction is Sionil José's declaration that the salvation of the Filipino race is not simple at all, but a difficult ethical imperative: to refuse the
temptation of the power and privilege and work in solidarity with the tao.

REVOLUTIONARY HOPE, REVOLUTIONARY FAILURE: BENIGNO AND CORAZON AQUINO

Dela Raza's commitment to Filipino emergent-nationalism is precipitated
through a series of events that link him personally to the contemporary history of his nation. The first of these is his relationship with Ninoy Aquino and
his reaction to Aquino's assassination. The second is his reaction to the resulting nonviolent mass revolution known as EDSA that toppled the Marcos
regime. Finally, and perhaps most important, he is shaped by Corazon Aquino's
betrayal of the ideals of EDSA. For Sionil José, Benigno and Corazon Aquino
represent both the potential and failure of People Power to effect a change in
the Filipino power structure.

Sionil José has Salvador meet Benigno Aquino in Honolulu in January
1981, when Aquino was living in exile in the United States during the Marcos era. Dela Raza predicts the assassination of Aquino and sees in the EDSA
Revolution the masa's potential to effect real political change. As a historian,
Salvador dela Raza finds EDSA gratifying in part because "he had finally seen
one great event in history; it had unfolded before him in all its human glory
and he was grateful that he was [t]here," witnessing the event in person rather
than excavating its records from dusty archives and turgid academic tomes.
More important, however, dela Raza rejoices at EDSA not only for himself
but also for all Filipinos: "long afterwards he would always remember this
moment of freedom, not for himself for he had always been free, but for his
people." To dela Raza, EDSA represented a fulfillment of the potential of
emergent nationalism: the victory at EDSA "reassured him not just of [Fil-
ipinos'] unity but of their capability for creating a nation" (223, 224).

However, the EDSA honeymoon did not last long. Pepe Samson, making
a repeat appearance from *Mass* as one of Ninoy Aquino's insurgent colleagues,
warns Salvador: "I am a pessimist. . . . So we will get rid of Marcos, but will
we also get rid of all the powerful Filipinos who have enslaved us?. . . . At
least, if [EDSA] succeeds, that's one Filipino tyrant that will be removed. But
when will Filipinos realize that it is themselves who are often their worst
enemy[?]" Samson doubts Corazon Aquino's willingness to effect real change,
since she came from one of the ruling families and is one of the wealthy land-
lords whose fortunes would be compromised if land reform were imple-
mented (221, 227). He is, of course, shown to be prophetic, as Corazon
Aquino betrays the revolutionary progress her husband's martyrdom initiated.

Immediately following the EDSA chapter, the tao, who so recently had
turned out to shout their acclaim for Cory Aquino, converge at Malacañan,

the presidential palace, to protest against Aquino as they had so recently protested against Ferdinand Marcos. Just as Salvador dela Raza witnesses the tao's joyful triumph at EDSA, he watches with horror as the soldiers under Cory Aquino's administration fire into the crowd. The EDSA revolution succeeded because the Filipino soldiers under Marcos had quailed at firing on peaceful protestors. The miracle of EDSA was that, at the critical moment, the soldiers held their fire. Corazon Aquino's betrayal of her husband's martyrdom lies both in her refusal to redistribute property more equitably while the government was in a state of temporary flux and in her government's murder of the same protestors that had brought her to power. The extent of Cory Aquino's betrayal of the People Power that catapulted her into office is demonstrated in *Viajero* by the fact that more protestors were killed during the Aquino administration post EDSA demonstrations than had been killed during Marcos's dictatorship: "not even during the most virulent demonstrations under Marcos were so many people killed" (243). In Benigno and Cory Aquino, Salvador dela Raza witnesses the greatest opportunity for, and failure of, revolutionary change both by and on behalf of the masa.

Benigno Aquino's dream of lasting change in the Philippines is blighted by his widow's refusal to break the oligarchy of the Philippine elite, but Aquino remains a generative force for emergent or anti-imperialist nationalism in the novel. Benigno Aquino posthumously convinces Salvador dela Raza to return to the Philippines and nurtures dela Raza's commitment to the tao—the two acts Sionil José posits as the political litmus test for Filipino nationalists. Although when they first meet in Hawaii dela Raza and Aquino found their friendship on the affinity they feel as exiles, Aquino insists that exile is ultimately wrong. Aquino insists that the fight for Philippine reforms cannot take place in America; he, and all true Filipinos, must return to the Philippines to work for change in their homeland. Fearing for Aquino's safety during Marcos's dictatorship, Salvador warns Aquino to wait to return, but Aquino is steadfast in his determination to return to the Philippines and he urges Salvador to go with him. Aquino also urges Salvador to reclaim his Filipino identity. On the night they meet, Aquino queries Salvador: "I take it you are an American citizen. Have you ever thought of becoming a Filipino. . . . We [Filipinas] need you. America does not" (187, 190).

Aquino's influence upon dela Raza increases after he dies on the tarmac in Manila. Salvador "dreamed of Ninoy th[e] very week the politician was killed, . . . [Salvador heard] his voice urging him not just in the dream but in the stern silence of his own conscience, go home, Salvador dela Raza. Go home!" (191). In his dreams Salvador debates Aquino over his ethnic/political identity and the ethical imperative to return to his homeland to fight for social justice:

Salvador: Why do you intrude so often in my life? Not only in my sleep do you bother me now, [but in] my waking hours as well.

Ninoy: It is not I, Buddy, who is bothering you. It is your own conscience, your own past, your race and your nation. . . .

Salvador: And what will I be if I went back? A voyeur? Just as I have always been? . . . So much crime in the streets, poverty, oppression, a dictatorship that is vicious, greedy beyond satiation. . . .

Ninoy: You are arguing precisely for the reasons that you are needed there. . . . No, Buddy, you are not being honest with yourself because you cannot face the truth. And that truth, American though you may be, is that you love Filipinas and the freedom and justice our motherland longs for, just like the many men whose lives you have studied. You are one of them, a traveller, and now you must go where your heart is. (191–92)

This passage makes clear that dela Raza, devoted as he is to his historical research, recognizes that for him, academia is legitimized voyeurism. Dela Raza realizes that academia provides him the psychological as well as ideological distance from the subject of his research, and, as this dream suggests, only a return to his historical origins can reposition him as an agent rather than a passive bystander.

It is this dream, in which the dead Aquino interrogates him on his Filipino identity, that finally pushes dela Raza to return to the Philippines, armed with a list of insurgent contacts Aquino had given him. Two of these characters, Father Jess and Pepe Samson, appeared in the last Rosales novel, *Mass*. By continuing the debates over identity, nationalism, and revolution that Salvador began with Benigno Aquino, and by taking Salvador through Manila and the provinces to see for himself the plight of the Filipino people, Father Jess and Pepe Samson foster dela Raza's emergence from the voyeuristic cocoon in which he had been comfortably ensconced.

Throughout the Rosales cycle, the majority of Sionil José's nationalist protagonists sever their ties to the tao. Several of these characters have ties to both the peasant class and the elites, and the difficult choice they must make, but never do, is to repudiate the privilege of the ilustrados. In Sionil José's nationalist cosmos, there are few hereditary members of the elite who reject the privilege of their birthright. *Viajero,* however, features two such characters in the figures of Leo Mercado's wife and Father Jess. As Father Jess tells Salvador, "I know whereof I speak. . . . I come from the same class I condemn[.] I was born very rich, in Negros. . . . I do not have to be here, if I may brag about it" (199–200). This is the matrix of Sionil José's nationalistic ethos: to voluntarily join in the hardships of the tao when one has a more comfortable alternative. For Sionil José, it is the choice, the deliberate decision to reject the self-colonization that is integral to the ilustrado elite and instead to embrace the cause of the poor, the dark-skinned, the peasants, that is the decisive factor in a nationalist commitment. Salvador recognizes that in returning to his homeland he has reached a point of ethical choice: he can either "return to the saccharine comfort of America, or linger in this hell hole which was his birthplace" (225). It is by bringing dela Raza, a privileged member of the diaspora, to this turning point that Sionil José powerfully elucidates in *Viajero* the political praxis that underlies his formulation of Filipino nationalism.

Throughout the Rosales novels, Sionil José's development of a model of emergent Filipino nationalism assumes that the ilustrados cannot make the changes the country needs because even its educated idealists live in a cocoon, buffered by the vast socioeconomic divide. Sionil José's political praxis aims to rectify this blindness. Dela Raza has his epiphany when he visits a remote rural village with Pepe Samson to acquaint himself with the realities of the lives of the poverty-stricken masa. Samson berates dela Raza for "indulging" in the "luxury" of his identity crisis, curtly observing, "You academics, you Americans—you are no different from our middle-class Filipinos wondering about who they are. . . . I have no time to ask such questions. None of us bother with that. . . . I am Jose Samson, I come from a small village in Pangasinan. I am Ilokano but, above all else, I am Filipino. I am also certain it is here, in my unhappy country, where I will die" (233). Almost immediately, government soldiers attack and kill several townspeople for supporting the insurgent cause, and dela Raza suddenly realizes that he must emancipate himself from the "comfortable prison" of socioeconomic privilege and inividualism (238). Salvador dela Raza fulfills the promise of his name when he breaks free of his cocoon of privilege and no longer considers himself as disconnected from the tao by realizing "the rich and the poor are yoked together!" (239). This moment of Filipino nationalist epiphany is doubly significant because Salvador dela Raza is not only a representative of the Filipino diaspora but is also an American by adoption. Salvador dela Raza's moment of self-identification is also a personal decolonization, a self-liberation from the American colonial influence. The diasporic wanderer, the Filipino who is an expatriate even at home, the United States' continuing colonial influence—Sionil José brings all of these epistemological gaps to closure in this moment of critical nationalist epiphany.

"Home, at Last": The Repatriation of Salvador dela Raza

For Sionil José, the nation and the individual reflect each other; the recuperation of national history is indivisible from that of the individual's family history. In order to become the effective teacher of the emergent-nationalist movement, dela Raza must recuperate the schisms within himself caused by the disruptions of his family. Dela Raza's repatriation to the Philippines is inextricably entwined with his repatriation within a nationalist paternal lineage. By imaginatively reconnecting with his lost father figures, dela Raza returns to Filipinas to take his own place within the patriotic patriarchy.

Returning to the Philippines, Salvador dela Raza completes his literal as well as figurative journey by traveling back to the place he thinks of as home: the mountain where he lived briefly but happily with his first adopted parents, Apo Tale and Inay Mayang. Although Apo Tale's hut is long gone, Salvador rejoices in finally coming home: "I was here, this is home, at last. Home—the sweet and honest word sank into his consciousness, his very flesh suffusing him with the brightness of discovery and belonging, as if in all his travels, he had finally found the end of it all. . . . Apo Tale, Inay Mayang—this is Badong returned to your embrace" (Sionil José 1993, 212). Salvador builds his home, a simple peasant's hut, on the site of Apo Tale's old house, and returns to a life of subsistence farming. Living a farmer's life, Salvador goes through an epidermal transformation that makes physiologically manifest his commitment to the tao: due to the long hours of agricultural work and exposure to the sun, "there is a peasant roughness now to my skin . . . I haven't been to Manila in weeks and the [provincial] telephone operator in the substation cannot quite believe what she sees; she says I have grown so dark" (264).

As he acquires the "peasant roughness . . . to [his] skin," Salvador also regains his mother tongue. In the same sentence in which Salvador notes his darker color, he also asserts, "I am now utterly confident with my Filipino. . . . I can now lecture in it" (264). And lecture he does, for Salvador's mountain homestead becomes an impromptu school for the nationalist cause. As young Filipinos come to dela Raza for guidance, he teaches them to look to the past for answers:

> They start coming to me, and they ask questions. I tell them what I know, relate to them stories about Filipinas, and they are so eager to learn. God and nation, people and justice—these are the givens in the equation. I go back to my reading of the Colorum Uprising in eastern Pangasinan in 1931 and repeat what the Colorums have said, that God created earth, water and air for all men, that land belongs to them who till it—and that it was against God's laws for one man, one family, one group, to own so much while the rest of the nation starves. I tell them that enlightening men's minds is the most difficult of all endeavors, much, much more difficult than violence and killing. (250–51)

His liberational theological bent notwithstanding, Salvador dela Raza embodies Fanon's man of culture cum nationalist champion by recuperating history for the decolonization of the nation and its people rather than as an abstract academic pursuit. By teaching the young cadres the lessons of their history and the duty they have to the present and future of their country, Salvador revives the insurgent movement. At the novel's beginning, Simplicio Verdad had admitted that dela Raza's formal membership in the insurgent movement was a matter of speculation (1, 4). Whether or not he had formally joined the movement, however, dela Raza's teaching young Filipinos the lessons of their history had revitalized the movement and swelled its ranks with new cadres. Dela Raza's lesson to his students that "enlightening men's minds is . . . much more difficult than violence and killing" subscribes to Pepe Samson's belief that the core of the insurgent movement's cause lies in education rather than in demonstrations or formal combat (250–51). Through his teaching, and the resulting increase in the numbers of new cadres, it is clear that dela Raza is not only a de facto member of the insurgent movement but also one of its leaders. Dela Raza demonstrates Sionil José's nationalist ideal by rejecting the empty status and inherent dilettantism of academic history and instead putting history to use to educate Filipinos on the imperatives of "God and nation, [the] people and justice," leading to the ultimate rejuvenation of "Filipinas."[5]

But dela Raza can only become the influential teacher and leader and thus fulfill his commitment to Filipinas by reconnecting with his various father figures. It is significant that dela Raza operates his mountain school from the modest subsistence farm he built to re-create Apo Tale's homestead; by doing so, dela Raza not only underscores his allegiance with the tao but also repositions himself with a critical, if imaginative, patriarchal lineage. Throughout the novel, dela Raza has been driven by patriarchal influences, consciously through the academic training he gained from James Wack and subconsciously by his need to find his lost native fathers: Apo Tale, the surrogate father Salvador revered, and the biological father he lost to the Japanese Occupation.

Having reconnected with Apo Tale by rebuilding his mountain home, Salvador also must make a connection to his biological father. Salvador learns that he was probably left by his biological father at Manila's Quiapo Church during the feast of the Black Nazarene. Visiting Quiapo Church, Salvador literally as well as figuratively returns to the beginning of his story, repeating "Again: Memory, help me!" (206). Learning that his father and mother probably died in the melee that came in retaliation for the murders of two Japanese officers, Salvador imaginatively reconstructs his father as a rebel soldier dying for the cause: "So this is what it means to finally know who you are— oh, my father, that I should have at least known you, absorbed your courage, defined your cause. He exalted in the knowledge, tenuous though it may be, that there in his blood, after all, was a tenacious strain of continuity, that his father had shed blood for Filipinas" (206).

Dela Raza's conviction that his biological father was a patriot martyred to the nationalist cause is suspect. One page earlier, Salvador "told [Leo Mercado] of his earliest memory, of his father and mother always running, run-

ning, from an unseen enemy, from danger, and in the telling, it suddenly
occurred to him that his father was a guerrilla, and that the Japanese who were
after him shot him because he had dared to fight them" (205). However, there
is no evidence from any account Salvador hears about that day to indicate that
his biological father and mother were guerillas, that the Japanese were specifically killing guerillas, or that guerillas were known to be in that area on that
day. The leap in logic Salvador makes to assume that his father was a guerilla
who died for the cause indicates the depth of his drive to locate himself in a
nationalist genealogy.

Having located himself in a continuum of nationalist insurgency by imaginatively reconnecting with both his biological father and Apo Tale, Salvador
himself becomes a figurative father in the nationalist insurgent movement. By
making his mountain home an unofficial but highly successful school for
young cadres of the insurgent movement, dela Raza becomes a patriarch of his
people. He repopulates the languishing movement, which Simplicio Verdad
had described at the beginning of the novel as having been "emasculated" (3).
Having reconnected with Apo Tale by rebuilding his simple farmer's hut and
reviving his modest farm, Salvador himself becomes an Apo to his students.
Apo is a term of respect for an older man, but its literal meaning is "patriarch."
The respect with which Filipinos regard dela Raza garner him the generic
honorific Apo, but dela Raza earns the patriarchal meaning of the title by
symbolically fathering a new generation of young nationalist activists.

All three of dela Raza's father figures are essential to his emergence as a
Filipino nationalist. His return to his home on Apo Tale's mountain and his
imaginative reconnection to his biological father are necessary elements of
dela Raza's repatriation. But James Wack, Salvador's adopted father, is also
critical to dela Raza's growth into a Filipino nationalist. When dela Raza
shows his adopted sister, Jessica Wack, his mountain hut, he talks about its significance in relation to James Wack, not to Apo Tale. "'[It] was here where
Dad found me, Jessie,' he reminded her, glorying again in the retelling," and
with that retelling, "those battered images that had littered his boyhood were
finally retrieved and made whole" (268–69). The recuperation of Salvador
dela Raza's fractured identity is incomplete without including James Wack's
paternal influence. On the most basic level, Wack saved the young, twice-
orphaned Salvador from probable starvation in the town of Raza, and through
raising and educating him in the United States, Wack gave the young dela
Raza the First World educational and economic privilege to become a historian,
a crucial step toward Salvador's ultimate repatriation. An academic himself,
Wack mentored Salvador as a historian and inculcated in him an awareness
that American history has been a history of racial domination—that the racial
inequalities in both the United States and the Philippines are the lingering
effects of Anglo-European imperialism.[6] This education becomes a key factor

in dela Raza's decision to go back to the Philippines and, ultimately, to devote his life to the tao.

James Wack is an unlikely representative of the United States, and his importance to the novel demonstrates its complicated engagement with the Philippine-American entanglement. On one hand, Wack represents American values and wealth by feeding the villagers of Raza and adopting the young Salvador. On the other hand, however, Wack also criticizes the United States by acquainting dela Raza with the underside of the American Dream: racial discrimination and its role in colonialism, the betrayal of the ideals of social and political equity and nationwide democracy. James Wack reveals the crucial gap between American democracy as an idealized abstraction and the betrayal of that ideal. James Wack's mentorship of dela Raza both reinforces and over-turns American colonial tutelage. On one level, the fact that dela Raza must learn these lessons from Wack, provider of American largesse, reenacts the ostensibly altruistic aims of American education, which was a key component of the U.S. colonial regime in the Philippines. On another level, however, Wack's lessons to dela Raza about the ironies of *American* history enable dela Raza to see the failures in *Philippine* history. By inculcating in dela Raza an understanding of the disjunction between the American Dream and its reality, Wack tutors dela Raza in the critical awareness necessary for dela Raza to make his commitment to the Filipino masa—thus, ironically, fulfilling American national ideals as much as Filipino ones. Democracy, political equality, and equal opportunity were neither precolonial nor colonial Filipino concepts. The Philippines absorbed democratic concepts as the result of American colonial rule (a lesson *Back to Bataan*'s redoubtable Miss Barnes dispenses to her young students). Thus, Salvador dela Raza's emergence as a successful Filipino nationalist is predicated on his commitment to traditionally American tenets of democracy and equality. Ironically, dela Raza becomes an ideal Filipino when he operates as an ideal American.

VIAJERO: AN AMERICAN NOVEL?

In this positing of the ideal Filipino as an ideal American, there seems to be a recurrence of the interpellation of neocolonial tutelage in *Back to Bataan*. However, although throughout *Viajero* various Filipino characters criticize the United States' continuing neocolonial influence over the Philippines, Sionil José portrays the United States as also providing important elements for the recuperation of Filipino nationalism. Thus, although the novel initially appears to simply reinscribe American neocolonialism in the Philippines, the ideological interplay between the United States and the Philippines in *Viajero* suggests that national identities are forged in the interstices of colonial and neocolonial encounters. The figure of Salvador dela Raza as "Savior of the [Filipino] Race" is not merely an example of the U.S. reassertion of colonial tutelage in the Philippines and thus the undermining of Filipino national sovereignty, but rather Filipino emergent-nationalism as developing through exchanges between subalterns in the metropolis and the (neo)colony. Thus a careful examination of *Viajero's* conclusion renders not the reassertion of American ideological hegemony in the Philippines, but the recuperation of both U.S. and Filipino emergent-nationalisms. Ultimately, *Viajero* offers the possibility for the nationalist rejuvenation of *both* nations through the same nationalist commitment to the uplift of both the American and Filipino peoples. Thus, *Viajero* suggests that the intractable Philippine-American entanglement is both necessary and ultimately beneficial to both nations, rather than manifesting a symptom of (Filipino) nationalist failure.

The complex commingling of Filipino and American nationalisms in *Viajero* first arises when Salvador dela Raza meets Benigno Aquino in Hawaii. When they first meet, dela Raza expects Aquino to excoriate the U.S. support of the Marcos regime. To dela Raza's surprise, Aquino instead "mourned the death of the American dream, the beliefs of the American founding fathers which have lost their meaning, not because the American people no longer had vision, but because they had become too comfortable with their status and with the dictators with whom they forged pragmatic, opportunistic alliances" (Sionil José 1993, 185). The words that Sionil José imagines for Aquino here are ironic in that the American Dream that brought the United States to the Philippines was Manifest Destiny, which cost hundreds of thousands of Filipino lives and cost the Philippines a half century of sovereignty. Throughout *Viajero* as well as the Rosales novels, Sionil José condemns American colonial oppression in the Philippines. *Po-on*, the first Rosales novel, was set during the Philippine-American War and ends with a statement by an anonymous Filipino *insurrecto:* "*Conquest by force is not sanctioned by God. The Americans have no right to be here. We will defeat them in the end because we believe this land they usurp is ours*" (Sionil José 1984, 204). This excoriation of the Americans' colonial conquest of the Philippines is more what one would expect in *Viajero* than Benigno Aquino acting as a late-twentieth-century apologist for the continuing validity of the American Dream or the democratic tenets of the U.S. Founding Fathers. Indeed, in other places in *Viajero* Aquino blasts the American government for supporting Ferdinand Marcos's dictatorship.

Aquino's apparent inability to divorce himself from a certain continuing identification with the former imperial master figures the paradigmatic conflict of postcolonial subjectivity. In his analysis of the early American colonial agenda in the Philippines, Vicente Rafael wrote, "While colonial rule may be a transitional state of self-rule, the self that rules itself can only emerge by way of an intimate relationship with a colonial master who sets the standards and practices of discipline to mold the conduct of the colonial subject. In other words, the culmination of colonial rule, self-government, can be achieved only when the subject has learned to colonize itself" (Rafael 2000, 22). On one level, Benigno Aquino's statement mourning the death of the American Dream appears to be a demonstration of this internal colonization. However, while on one level Aquino's statement appears to simply rearticulate the paradigmatic postcolonial dilemma, on another level Aquino's statements, when carefully examined, furnish an oblique criticism not only of the American people's failure to live up to their own patriotic ideals but also of exactly the same failure on the part of the Filipino people. Aquino's excoriation of the American people "not because . . . [they] no longer had vision, but because they had become too comfortable with their status and with the dictators with whom they forged pragmatic, opportunistic alliances" is a denunciation that is more germane to the Filipino people than it is to Americans. While Aquino's statement may be true of the American people, it is equally applicable to Filipinos—a fact to which not only Aquino but also other nationalist spokesmen such as Father Jess and, particularly, Pepe Samson attest.[7] It is Filipinos, not Americans, of whom one more immediately thinks when considering the problem of "dictators"; it is precisely the formation of "opportunistic alliances" with dictators that marks Sionil José's series of failed nationalists in the Rosales novels. Aquino's apparent statement on the death of the American Dream is in fact a displacement of his mourning for the death of the Filipino dream: the dream of at last renouncing opportunistic alliances with dictators and their henchmen, the ilustrado elite (this, of course, being Sionil José's nationalist paradigm), and regaining their national(ist) "vision."

Aquino's statement on the failure of the American Dream, then, is a misdirected diagnosis of the Philippine nationalist malaise, and Aquino's displacement of the blame from the Filipino to the American people sets up *Viajero* as predicating the resolution of the dilemma of Filipino nationalism on an American model. And this is exactly what happens. While *Viajero* is, as Sionil José's subtitle claims, "A Filipino Novel," it is just as much a novel of America as it is a novel of the Philippines. Over the course of the novel, Salvador struggles to choose between his lost, originary Filipino identity and his adopted American identity, while simultaneously grappling with American race politics through the experiences of his African American adoptive family. Despite the fact that Salvador learns that ultimately he must reject his American identity in order to assume his nationalist responsibility as a Filipino, Sionil José ends the novel with the striking claim that dela Raza gained his nationalist vision only by standing on his American father's supporting shoulders.

On the last page of the novel Salvador psychologically returns to his rescue by James Wack: "Here I am, a waif in tatters, barefoot, hungry and sick, and this gentleman with curly hair, this tall American officer in khaki, two silver bars on his collar, picks me up. Oh, my father, look at your wandering son returned to his home, to his first memory" (Sionil José 1993, 277). Salvador remembers Wack having soldier's clothes scaled down for him and trading military goods for a pair of small leather shoes. He remembers first wearing shoes and the pain they caused: "I show him the raw blisters which, he says, will heal. His eyes are merry, [as] he tousles my hair. 'This is the price you have to pay for civilization,' he tells me, then hoists me on his shoulders" (278). Although the American colonialists brought much-touted gifts to their Pacific colony—roads, sanitation systems, public education—such civilization had its price: the Filipino-American War and a half century of economic exploitation and political control, and a twilight neocolonialism in which the shadowed hand of American dominance holds Philippine politics and the economy with a light but resolute grasp. These are facts of which Sionil José is, of course, well aware—and so is his Filipino audience. And yet Sionil José ends his Filipino novel with the American soldier (who, as discussed in chapter 3, liberated the Philippines from the Japanese Occupation to return the Philippines to one more year of commonwealth dependency before officially granting independence in 1946) tousling the hair of his Filipino dependent and teaching the lesson of American benevolent assimilation: "This is the price you have to pay for civilization." And then Wack lifts the young Salvador on his shoulders. Salvador's response, and the novel's final words, are, "I am very glad for up there, I can see much more" (278). For Salvador dela Raza, it is his American background—the financial, educational, and social uplifting he got from James Wack's money and, most important, his lessons in American history—that allow him to see further than he could if he had (literally, as well as figuratively) stayed on Filipino ground. Thus Sionil José ends *Viajero*, a novel about the achievement of Filipino emergent-nationalism, with an allegorical reaffirmation of American colonial tutelage. It is the "vision" dela Raza gains from America that allows him to develop the critical awareness of both U.S. and Philippine histories, which in turn leads to his realization of and dedication to the cause of Filipino nationalism, a nationalism which must, in Sionil José's view and the view of many contemporary Filipino nationalist leaders, be defined apart from the United States.

Through integrating dela Raza's American and Filipino selves on Philippine soil, Sionil José brings his Filipino novel to a positive conclusion that Filipino literature—whether as exilic literature in the United States or as repatriate literature in the Philippines—strives toward but seldom finds. The diasporic exile returns and is reunited with the homeland, Inang Bayan (Filipinas, the motherland) and *kababayan* (countrymen). When one scans Filipino literature, from José Rizal's *Noli* and *Fili,* to the literature of *pensionados* (for example, Bienvenidos Santos), to Carlos Bulosan, to contemporary Filipino authors such as Jessica Hagedorn, one sees repeated themes of dislocation, exile, fractured families and identities, and a country in which one cannot live successfully but cannot leave behind any more successfully. In *Viajero*, Sionil José at last portrays the protagonist as the successfully repatriated exile, the son returned to his fathers (all of them!), the Filipino who chooses to live with and work on behalf of the tao instead of resting comfortably in his privileged cocoon. But Salvador dela Raza must integrate both parts of his identity, American and Filipino, to be psychologically whole and politically effective. It is by integrating the part of him that is Filipino with the part of him that is American—and only by doing *both*—that Salvador dela Raza fulfills the promise of his name.

"Truly Brother and Sister Now": Indio/American Indian Comes Full Circle

Dela Raza's American background—both the economic privilege dela Raza gains through his adoption by James Wack and, just as important, Wack's political and intellectual mentoring of dela Raza—supply elements critical to dela Raza's ultimate commitment to Filipino emergent-nationalism. Wack serves both as a representative of the American colonial master and as a challenge to American hegemony. As a soldier, Wack represents American military might and, in giving food to the starving residents of Raza, American plentitude and generosity. But as an African American, Wack represents ethnic minorities in the United States. While as a soldier Wack represents America-in-the-Philippines, as a black man he represents, at a symbolic level, the Philippines-in-America—the brown man who historically has been both marginalized and exploited by the Anglo majority power structure. After the war, in addition to becoming a respected academic, Wack becomes a devoted civil rights activist, determined that "his children must not relive the damnation of his [own] experience" as a black man in America (Sionil José 1993, 22). In his own way, Wack also makes the nationalist commitment to the American tao.

Mentoring Salvador in historical research, Wack teaches dela Raza to grasp as a gestalt the multivalent history of racial exploitation and discrimination that Western nations such as imperial Spain and the United States imposed on the darker-skinned natives in the lands those imperial powers conquered, thus connecting the Wack's family history to the history of the Philippine indio. Studying Spanish colonialism across the globe, Salvador meditates,

> The elites of a colonized nation usually inherit the vices—not the virtues—of the colonizer, and this truism was now blatantly evident in the elites of the former Spanish colonies, in Filipinas as well, where power was mostly in the hands of mestizos, who in turn discriminate and look down on the native population. The Indios, [he] was convinced, were

willing victims long after the conquistador had gone, and the legacy of cruelty and intolerance still prevailed. In many ways, he now came to realize, there was not much difference between the black Americans suffering white prejudice in the United States and the Indios of Filipinas under their [Spanish colonial] elites. (102)

Dela Raza's realization of the figurative fraternity between American minorities and Filipino indios brings full circle the longstanding American Indian/indio connection. At the end of the nineteenth century, José Rizal laid the groundwork for the establishment of a Filipino national consciousness and solidarity through his recuperation of *indio*, the Spanish colonizers' derogatory term for native-born Filipinos. Rizal founded his recuperation of the Philippine indio on his admiration for American Indians. Thus Rizal established a positive association between American Indians and Philippine indios, an association that was ironic both because Rizal based his *Indios Bravos* on a theatricized portrait of American Indians in the Wild West show, in which the show Indians daily reenacted their subjugation by Anglo America as fulfillment of the U.S. Manifest Destiny, and because the show Indians' subject position as war trophies for the U.S. continental Indian Wars prefigured Philippine indios' similar conquest through the Philippine-American War. Thus the indio/Indian connection encapsulates the complex, conflicted Philippine-American entanglement.

While it is dela Raza who makes the cognitive connection between the oppression of American ethnic minorities and Filipino indios, it is through Jessica Wack, Salvador dela Raza's adopted sister, that Sionil José resolves the issue. Dela Raza's nationalist commitment derived from the influence of his American surrogate father, but Sionil José also makes Salvador's commitment to the Filipino people analogous to Jessica Wack's commitment to an American masa. Commitments to both movements are necessary elements of Salvador dela Raza's maturation into the revitalizing force for Filipino emergent-nationalism.

While dela Raza is caught between the pull of his Filipino heritage and his upbringing as an American, Jessie also is torn by America's racial tensions. Because of their father's wealth, both Jessie and Salvador have economic freedom, but both suffer cultural dislocation. Although both her parents were sufficiently light-skinned to pass for white, Jessie is undeniably brown. The symbolic fraternity between Salvador and Jessica is manifested in their shared skin color; although Jessie is African American, Salvador describes her as a "mestiza Negra" (136). The politics of the color line straddle both sides of the Pacific, for when dela Raza is in the Philippines Pepe Samson advises against Jessie coming to visit because even in the Philippines, Jessie's dark skin would expose her to prejudice and discrimination. "In this country," Pepe warns dela

Raza, "the higher you go, the whiter it becomes. . . . Maybe some other time, in the future, when there is peace and justice here [Jessie can come to the Philippines]. It may not come at all, though," Pepe concludes sadly (228–29).

Rejected by dark-skinned and light-skinned Americans and Filipinos alike, Jessie spends her life drifting. At the end of the novel, Jessie tells Salvador that she has fallen in love and plans to marry. In response to Salvador's skepticism Jessie explains:

> "Finally, I am truly in love. And I'm marrying him. . . . I've always been, as you said, self-centered. But I could sacrifice for this man. Money is important to him, it is to all of us, but he wants to spend money not just for himself but"—a meaningful pause here—"for others, for his own people."
>
> "He's not American?"
>
> "He is. Sammy Neqwatewa is Hopi." (265)

Jessica explains that she and Sammy will live in New Mexico, working for a foundation that helps "the underprivileged get education. Indians, blacks, poor whites" (268).

The ethical imperative for Salvador throughout the novel is to reject the privilege and dilettantism made possible by his American education and financial resources and commit himself to the uplift of his (Filipino) "people." Dela Raza finalizes his break with his American identity when Jessie renounces her privileged status and, through Sammy, devotes herself to "his . . . people." It is highly significant that Sammy Neqwatewa is Native American. By making Sammy Native American, Sionil José recuperates the (Native American) Indian and (Filipino) indio dichotomy. Earlier in the novel Salvador dela Raza notes imperialism's historical continuum of racial oppression of indios by the Spaniards, both in the Americas and in the Philippines and, further, the U.S. continued racist oppression during its own colonial tenure, starting with its decimation and colonization of American Indians at home and continuing to the Philippines. Jessica's marriage to Sammy both joins and resolves the Indian/indio dynamic. In not just joining together but by "marrying" the United States' many exploited minorities—not limited to racial minorities but also explicitly including "poor whites"—Sionil José defines an American version of the masa.

The significance of Jessie's marriage to Sammy and her devotion to the mission of racial uplift in the United States—a parallel to Salvador's nationalist/populist commitment in the Philippines—is made clear through Salvador's realization that with Jessie's devotion to a worthy racial cause, he feels that they "were truly brother and sister now" (266). There had always been a subtle sibling rivalry between Jessie and Salvador as they competed for James Wack's attention. In this sibling competition, each had an advantage: Jessie because she was Wack's biological daughter; Salvador because he became an academic and thus enjoyed Wack's intellectual mentoring. But with Jessie and Salvador's ultimate dedication to the cause of their respective tao, the sibling rivalry dissolves and a "true" family relationship can blossom between them.

The interrelated nature of Jessica and Salvador's decisions to devote their lives to their respective tao is further evidence of the interconnectedness of American and Filipino nationalisms. Jessie's dedication to her people facilitates Salvador's final commitment to *his* people; it is not until Jessie has found a safe harbor that Salvador can finally tell her that he intends to spend the rest of his life in the Philippines, thereby severing his last tie to the United States (265). Both by making Salvador's ultimate commitment to the Filipino masa connected to Jessica's similar commitment to an American masa and by specifically making Jessica's devotion to the American tao the factor that finally makes Salvador and Jessica truly brother and sister at last, Sionil José constructs the fulfillment of a true Filipino nationalism linked to a similar nationalist commitment in the United States. The establishment of a "true" fraternity between Jessica and Salvador symbolically overturns the "false" fraternity encapsulated in the little-brown-brother ideology. Sionil José's connecting dela Raza's definitive commitment to the Filipino tao to a similar commitment on Jessie's side to the American tao appears to reinforce the United States' continuing ideological dominance over Filipino nationalism. However, here again Sionil José posits the attainment of Filipino emergent-nationalism as mutually dependent upon a similar form of American nationalism. Further, in the connection between dela Raza's/Jessica Wack's commitments to the nationwide betterment of their respective peoples, Sionil José once again portrays the emergent-nationalist matrix as arising out of the interstices of (neo)colonial exchange.

Throughout *Viajero* the ethical imperative is for Sionil José's protagonists to renounce privilege and devote themselves to the people. *Viajero* suggests that not only is the fate of the Filipino ilustrado inextricably linked to that of the tao, but also that the fates of the racialized underclasses of the United States and the Philippines, produced out of parallel trajectories of imperial oppression, are intangibly but indivisibly linked.

Viajero performs a series of important recuperations of the ideological, political, and racial conflicts raised in this book's previous chapters. It postulates Salvador dela Raza as the long-awaited representative of a (specifically anti-American) politically independent Filipino nationalism. It brings full circle the more than century-long affiliation between the Filipino indio and the American Indian as connected facets of Euro-American imperialism. It repudiates the false fraternity of the little-brown-brother colonial ideology and replaces it with a true fraternity between symbolic political equals. Sionil José's treatment of neocolonial tutelage complicates earlier infantilizing representations of Filipinos relative to their American mentors. These significant advances are not obtained through a definitive break from the United States, but instead through a reinvention of the Philippine-American dynamic as mutually integral for the recuperation of both nations. While on the surface appearing to break the century-long Philippine-American entanglement, *Viajero* instead demonstrates its continuing endurance and at the same time finds within that dynamic the potential for the long-awaited attainment of Filipino self-determination.

The Battleground of History

THE BALANGIGA BELLS

ON JUNE 12, 1998, the Philippines celebrated the centennial of the Philippine Declaration of Independence, a culmination of five years of centennial commemorations. The main event was a reenactment of Emilio Aguinaldo's declaration of Philippine independence from the balcony of his house in Kawit, Cavite. The government-sponsored event was attended by political and cultural dignitaries of the Philippines as well as representatives of the international diplomatic community.

As part of the celebration, the National Centennial Commission originally planned to "ring in" the centennial by pealing the bells of Balangiga. "At . . . 4:20 in the afternoon, the exact moment when General Emilio Aguinaldo declared Philippine Independence from almost four hundred years of Spanish rule and when he unfurled the Philippine flag at the terrace of his Kawit mansion, the bells of Balangiga, [were to] trigger the start of the celebrations," Richel Langit wrote in a *Manila Times* article on preparations for the June 12 centennial celebrations (Langit 1998). Instead, as David Lamb of the *Los Angeles Times* succinctly put it, "When the Philippines celebrat[ed] the centennial of its independence from Spain on June 12 [1998], one of its most symbolic artifacts—much to the nation's chagrin—[was] on display at a military base in Wyoming" (Lamb 1998).

The Balangiga bells were taken as war booty by American soldiers following the "massacre" of American troops at Balangiga, a small town on the island of Samar, during the Philippine-American War. Early in the morning of September 28, 1901, Filipinos launched a surprise attack on the U.S. Ninth Infantry, Company C, stationed at Balangiga. The town church bell pealed at the beginning of the attack, and in a short time, around fifty American soldiers were killed. A handful of survivors escaped to the American camp at Basey, bringing back a retaliatory force that virtually leveled the town of Balangiga. The Filipinos' "sneak attack" enraged American military leaders, prompting Brig. Gen. Jacob "Hell-Roaring Jake" Smith to order a brutal scorched-earth campaign across Samar during which American soldiers killed thousands of noncombatants. Smith achieved his ambition to transform Samar into a "howling wilderness" in retaliation for the Balangiga "massacre." As a final punitive gesture, the Americans took the Balangiga church bells, sending them home as war trophies to F. E. Warren Air Force Base in Cheyenne, Wyoming, where they reside to this day.

These are the basic, undisputed facts of the Balangiga incident. Very little else about the history of the Balangiga incident remains undisputed. The Balangiga bells present a case study in the fabrication of historical fact and legend codified into national history. The events preceding and succeeding September 28, 1901, have been woven into legend, interlarding questionable interpretations, historical inaccuracies, shady or absent provenance, and the inevitable complications of secondhand historical scholarship. "History brought the bells to F. E. Warren," declares Wyoming Sen. Craig Thomas (Thomas 1998b). Exactly what history—or, more important, whose history—brought the bells to rest in the "Trophy Park" of a U.S. military base is the subject of a contentious historical as well as historiographical battle, one that is less bloody but no less vituperative than the one that raged across the small town of Balangiga a century ago. The controversy over the Balangiga bells manifests the collision of opposing versions of Philippine and American history and nationalism in which historical hegemony is concomitant with physical possession. Over a century after the (U.S.) official declaration of the conclusion of the Philippine-American War, Americans and Filipinos continue to fight the battle of Balangiga.

For over forty years, Filipinos have sought the return of one or both of the bells currently in Cheyenne. A handful of U.S. veterans, however, have staunchly resisted returning the bells, invoking the inviolability of national monuments. Over the past five years, debates over the bells' disposition have become a cause célèbre, generating enormous attention in both the United States and the Philippines. Editorials and letters to the editor about the bells burgeoned, first locally in Wyoming and then across the United States as well as in the main Philippine newspapers. Like the journalistic storm surrounding the July 4, 1996, commemoration of "Phil-Am Friendship Day," debates about the bells reveal the continuing tensions between Filipinos and Americans that belie the states' official protestations of Philippine-American "friendship."

For both sides, the bells are much more than mere physical artifacts from September 28, 1901. For anticompromise Americans, they are a symbol of the inviolability of soldiers' memorials: a symbolization of the unimpeachable rightness of the U.S. military cause, a belief veterans hold as an article of faith that has as much to do with contemporary U.S. military engagements as it does with a hundred-year-old incident on the other side of the world. For procompromise Americans, the bells are a symbol of healing and sharing: an acknowledgment of, and implicit apology for, American imperialism in the Philippines as well as an acknowledgment of the similarity between the American and Philippine revolutions. The bells are a symbol not just of the Balangiga church but also of the Philippine Revolution itself, a symbol, like the U.S. Liberty Bell, of the entire nation's aspiration to freedom and political sovereignty. For many Filipinos, the United States' taking of the bells is a symbolic encapsulation of the theft of Filipino independence; many American veterans' insistence that the men of Company C were in Balangiga as "peacekeepers" and were the "innocent" victims of an unfair "sneak attack" by "insurgents" continues to rankle. The reclamation of the Balangiga bells, therefore, presents the symbolic reclamation of Filipino national agency.[1] The Balangiga bells have become a site of memory, a synecdoche for the unresolved tensions over U.S. historical narratives that continue to designate the Philippine Revolution an insurrection.[2] The Philippine-American War is being fought all over again on the symbolic front through various arguments over who owns the bells, who controls or rightfully tells the history of the Philippine-American War, what constitutes historical authenticity, and how the bells play into current U.S.-R.P. political issues such as the Visiting Forces Agreement and Filipino Veterans Benefits. For both countries, what is at stake is the nationalist symbolism inherent in monuments: the veneration and maintenance of a particular nationalist historical narrative, which both looks to the past (by memorializing the event) and the present (by making claims on ensuing generations to sustain historical memory/veneration of the national narrative symbolized in the moment).[3] Thus the debates and negotiations over the Balangiga bells reflect Filipinos' and Americans' visions of their national legitimacy both past and present.

THE BALANGIGA "MASSACRE,"
SEPTEMBER 28, 1901

American historical orthodoxy labels the events that took place on September 28, 1901, the Balangiga "massacre"; in fact, it is the interpretation of the incident as a "massacre" that engenders some of the anticompromise Americans' resentment over the incident even today, thus fueling their opposition to returning the bells. The *VFW* (Veterans of Foreign Wars) magazine called the incident the "Balangiga Massacre" in the issue commemorating the centennial of the Philippine-American War. "A Combat Chronology" of "Philippines War" notes that during the "Balangiga Massacre" "the U.S. Army sustain[ed] its single largest KIA count of the entire war," citing around seventy American casualties (Kolb 1999b, 35).

This incident was listed by the *VFW* as a "massacre" despite the fact that even it acknowledges that 250 Filipinos were killed that day. The fact that, even by pro-American estimates, around fifty American soldiers died at

Balangiga, with almost half that number again either MIA or wounded, while five times that number of Filipinos died on the same day, provokes some meditation on the use of the term *massacre*. A massacre usually implies that either a very large number or the vast majority of combatants on one side was killed by a large force on the other side (for example, 90 percent of one force killed by their opponents). And it is true that the majority of the U.S. Ninth Infantry was either killed or wounded at Balangiga; only four of the seventy-four Americans escaped that morning without injury, and most died. While it is true that Company C was "massacred" in the numeric sense, what is largely suppressed or treated as irrelevant is that despite the striking casualties on the American side, the seventy-four men of Company C killed some 250 Filipinos that same day.[4] That fact might lead one to assume that the use of the term *"massacre"* refers to Filipino rather than American casualties. But that is not the case. The American use of *massacre* invariably implies that it was the Filipinos that slaughtered the Americans, not the other way around.[5]

Another basis for the use of the term *massacre* is the savagery of the wounds/deaths inflicted, as opposed to their sheer number. Pro-American accounts of the Philippine-American War habitually highlight the more gruesome aspects of the Balangiga incident, including spectacular overkill (for example, American soldiers being stabbed dozens of times, long past the fatal blow); beheadings and other dismemberments (the *VFW* centennial article "Remember Balangiga!" reprints typically sensationalized elements of the incident, quoting William Sexton's account in *Soldiers in the Sun*: "Hopelessly outnumbered, the Americans were butchered like hogs. . . . American brains and entrails strewed the plaza and barracks" [Kolb 2001, 41]); and the survivors' ordeal in escaping Balangiga to reach reinforcements at the American camp at Basey, thirty miles away, which necessitated a harrowing journey through shark-infested waters without food, water, or medical supplies. In addition to such sensational details, pro-American sources portray the Americans as innocent peacekeepers viciously betrayed and slaughtered by ungrateful and treacherous Filipinos, as in the following description of the "massacre" in John Basset Moore's 1906 *Digest of International Law:*

> The [Filipino] natives had been treated with kindness and confidence [by the men of Company C], liberty and self-government had been given to them. Captain Connell, the American commander, was of the same faith and had been worshipping in the same church with them. With all the assurance of friendship our men were seated at their meal unarmed among an apparently peaceful and friendly community, when they were set upon from behind and butchered and their bodies when found by their comrades the next day had been mutilated and treated with indescribable indignities. (Drinnon 1980, 321)[6]

Such traditional American accounts emphasize the U.S. soldiers' plight: they were unarmed, just going to breakfast, reading their first mail from home in months, on a peaceful Sunday morning when the Filipinos attacked. Such accounts focus on the Filipinos' treacherous "sneak attack," having infiltrated the town by deception (Filipino "rebels" disguised as women mourning children who reportedly had died of cholera smuggled bolo-filled coffins into the town church). Such accounts of the Balangiga "massacre," then, paint the Americans as innocent victims of a vicious attack by treacherous, deceitful savages.

Few American accounts debunk the myth of the placid American peacekeepers viciously slaughtered on a quiet Sunday morning, despite firsthand survivor accounts that describe a vigorous American defense of Balangiga. James Taylor's *The Massacre of Balangiga: Being an Authentic Account by Several of the Few Survivors* (1931) gives firsthand accounts of the Balangiga attack. Although one must take these survivors' narratives with a grain of salt, since they were compiled three decades after the attack and some ex post facto revisionism must have taken place, the various survivors' stories are remarkably detailed and remarkably consistent. The survivors' accounts include sensationalized rhetoric such as Dr. Meyer's declaration that "for weeks after the massacre ghastly panoramas of my butchered messmates would cross my mental vision" and employ the racist language of the time, referring to Filipinos as "savages," "devils," "goo-goos," and "barbarous head hunters" (Taylor 1931, 1). Several survivors' accounts pointed out the Americans' plight at being caught unarmed at breakfast, forcing them to defend themselves with whatever objects they could press into service for defense, including rocks, saucepans, shovels, baseball bats, and even their table cutlery (one survivor noted that the dead were found later "with blood-stained mess knives or forks in their hands, showing that they had sold their lives as dearly as possible" [11, 28]). Such minutiae of the Americans' desperate defense are often repeated; what is not routinely repeated is their vigorous, and effective, counterattack. Dr. G. E. Meyer related that he and Corporal Burke reached their weapons, "and together we started pumping lead into the 'googoos.' . . . In a few minutes seven of us were firing on the enemy. . . . As fast as they appeared we shot them, many being dead before striking the ground" (6–7). Arnold Irish boasted that "we just killed them as fast as they fell to the ground" (17). Sergeant Markley, known in the company as a sharpshooter, was particularly remembered by several men as mounting a deadly counterattack. When Melwin Wall returned the next day with reinforcements from Camp Basey, he "found that two hundred fifty natives had been killed in the fight. They were lying four feet deep on the ground. We never knew how many had been wounded, but the number must have been large" (37). Then, according to Arnold Irish, "we shot all the natives in town except those whom we took [as] prisoners and forced to help bury our dead" (17). While pro-American histories of the Balangiga "massacre" such as Col. E. G. Peyton's "Facts Concerning the Massacre of Company, Ninth Infantry, at Balangiga . . ." focus on the Americans as "fighting . . . [a] soldierly and valiant struggle for supremacy over a relentless and savage enemy greatly superior in numbers" brutally massacred "by [a] cowardly mob, led by men at whose hands their confiding victims were entitled to receive naturally human return in exchange for [their] kindly and considerate treatment," the fact was that the Americans, although the subjects of a surprise attack, killed at least five times as many Filipinos as the Filipinos killed Americans (and the number of Filipino dead is likely higher, since, as Melwin Wall notes, many Filipinos must have been seriously wounded that day but escaped or were evacuated from Balangiga, to die somewhere else [40–41]). Moreover, the next day the returning Americans, by their own accounts, killed almost the entire remaining population of the town, sparing only those they pressed into labor, and burned the entire town to the ground. These facts, routinely left out of pro-American military accounts, cast considerable doubt on conventionally referring to September 28, 1901, as the "Balangiga Massacre."

Historical inaccuracies abound regarding the attack. Part of the traditional American account of the attack is that it occurred on a peaceful Sunday morning. But September 28 fell on a Saturday in 1901. This historical error is easily checked, but American sources often repeat the inaccuracy. In "Balangiga and Bad Historians," Bob Couttie (2001a) exposes many of the historical inaccuracies that have become part of the Balangiga orthodoxy. Most historians, especially Americans, have looked to Joseph Schott's *Ordeal of Samar* (1965) as the main source for the Balangiga incident. "Closer examination of Schott's sources show that the book is far from authoritative, and, although extensive, is not extensively factual," Couttie contends. "Both American and Filipino historians and writers cite the book, sometimes as the sole reference, perpetuating its grand array of errors of commission and omission." All together, Couttie concludes, "Schott managed to be both selective in his use of the core materials available to him and uncritical of their content. It was simply poor history." Couttie interrogates a broad array of supposed "facts" of the Balangiga attack. Most damning of these is Couttie's analysis of the provenance of Balangiga Mayor Pedro Abayan's reputed letter to the Americans asking "U.S. military authorities for U.S. troops to be stationed at Balangiga to provide protection from bandits and Moro pirates," a "fact" often cited in pro-American accounts of the Balangiga incident as proof of the Filipinos' perfidy. "No such letter has ever been found," writes Couttie.

Despite the usefulness of such a letter to the American authorities after the incident, when they wished to show the treachery of the natives, none has ever been produced, nor referred to in any official or unofficial report. . . . Its sole source appears to be an article by George Meyer, one of the survivors, published in 1935. Meyer was merely a musician, not yet 20 at the time, and therefore unlikely to be in a position to know the background to the Company's movement orders. . . . In fact, as First Lieutenant Edward Bumpus says in a letter to his family, Company C w[as] in Balangiga to prevent the use of the port to smuggle supplies to the Filipino guerillas. (Couttie 2001a)

Another piece of the Balangiga orthodoxy Bob Couttie dismantles is the gruesome postmortem mutilations allegedly inflicted on the men of Company C. "A part of the legend of Balangiga, and one which no Filipino historian has dealt with and which every American historian has taken as a given, is the mutilation of the bodies of Co. C. Yet there is surprisingly little evidence for it," Couttie attests (Couttie 1998b). Richard Kolb's "Remember Balangiga!" for the *VFW* magazine issue commemorating the centenary of the Balangiga attack is a typical example. Kolb quotes Stanley Karnow's account of the Balangiga attack, which noted that the dead of Company C "had been mutilated beyond belief, as if an arcane rite had driven the townsfolk into barbaric frenzy. . . . Disemboweled bodies had been stuffed with molasses or jam to attract ants" (Kolb 2001, 42; see Karnow 1989, 189–91, for his account of the Balangiga attack). Such graphic descriptions of mutilated bodies prompted Secretary of War Elihu Root to state that "*all* of the dead had been mutilated and treated with indescribable indignities" (Kolb 2001, 42; emphasis added). But as Couttie observes, there is little evidence to support the nearly universal retelling of horrible postmortem mutilations. The survivor accounts compiled in Taylor's *The Massacre of Balangiga* concur in remarkable detail about the events of the attack itself, and several of the survivors returned the next day with reinforcements from Company G, Eleventh Infantry Regiment, to bury the dead. But the survivors' accounts recall few instances of mutilations. George Markley does describe one specific instance of postmortem mutilation, remembering that "the eyes of Lieutenant Bumpus had been gouged out and jam smeared over same to attract the ants" (Taylor 1931, 32). Dr. Meyer describes "our dead" as being "horribly mutilated," but that mutilation, even from his own description, entailed the corpses' clothing being gone and their hair being burned—perhaps not surprising given the fact that, as Meyer mentions, the village had been burned to the ground. The one example of an actual postmortem mutilation Meyer describes was perpetrated on the company dog, who was killed and "his eyes dug out and stones put in place of them" (16). Arnold Irish does state that "the dead were terribly mutilated and all their clothes [were] stripped from their bodies" but does not give specifics (18). Yet several of the men recount the method they used to identify the corpses before burial: each man's name was written on a slip of paper, which was sealed in a bottle and buried with the corpse (16, 32, 61).[7] The concurrence of the burial details shared by so many of the survivors suggests that if the men of Company C truly had been "horribly mutilated," those mutilations would have been recalled in their peers' memoirs, as were the graphic details of the injuries inflicted during the attack itself.

While a careful analysis of survivors' accounts thus casts doubt on atrocities inflicted upon the American dead at Balangiga, an important factor on the Filipino side must also be taken into account. Filipino culture forbids post-mortem mutilation. As Eugenio Daza, one of the Filipino survivors of the Balangiga incident, attests, "the Filipino is a Catholic, religious by nature, and fanatic with respect to the dead. The Filipino believes that the profanation of the dead necessarily brings bad luck and misfortune. Besides, it would not reasonably be expected that during an extraordinary event as that which took place at Balangiga, anyone could have entrained the thoughts of profaning the dead: there was no time to lose for such acts" (Daza 1935). Contemporary Filipino historian Rolando Borrinaga concurs, explaining, "Our strong belief in *kalag* [spirit of the dead] and the revenge of the human soul deter us from physically harming a dead person's corpse. The bolo wounds on the American dead in Balangiga were presumably inflicted during actual fighting, and not after they were killed" (Borrinaga 1998b). But reports of "horrible" mutilations of the American dead were useful in bolstering public support at home for the war; as Kolb notes, "The [American] public was outraged, especially because all the American corpses were horribly mutilated" (Kolb 1999a, 24). Today the myth of Filipino-inflicted mutilations continues. At the centennial ceremony held on September 28, 2001, at F. E. Warren Air Force Base in Cheyenne, retired Gen. Robert Scott emphasized the violence of the attack in his oral summary of the Balangiga incident, declaring that the men of Company C "died terrible deaths, and mutilations." While the myth of post-mortem atrocities was useful one hundred years ago to garner support for the U.S. military campaign in the Philippines, the myth continues to be invoked by contemporary Americans as an implicit rationale for why the bells should not be returned to Balangiga. The sensationalized "facts" of September 28, 1901, are employed today in the same way, and for the same reasons, as they were a hundred years ago.

As Bob Couttie has observed, American historians such as Joseph Schott are "not alone" in perpetuating historical inaccuracies and generalizing allegations of wartime atrocities. "Filipino historians, too, have made errors," writes Couttie (2001a), noting such legends as guerillas being smuggled into Balangiga during a cockfight. The most serious inaccuracy, however, is the persistent myth that the Americans practiced the infamous "water cure" on suspected insurrectos in Balangiga.[8] As Couttie notes, accusations were made of the Americans' use of the "water cure" in Catbalogan, not Balangiga (Couttie 2001a). When ""Brig. Gen. Jacob "Hell-Roaring Jake" Smith launched his scorched-earth campaign across Samar in retaliation for the Balangiga massacre, he infamously commanded his men to "kill and burn! The more you kill and burn the better it will please me," and ordered his soldiers to kill male children above the age of ten (Miller 1982, 220).[9] Anti-imperialists publicized Smith's orders, and Americans were shocked and repelled by the news. Like the reports of ghastly mutilations perpetrated by savage Filipinos in the Balangiga "massacre," Brigadier General Smith's orders to "kill and burn" and to kill male children over the age of ten have become part of the Balangiga legend, not only reliably repeated but also generalized beyond historical fact. For example, two contemporary articles devoted to the Balangiga bells recount Smith's infamous orders. Margaret Laybourn writes that "the [American] retaliation [on Samar] also included burning the [Balangiga] church to the ground and killing *every* male resident over ten years old," and Julie Chao further enlarged the legend of Smith's insatiable thirst for juvenile blood, claiming that "American Brigadier General Jacob Smith essentially ordered his troops to kill *everyone* on the island of Samar over the age of ten" (Laybourn 1999; Chao 1998; emphasis added).

In addition to stretching historical fact, such accounts of the brutality of Smith's Samar campaign focus selectively. It is true that the American campaign on Samar was a brutal one, during which Americans killed thousands of Filipinos, insurrectos and noncombatants alike, ultimately reducing Samar's total population by as much as a third (Rodis 1997). However, as Reynaldo Imperial wrote, the Samar campaign became a no-holds-barred fight on both sides. Neither side showed pity for the enemy as the violence escalated. "After five months," Imperial notes,

> the battles in Samar were being fought to the last man. Neither of the forces took prisoners. . . . The guerillas mounted massive counterattacks against American . . . squads, surprising them with ambuscades. The guerillas pursued every soldier and slashed him to death. . . . General Smith was convinced that the war of pacification and the strategy of killing and burning in Samar were not enough to undermine the steadfast position of the guerillas. So he said: "Neutrality must not be tolerated. The time has now arrived when all natives in this brigade who are not openly for us must be regarded as against us. In short, if not an active friend, he is an open 'enemy'". . . . With this as [a] guiding principle, the American forces in Samar mounted an operation characterized by escalating terror. . . . This massive counter-offensive . . . easily degenerated into mass slaughter and wanton destruction of anyone alive. The Americans chased poorly armed bands of guerillas but failed to capture or kill

them. In anger, they turned on the civilian population and punished entire villages they chanced upon, in what General Smith termed . . . "protective retribution." . . . One soldier, after his active service in Samar, [. . . wrote] ". . . there would be no prisoners taken. It meant we were to shoot everything that came in sight—men, women or children." (Imperial 1998)

General Smith's infamous order for American troops to kill Filipino children stimulated outrage at home and continues to do so today, but at least two Filipino sources document children's role in the Balangiga attack, thus rationalizing to some extent Smith's belief that children were active Filipino insurrectos. Imperial notes that Smith's order "was a reaction to reports that some of those who attacked Company C were barely children," and Eugenio Daza noted in his memoir that "the pre-arranged signal for the attack was the ringing of the bells by . . . children, at the [Balangiga church] belfry" (Imperial 1998; Daza 1935).[10] The Samar campaign as a whole, then, should be considered in the larger context of the Philippine-American War—as should the Balangiga attack. Such a more comprehensive view would render the Americans' actions on Samar both more and less sympathetic than the current American orthodoxy preserves. On one hand, it would make the men of Company C appear less innocent. Defending the Americans at Balangiga, Bob Nab of the American Legion complains, " 'All of a sudden it seems to be turning to the point where the American military is the bad guy. . . . The only thing we did was try to retaliate and try to protect the military people who were left there," as though Captain Connell and his men were shipwrecked or accidentally lost on Samar (Drake 1998). The men of Company C were neither shipwrecked nor lost; they were there fighting on the American side of the war. For all that they were "innocently" engaged in their normal early-morning activities on September 28, 1901, the men of Company C were in Balangiga as soldiers. On the other hand, a more comprehensive view of the Samar campaign may render Smith's retaliatory campaign more understandable, since even Filipino sources support Smith's central concern: that ostensibly peaceful Filipino villagers and even children were actively involved in the Filipino cause and thus might reasonably be treated as combatants.

If the apologists for the American military are highly selective in their portrayal of the events surrounding the Balangiga incident, the same may be said for those on the pro-Filipino/anti-American military side of the historical fence. While the pro-American advocates focus almost exclusively on the events of September 28, 1901, their opponents focus on the preceding and succeeding events that provide a rationale for the Filipino attack on Company C; for example, (1) the Filipinos had fought their own revolution for political sovereignty from Spain from 1896 to 1898 and had virtually won that war

when Spain ceded the Philippines to the United States in the Treaty of Paris;
(2) the Filipinos had declared their independence on June 12, 1898, in the
political tradition of the United States' own Declaration of Independence; (3)
the attack itself was a legitimate act of war within the context of the Philippine-American War as opposed to an "insurrection" waged by "rebels" and
"bandits";[11] (4) the American soldiers of Company C had pressed the men of
Balangiga into forced labor in the days preceding the September 28 attack; (5)
Captain Connell's orders to cut down the town's root crops and confiscate
foodstuffs (to prevent food going to the insurgents) confronted the Balangiga
townspeople with a food shortage so severe that starvation was a real possibility;[12] (6) the Americans had repeated warnings that the Filipinos were plan-
ning some kind of attack (indeed, the night before the attack Adolph Gamlin
observed women and children evacuating the town and reported it, but he
was ignored [Couttie 2001c]); and (7) the deaths of fifty-odd American soldiers hardly compare to the many thousands killed all over Samar during Brig.
Gen. Jake Smith's retaliatory campaign. In short, both pro- and anti-Americans
focus selectively on the September incident: the pro-American faction focuses
on the attack that September morning, and especially on its gruesome details,
while those critical of the Americans' presence in the Philippines focus on the
circumstances before and after the attack, putting the incident in the larger
context of the Philippine-American War and for the most part studiously
ignoring the details of the September 28 attack itself. In the exaggerations of
war atrocities, the sedulous selectivity of each faction's version of the
Balangiga incident, and the perpetuation of historical inaccuracies, September
28, 1901, has become a historical palimpsest. Each side highlighted, elided,
and even fabricated elements of the historical record in support of a rationalization of Americans'/Filipinos' actions during the Samar campaign.

ENTER THE BELLS

While the debates about the Balangiga "massacre" continue on both sides
of the Pacific, tensions have been distilled into the Balangiga bells. The survivors of the September 28, 1901, attack escaped to the American camp at
Basey and returned the next night with reinforcements. Two companies of the
Eleventh Infantry went back to Balangiga to secure the American position and
bury the American dead. The Balangiga town church, as well as most of the
town, was burned to the ground, and when the Eleventh Infantry left
Balangiga, they took the church's bells as war booty. The bells accompanied
the Eleventh Infantry to Fort D. A. Russell, Wyoming, in 1904. When Company C mustered out of Wyoming, it took one of the bells to its subsequent
postings (Madison Barracks, New York; Fort Sam Houston, Texas; Fort Lewis,
Washington; Fort Ord, California, and, since the early 1950s, near Tong Du

Chon in South Korea), leaving two bells at the Wyoming base, which was later renamed F. E. Warren Air Force Base (Couttie 2001b; Kelly 1997a).

The Balangiga church bells have become and remain the center of a protracted controversy between Filipino and American civilians, their respective governments, and a small but vociferous group of American veterans. Both Filipinos and Americans have suggested returning the bells to Balangiga for almost a century. In 1911, Maj. Gen. Franklin Bell, who had served as U.S. Army chief of staff 1906–10, wrote from U.S. headquarters in Manila "question[ing] the propriety of taking (even as a souvenir) a bell belonging to the Catholic Church simply because a recreant native priest either used it or permitted it to be used to sound a signal of attack on American soldiers" (Herman 1997). Eugenio Daza, whose memoir is the best-known firsthand Filipino account of the Balangiga incident, closed his 1935 affidavit with a plea for the bells' return: "one of the bells which were rung on that memorable day of the heroic battle, was taken by the Americans to the United States. Could we secure its return? That depends on the patriotism of our leaders and the good will of the American people" (Daza 1935). However, such early suggestions to return the bells were ineffective, and during the decades after the conclusion of the Philippine-American War, the Balangiga bells were forgotten by Americans and Filipinos alike. For years two of the bells resided on the parade ground of Fort D. A. Russell (now F. E. Warren), long after the Eleventh Infantry moved on. With the men who took them gone, the bells seemed obsolete; as Gerald Adams, retired colonel and base historian for F. E. Warren remarked, base officials "wanted to get rid of them. . . . [The bells] just didn't seem to have any strong meaning" (Tomsho 1997).

That changed, however, as soon as representatives of the Philippine government asked for their return. For over four decades, the Philippine government has sought the return of both bells. Fidel Ramos, president of the Philippines from 1992 to 1998, first became interested in the U.S. possession of the bells when he was at West Point in the 1950s (de la Cruz 1998). He requested a return of the bells in 1986 when he served as Philippine secretary of defense under President Cory Aquino. In 1987 he approached U.S. Secretary of Defense Dick Cheney, a former Wyoming congressman, about returning the bells, but that request went nowhere. In 1994 efforts to return the bells to the Philippines intensified in an effort to regain the bells for the July 4, 1996, commemoration of the U.S. formal grant of independence. As president, Ramos made recovering the bells a major point during Bill Clinton's presidential visit in 1994, but evidently realizing that getting the bells back might be a lengthy process, Ramos requested the bells as "a good [will] gesture in 1998 to commemorate 100 years of U.S.-Philippine relations" (Rodis 1997). But the bells did not reach the American public's eye until 1997, when

27. The Balangiga bells at F. E. Warren Air Force Base, circa 1931. Photo courtesy of Wyoming Representative Jayne Mockler.

Philippine Ambassador to the United States Raul Rabe visited Cheyenne and spoke at the local Rotary Club about them. At that meeting, he showed *Savage Acts: Wars, Fairs, and Empire, 1898–1904*, an American video about the U.S. actions in the Philippines during the Philippine-American War that did not present the American interest in the Philippines as one of benevolent assimilation. A storm of controversy arose over whether one or both bells should be returned. The issue has provoked more letters to the editors of the Cheyenne newspapers than has any other issue, and the story spread across the United States, sparking articles and editorials from the *Los Angeles Times* and *San Francisco Examiner* to the *Wall Street Journal* and the *Washington Times,* as well as Philippine journals such as the *Philippine Daily Inquirer,* the *Manila Times,* and ABS-CBN News.

In 1997, the Philippine government proposed a compromise: to reproduce the bells so that each country could retain one original bell and one reproduction, thus symbolizing the two countries' economic and political ties. Those who support the compromise see sharing the bells as symbolizing a shared history, both positive and negative.[13] " 'By sharing the bells,' said [Philippine] Foreign Secretary Domingo Siazon, 'we share the agonies they represent, and then we can close this chapter of our history' " (Lamb 1998). An editorial for the *Wyoming Gillette News Record* on July 6, 1997, urged the compromise because "in that spirit of sharing, they can symbolize not only a tragic past but a hopeful future" (Rodis 1997). On November 7, 1997,

Robert Underwood, U.S. congressman from Guam, introduced House Resolution 312 supporting the proposed Philippine compromise. Citing the U.S./Philippines' "shared historic and political ties for over one hundred years" and recognizing the significance of the 1998 Philippine Centennial, Underwood's resolution ends by urging the compromise "as a measure of friendship, good will, and cooperation" (U.S. House 1997, 1–2). In his February 12, 1998, congressional speech in support of the resolution, Underwood stated, "My purpose is neither to glorify any of the actions taken nor condemn any of the atrocities committed at the time the bells were taken. . . . Instead of a solitary reminder of death, destruction, suffering and treachery, the bells would be converted into fitting monuments located on both sides of the world dedicated to the peace, friendship and cooperation between the United States and the Filipino people" (Underwood 1998b). In February 1998, Wyoming state representatives Jayne Mockler and Jeff Wasserburger circulated an informal resolution in the state legislature recommending that the U.S. Congress support the proposed resolution to share the bells with the Philippines. The Wyoming resolution "specified that the Philippines pay all costs, and it would recognize that both nations committed atrocities." More than two-thirds of the Wyoming state legislators signed the resolution, which had no force of law; if a majority of the legislators signed the resolution, it would be forwarded to the U.S. Congress only as a recommendation (Herman 1997).

A small but vociferous group of (mainly Wyoming) veterans stoutly oppose all proposals to return any of the bells to the Philippines or even to remove the bells from the current monument at F. E. Warren so that they can be replicated.[14] Wyoming veterans objected to being shut out of the legislative process by Mockler and Wasserburger's introduction of their resolution to the state legislature (informal resolutions do not normally come up for a vote; individual legislators simply sign the resolution or not, according to their opinion on the issue), claiming that Mockler and Wasserburger's resolution "amount[ed] to the same kind of sneak attack that resulted in the loss of fifty-four American soldiers at Balangiga in 1901" (Drake 1998). Kenneth Weber, commander of the VFW Department of Wyoming, gave an overview of the anti-return veterans' position when he stated, "The members of the Veterans of Foreign Wars will not stand idle and allow a sacred memorial to those soldiers killed while doing their duty [to] be dismantled" ("VFW Strongly Opposes Compromise on Bells" 1997). As retired Air Force Col. Joe Sestak argues, "[t]o dismantle a memorial to our own is to desecrate their memory and to diminish their heroic deeds" (Sestak 1999b). Jim Lloyd, president of the United Veterans Council of Wyoming, declared that the compromise is "an affront to the soldiers who died, and their survivors" (Peterson 1998).[15] Retired Air Force Gen. Robert R. Scott agrees, asserting, "It would be a breach of faith to the

men who gave their lives to now take one of the bells and give it back"
("Ambassador Offers Bell Compromise" 1997). Kenneth Steadman, executive
director of the VFW, wrote to Douglas K. Bereuter, chairman of the Congressional East Asia Subcommittee, Committee on International Relations:

> the VFW opposes and rejects any compromise or agreement with the
> government of the Philippines which would result in the return of any of
> the Bells of Balangiga to the Philippines. The church bells were paid for
> with American blood in 1901 when they were used to signal an unpro-
> voked attack by insurrectionists against an American Army garrison
> which resulted in the massacre of forty-five American soldiers. The Bells
> serve [a]s a permanent memorial to the sacrifice of the American soldiers
> from Fort D.A. Russell (Wyoming) who gave their lives for their country
> while doing their duty. . . . To return the bells sends the wrong message
> to the world. (appended to Thomas 1998b)

The significance of the bells lies in their symbolism of the U.S. commitment
to contemporary troops. More than the memory of the men of Company C
per se, the veterans insist that the bells are a reflection of present rather than
past American nationalism as embodied in military personnel. To ensure that
the bells were not sent back, in the summer of 1999 Senators Craig Thomas
and Michael Enzi of Wyoming attached a rider bill (S. 404) to the FY-2000
Defense Authorization Bill. "A bill to prohibit the return of veterans memorial objects without specific authorization in law" is known as the Thomas
Bill.[16] Although the formal title of the bill implies that it is a policy statement,
referring to veterans memorials in general, the Thomas Bill specifically addresses
the bells, noting the importance of the bells as a monument to the American
casualties at Balangiga, asserting, "to the veterans of Wyoming, and the United
States as a whole, the bells represent a lasting memorial to those fifty-four
American soldiers killed as a result of an unprovoked insurgent attack in
Balangiga" (Thomas 1998b). However, the Thomas Bill links the bells' symbolic significance in preserving reverence for the casualties of Company C to
safeguarding respect for contemporary American military personnel by attest-
ing "that American troops who serve around the world will not be forsaken"
(Thomas 1998b).[17]

What is at stake for the anticompromise veterans is a particular portrait of
the American soldier in the Philippines. Joe Sestak (2001) characterized
Philippine Ambassador Raul Rabe's address to the Cheyenne Rotary Club on
the subject of the Balangiga bells as "inflammatory. . . . making American soldiers [out to be] terrorists, practically. We took exception to the way the
American soldier was portrayed." Sestak and fellow veteran Robert Nab insist
that far from being "terrorists," "the U.S. military was acting as 'peacekeepers'
for both countries during this period of time" (Sestak and Nab 1997). Veter-

ans maintain that the Americans were "peace keepers deployed to the Philippines after the Spanish American War," according to retired Air Force Col. Gerald Adams (Kelly 1997b). Characterizing American soldiers in the Philippines from 1898 to 1902 as peacekeepers begs the question of whose peace they were keeping; with U.S. attitudes toward Filipino insurgency such as that expressed on February 11, 1899, in the *New York Criterion* opining that "whether we like it or not, we must go on slaughtering the natives . . . and taking what muddy glory lies in this wholesale killing until they have learned to respect our arms," it was clear that U.S. peacekeeping in the Philippines held little peace for Filipinos (Roth 1981, epigraph).[18]

Advocates of the United States as "peacekeeper" consider the Philippines only from the perspective of the United States and similarly consider 1898 as historically significant only in relation to the U.S. victory in the Battle of Manila Bay. In this view, there was no Philippine-American War; the Philippines came to the United States following the Spanish-American War, and those opposing the compromise to share the bells dismiss Philippine revolution as either "an insurrection," as Sen. Craig Thomas characterized it in the Thomas Bill, or "a bloody civil war," as the Wyoming Delegation (Sen. Craig Thomas, Sen. Michael Ezni, and Congresswoman Barbara Cubin) characterized it in a January 9, 1998, letter to President Clinton (appended in Thomas 1998b). For anticompromise veterans, the Balangiga bells have nothing to do with the issue of Philippine independence or its putative centennial on June 12, 1998. As VFW Executive Director Kenneth Steadman explains, "The Bells of Balangiga played no part at all in Admiral Dewey's defeat of the Spanish Navy at Manila Bay in 1898. Subsequently, that naval defeat forced the Spanish to relinquish control of the Philippine Islands to the United States. The soldiers killed were from Fort D. A. Russell and were ordered to the Philippine Islands because a savage guerrilla war had broken out after the conclusion of the Spanish-American War of 1898. Therefore, we believe the bells have no significance or connection to the celebration of Philippine independence" (Thomas 1998b).

Joe Sestak clarifies the question of Philippine independence: "The Balangiga bells had nothing to do with independence, freedom or liberation in the Philippines; they signaled a massacre. . . . The Philippines were given their independence by the United States on July 4, 1946, not in 1898 when Admiral Dewey defeated the Spanish Armada" (Sestak 1999a).

For anticompromise veterans and legislators, the subject of Philippine independence is a touchy one; from their perspective, Philippine refusals to acknowledge the gift of independence from the United States in 1946 constitute egregious, and puzzling, ingratitude. Senator Thomas complained without a trace of irony that Filipinos "act like we didn't do anything at all for their independence over the years and I don't think that's the way it is at all" (Drake and Rea 1998). Wyoming Representative Barbara Cubin agrees, arguing with an equal lack of irony, "the Bells of Balangiga memorial represents the blood and sweat invested by America to secure an independent Philippines" ("Congressional Delegation Writes Bill to Protect Bells" 1998). Those opposing the compromise intractably subscribe to a version of U.S. history that maintains American moral righteousness in the Philippines, positing the American soldiers as peacekeepers rather than agents of U.S. imperialism, intervening in a bloody civil war rather than preempting an anticolonial revolution, and granting Philippine independence in 1946. Any other interpretation of the events of 1898–1902, in this view, constitutes historical and national heresy.

While those opposing the proposed compromise tend to have a fairly homogenous viewpoint on the bells as a synecdoche for the United States and its soldiers' actions during the Philippine "insurrection," Americans who support the return of one or both bells to the Philippines do so for a variety of reasons. Some support the compromise to acknowledge Filipinos as faithful American allies throughout the twentieth century. As Guam Representative Robert Underwood notes, "Let us . . . not forget that . . . these very same people and their descendants suffered, fought, and died fighting with our troops for a common cause in the battlefields of Bataan, Corregidor, Korea and Vietnam, making the Philippines the only Asian country that has stood with the United States in every conflict in this century" (Underwood 1998a). Others focus on the issue of religious sacrilege, condemning Americans' taking sacred objects as war booty. A spokesman for the Jewish War Veterans of the U.S.A. asserted that "the taking of the bells from Philippine churches for an American vets 'memorial' would be like Germans taking Torahs as 'war trophies' from synagogues burned down somewhere in Poland for a 'memorial' to German soldiers killed in the 1943 Warsaw Jewish Ghetto Uprising," and Ruby Potmesil argued, "No one dismantled a Buddhist temple in Vietnam to place beside the Vietnam War Memorial" (Swallow 2000; Potmesil 1998). Jim Helzer researched the rules of conduct regarding the taking of war booty and decided,

> the taking of [t]he Bells was in fact legally wrongful in 1901, just as the taking of the bells would be wrongful today. Both the Philippines and the United States were signatories to the 1899 Hague Convention which as a treaty had the force of law under our Constitution. . . .
>
> The 1863 Lieber Code, the set of formal guidelines providing a code of conduct for the U.S. Army in effect in 1901, provided that "property belonging to churches . . . is not to be considered public property" and that private property could "be seized only by way of military necessity." . . . There is no doubt that the bells were religious objects, the taking of which was clearly not demanded by any necessity of war. (Helzer 1998)

While a variety of opinions motivates many Americans to support returning at least one of the bells, for most procompromise Americans, the returning of the Balangiga bells is dictated by a sense of national obligation stemming from the values axis of nationalism. From this perspective, the keeping, if not the taking, of the Balangiga bells betrays the national character. As Jim Helzer put it,

> History, as I was taught it, cast Americans in the role of liberators from the Spanish. We weren't told that when Admiral Dewey arrived at Manila to annihilate the Spanish fleet, the Spanish were in control of little more than the Manila area, the Filipinos fighting for independence were in control virtually everywhere else. . . . No matter how America saw itself, the Filipinos saw us as simply a new colonial master. . . . It's time for us to face up to our obligations to this period of history. Keeping the bells of Balangiga dishonors us all and tarnishes the memory of our soldiers who died nearly a century ago. Returning them would be in the greatest traditions of America and of Wyoming (Helzer 1997)

Theodore Gostas, a Vietnam veteran, invoked U.S. national honor as dictating the return of the bells, arguing, "The return [of the bells] . . . symbolizes the great forgiving nature and compassion of the American people. These traits are truly aspects of why this nation is so highly regarded by all free people of all lands upon this earth" (Gostas 1999, 3). Rodger McDaniel (1998) agrees, stating, "I think we would do greater honor to the real values of our nation . . . by graciously returning [the bells] to a people to whom such a gesture would say a great deal about who we are."

Opposing invocations of U.S. national ideals, values, honor, and/or character recapitulate arguments made by both imperialists and anti-imperialists a hundred years earlier regarding the U.S. annexation of the Philippines and its involvement in the Philippine-American War. As noted in this book's introduction, anti-imperialists and imperialists alike appealed to the national character and to national ideals/values (for example, those contained in the Declaration of Independence, the American Revolution, and the Constitution). Those supporting the bells compromise employed the same nationalist arguments as had the anti-imperialists. As with the anti-imperialists a century before, the U.S. Declaration of Independence provides a compelling nationalist touchstone. Wyoming businessman Jim Helzer appealed to the U.S. Declaration of Independence as a governing principle for American nationalism when he asserted, "I like my history simple: I begin with the premise right out of our own Declaration of Independence, that people have a right to be independent and free as long as they have the means to express those aspirations democratically" (Helzer 2001). Once again invoking the doctrine of government only by consent of the governed, Steve Richardson attested,

"The United States of America has for two centuries served as the world's finest example of the value of independence. The spirit of the rebels at Balangiga is reminiscent of our own Revolutionary War in its resistance to armed occupation by a foreign state. Just as we proudly display the Liberty Bell in Philadelphia to symbolize our call to arms, the Filipinos wish to celebrate the bravery of those ancestors who risked their necks to declare independence from a fearsome power" (Richardson 1997).

Veteran Wayne Frisby also pointed to the political similarity between American and Filipino revolutionaries, affirming the "appropriate[ness of] . . . compar[ing] Philippine freedom fighters' actions to Washington's combat actions against the British. . . . How could our country, which had fought for self-government in such a prolonged revolution, resort to imposing colonial rule by force on a smaller nation . . . ?" (Frisby 1999, 2). Procompromise Americans also employed the analogy between the American and Philippine Revolutions to justify the Balangiga attack. Anti-return veterans, conversely, nurse continuing resentment over the Filipinos' sneak attack of the Americans at Balangiga: as retired Air Force Col. David McCracken said, "Part of this issue, as least with me as an old military guy, is the way the attack was conducted. It was underhanded," and L. D. Cleveland called the Balangiga attack a "dastardly deed" (Susman 2001; Cleveland 1998). Pro-return advocates responded by pointing out that Americans view George Washington's sneak attack against the British during the American Revolution a military triumph rather than a dastardly deed. Sydney Spiegel points out, "If [the Americans at Balangiga] were surprised while eating or sleeping, with the guns stacked in a corner of the room, then they were taken by surprise while their guard was relaxed—a legitimate and resourceful military tactic also used by George Washington at dawn on Christmas day when he attacked the sleeping Hessian allies of the British at Trenton, New Jersey, in 1776" (Spiegel 1999).

Wyoming Representative Jeff Wasserburger (1997) agreed: "Special interest groups have stated that the attack on the 9th Infantry was a surprise attack. This is true, but what rule of war requires an army to send written invitation to the opposing army of a pending attack? We certainly didn't expect George Washington to send an invitation that he was going to surprise the British at Trenton and Princeton in our fight for independence during the American Revolution. We, in fact, honor Washington's treachery at Trenton and Princeton and call his victories major turning points in the war." Joseph Hart, bishop of the diocese of Cheyenne, argues that the bells should be returned to Balangiga to be used for their original purpose: to call the faithful to worship. However, he also appealed to Americans' veneration of Revolutionary history and its artifacts to argue for the bells' return, stating, "The Old North Church in Boston was used to signal Paul Revere of the British intentions as they marched on Lexington and Concord. What if the British had burned down the Old North Church and taken back the bell or other remnants of the church to London for display? Americans would rightly have been outraged. How, then, can we justify the actions of American troops in burning down a church dedicated to the worship of God and justify our theft of artifacts from that church as being in honor of those slain?" (Hart 1998).

Several people advocating the bells' return to the Philippines cite the Balangiga bells as an analogue to the American Liberty Bell. A typical example of this argument appears in a 1998 letter to the editor of the *Chicago Tribune:* "in the Philippines . . . the bells are regarded as the equivalent of our Liberty Bell—symbols of a heroic effort to shake off colonial rule" ("Return Bells to Philippines" 1998). For both pro- and anticompromise advocates, the disposition of the bells symbolically recapitulates the U.S. co-optation of the Philippines and thus, perhaps not surprisingly, those condemning or defending the U.S. acquisition of the Philippines utilized remarkably similar arguments to condemn or defend the U.S. retention of the Balangiga bells a century after the Balangiga incident. In 2001, as in 1901, both sides were motivated by their own views of national honor, and the ethical obligations entailed in upholding each side's version of the national values, thus touching on the interplay between the identity and the values axes of nationalism. That dynamic in turn stimulated the interplay between individual citizens and the state, both through individuals' private actions lobbying the state to either return or retain the bells and through the involvement of legislators, even the national and state legislatures, on informal and formal political actions regarding the bells. Thus the Balangiga bells not only provide an intriguing example of the contentious dialogical construction of a site of memory but also offer a compelling case study in the interplay between the tripartite axes of nationalism on both sides of the Pacific.

"HISTORY BROUGHT THE BELLS": NATIONAL HISTORY AND THE BALANGIGA BELLS

Veterans who oppose returning the bells cite their historical significance both in relation to F. E. Warren Air Force Base and as a memorial to the Balangiga casualties. Retired Air Force general and former F. E. Warren commander Robert Scott notes that the fort "is the oldest continually active military installation in the United States. . . . It's a national historic site, and as such you don't remove artifacts" (Drake 1997). Retired Air Force Col. Gerald Adams has argued that the bells are "part of [F. E. Warren's] historical integrity," but that claim is debatable (Rodis 1997). Bob Couttie "challenge[d] [Wyoming VFW Commander Weber to name a single Wyoming man who was even present at Balangiga. . . . [or] produce any evidence that Company C had any significant connection with Fort Russell/Warren" (Couttie 1998a).

While anticompromise veterans' insistence that the bells are critical to F. E. Warren's "historical integrity" can thus be challenged, the bells' own "historical integrity" has become suspect as well. Some have claimed that at least one, and possibly both, of the bells currently on display at F. E. Warren's Trophy Park are not the bells from the Balangiga church (see figure 29). The bells' provenance is questionable because of an old photograph taken of some of the American survivors of the Balangiga attack grouped around a small bell, presumably one they took from the Balangiga church. The bell in that picture does not resemble either of the bells on display in Cheyenne (Borrinaga 1998b). Several critics have questioned the Cheyenne bells' provenance (for example, Swallow 2000; Kelly 1997a). As Rolando Borrinaga notes, "careful rereading of Pvt. Gamlin's and Pedro Duran's accounts also show that only one bell was rung to signal the attack on the American garrison in Balangiga. Even Daza's account mentioned only one bell taken by the Americans from Balangiga. It thus seemed like Balangiga only had one church bell at that time" (Borrinaga 1998b). One of the bells currently at F. E. Warren is marked "Se Refundio siendo cura Parroco el M.R.P.F. / Agustin Delgado año 1889." Since Agustin Delgado was the Balangiga parish priest in 1889, the inscription on the 1889 bell provides a strong case for the bell's Balangiga provenance (Balangiga Research Group 2002). The other bell at F. E. Warren is marked "San Francisco ano E. 1863," and there is no proof that it came from Balangiga. Gerald Adams, F. E. Warren base historian, told me in an interview on September 27, 2001, that he believes that the smaller bell currently at Warren was never in Balangiga. So at least one of the bells currently at F. E. Warren is probably not from Balangiga, and, as John Swallow posits, "It is entirely possible neither bell at Warren AFB is from Balangiga, but from other towns burned down in U.S. retaliation for the Balangiga Massacre," and "if the ones in Wyoming were from other towns the U.S. burned down, then [the American vets have] no moral claim [to those bells] since they are not honoring the dead of the Balangiga Massacre" (Hart 1998; Swallow 1998, 1999). But despite mounting evidence that at least one of the bells on display in Cheyenne is not from Balangiga, the veterans refuse to return either of the Cheyenne bells to the Philippines. "'To us it really doesn't make any difference,' said retired Air Force Col. Joseph Sestak, who heads the American Legion in Wyoming. '[The Cheyenne bells] may or may not have been rung at Balangiga. But the fact is, we've put them into a memorial. . . . We're not going to dismantle a memorial to our soldiers for anything'" (Susman 2001).

The anticompromise stance of many American veterans and legislators is puzzling in its intractability. As shocking as the Balangiga incident was, it was no more shocking to Americans than was the Japanese attack on Pearl Harbor or the revelation of Nazi atrocities in Europe during World War II. Yet many Americans have reconciled with their former Japanese and German enemies.

28. Company C survivors.

Stan Hathaway, former governor of Wyoming, wrote on March 13, 1998, to Sen. Craig Thomas:

> As I have studied this matter, I come to the conclusion that the position of the Veterans of Foreign Wars and American Legion is wrong on this issue. As a member of those organizations and as a combat veteran of World War II, I think I have a right to express that opinion. If we adopted the same philosophy with respect to Germany and Japan and have no forgiveness of military acts between our nations, we would indeed be asking for more trouble. The Germans have forgiven us for killing 300,000 people in the Dresden bomb raid of 1945. I was on that mission. To hang on to some undefined military principle after one hundred years doesn't make any sense to me or most people of Wyoming. (Hathaway 1998)

The intensity and longevity of the veterans' resentment over the Balangiga attack is particularly striking because there are no living survivors on either side who have firsthand experience of the incident. Presumably, reconciliation would be much more difficult between firsthand survivors of such an attack, since the participants likely would have sustained injuries and/or have lost

29. Balangiga bells at F. E. Warren Air Force Base, Cheyenne, Wyoming, on the centennial of the Balangiga incident, September 28, 2001. Photo by author.

comrades during the attack. Yet the living survivors of World War II have been able to achieve reconciliation with former enemies whereas the anticompromise veterans, who at best have only a third party role in the Balangiga incident (being neither firsthand participants nor their direct descendants, who may have a secondhand interest in the issue), staunchly refuse reconciliatory overtures by Filipinos and mounting opposition by their fellow Americans, including many veterans. The intransigence of the Wyoming veterans regarding the Balangiga bells demonstrates the importance veterans invest in their role as guardians of American militarism-cum-nationalism. In some ways, their self-assumed responsibility is more compelling because it is, at one level, disinterested: *because* they were not firsthand participants in the incident, they feel all the more strongly the righteousness of their self-appointed role as protectors of the U.S. national honor. They are preserving the historical integrity of a group of men who cannot do it for themselves and, in so doing, safeguarding the national honor a century after the fact.

The irony is that their nationalist devotion may be misplaced. Increasingly, critics are arguing that the "real" bell—the bell in the survivors' photograph—is the bell that followed the Ninth Infantry throughout its travels and now resides at the First Battalion/Ninth Infantry Division headquarters in South Korea. Bob Couttie observes that the Korea bell is dated 1896 and marked with the name Fr. Aparecio, who was the Balangiga parish priest of that time, so it is likely that it and the 1889 bell came from Balangiga. Filipinos and Americans alike have, at different points, been willing to negotiate on returning the Korea bell. In 1998, Sen. Craig Thomas, sponsor of the Thomas

Bill, offered to help return the Korea bell to the Philippines if the Philippine government would cease lobbying for the return of the two Cheyenne bells. But Fidel Ramos refused to give up a claim to even one of the Cheyenne bells—"a costly mistake," as Rolando Borrinaga (2001a) observes. Thus Filipinos and Americans alike have fetishized the two bells on display at F. E. Warren, insisting on retaining or regaining them despite the likelihood that at least one of those bells did not come from Balangiga—and thus have discounted the Korea bell, which likely *did* come from Balangiga. Both sides' intractable claims on the historical integrity of the two Wyoming bells ironically have resulted in their ignoring both the relative availability as well as the probable authenticity of the Korea bell.

Both sides' insistence on retaining/regaining the Wyoming bells despite their provenance reveals the extent to which the bells have become overdetermined repositories of Philippine/American nationalism. Ultimately, the bells themselves, as physical artifacts, are not the real issue. For both sides—indeed, for everyone except those who simply believe the bells should be used for their original purpose, to call Catholics to Mass—the real issue is national history. For both sides, but especially for the American veterans adamantly opposed to returning either of the two bells currently reposing in Wyoming, what is ultimately at stake is each nation's legitimacy, present as well as past. For each country, what is at stake is not simply the bells as a symbol of war booty. What is at stake even today, is history itself: who was the putative villain or victim in the Balangiga incident and, ultimately, in the Philippine-American War.

In *The War of 1898: The United States and Cuba in History and Historiography*, Louis A. Pérez Jr. outlines several remarkable similarities between the United States' actions in Cuba and in the Philippines in 1898.[19] Pérez notes the role historical hegemony played in both U.S. and Cuban relations in the century following the "splendid little war," observing, "U.S. hegemony insinuated itself into all facets of [Cubans'] daily lives and nowhere perhaps with more discernible effects than in notions of the past." Pérez details the ways in which the unresolved tensions of 1898 were resurrected in Fidel Castro's campaign of 1959, which was portrayed as a reclamation of the Cuban Revolution: "The year 1898, Cubans understood, was the point of pre-emption; 1959, they believed, was the moment of redemption. One of the objectives of the revolution was to make Cuba for Cubans, and this necessarily had to begin with history, to recover a usable past in which the Cuban presence mattered. In reconfiguring the way they saw themselves, Cubans also redefined the ways others saw them. After 1959 it was not uncommon for U.S. histories to view the war as the 'Spanish-Cuban-American War.' Cubans had regained their past" (Pérez 1988, 125, 131).

The similarities between the Philippines' and Cuba's treatment by the United States in 1898 are remarkable, and these similarities continue into the second century of U.S./Philippine/Cuban relations. As the debates over Philippine-American Friendship Day in 1996 and the disposition of the Balangiga bells reveal, Filipinos continue to struggle with the same unresolved resentments over the legacy of U.S. liberation that smoldered in Cuba until 1959. In 1959 Cubans claimed their agency in U.S. historical narratives—an ideological victory that was as important as any actual military engagement. Filipinos, however, have not been as fortunate. What is at stake in the debates over the Balangiga bells is as much historical—and historiographical—as it is the bells as physical artifacts. The bells of Balangiga function as a synecdoche of the Philippine-American War, and both sides, in asserting their argument for where the bells rightfully belong, assert the legitimacy of their version of the Philippine-American War. Even after a century, a fundamental struggle continues over whether the 1989–1902 conflict between the United States and the Philippines was the "Philippine-American War" or the "Philippine Insurrection." Wyoming Sen. Craig Thomas specifically referred to the bells as "a lasting memorial to those fifty-four American soldiers killed as a result of an unprovoked insurgent attack in Balangiga" and referred to the 1898–1902 conflict in general as an "insurrection" (Thomas 1998b). Filipinos continue to fight for American acknowledgment of the 1898–1902 conflict as the Philippine-American War. During his April 1998 presidential visit to the United States, Fidel Ramos optimistically opined that "I think history has been corrected in the sense that this was not the Philippine insurrection as it is recorded in some American history books. This was the Filipino war for independence against the Americans" ("Ramos to Call" 1998). Felipe Romanillo, executive director of the National Historical Institute, took a less rosy view when he observed that "in US history books, there is no mention of the Philippine-American War but only the Philippine 'insurrection.' For a hundred years, the Americans have branded Filipino freedom fighters as nothing more than bandits or rabble-rousers instead of genuine revolutionaries defending their homeland" ("For Whom the Bells of Balangiga Toll" 2001). The extent to which people see the Balangiga bells as emblematic of the Philippine-American War is revealed in Rene Sguisag's (2001) report on the Balangiga incident centenary when he cautioned, perhaps humorously but perhaps not, "we have to be careful we do not start a second Filipino-American War over the bell."

For those opposing the compromise, the bells symbolize the moral rectitude of the U.S. actions in the Philippines at the turn of the century, what Edward Linenthal calls a "patriotic orthodoxy" that has been codified in the national history (Linenthal 1991, 143).[20] These Americans protest historical revisionism as an attack by liberals on the national past. "There is a tendency by modern historians to rewrite history to meet their agendas, especially if the military is involved," complained Scott Jones (2001). Writing to former

Wyoming Gov. Stanley Hathaway on March 24, 1998, Sen. Craig Thomas wrote:

> In my view, history brought the bells to F. E. Warren and there they should stay. We should not . . . rewrite the past. . . . The "campaign" to return the bells is part of the revisionist movement happening within the humanities. Would we, following the same revisionist approach, return other U.S. holdings brought here by whatever historical circumstance, be it war, migration or antiquities expeditions because the items originated in another country with an upcoming anniversary? The Smithsonian is filled with such pieces. Where would it stop . . . ? . . . I just can't adopt the revisionist approach to history. (Thomas 1998a)

Timothy Vaughn also sees historical revisionism as attacking American nationalism:

> Does America have some reprehensible periods in its own history? Yes, it does. But there is not another nation on earth that tries as hard as we do to correct past wrongs, and to make amends. . . . However, the movement to return the Bells of Balangiga is not about making amends. It is part of the radical multicultural movement sweeping the nation in which our history is being rewritten by America-hating revisionists to portray the United States as evil and oppressive, our heroes trashed, our monuments torn down, and our institutions renamed. . . . It seems that we Americans are the only people on earth who are expected to feel guilty and ashamed of, and apologize for our past. . . . Ironically, it is precisely because we Americans are the most generous, compassionate and fair-minded people in the world that we are so easily duped into assisting the America-haters in their campaign to destroy our country. (Vaughn 1998)

Those supporting sharing the bells hurl their own charges of historical inaccuracy-cum-nationalism as regards the bells. To the accusation that she was attempting to rewrite history, Wyoming Representative Jayne Mockler responded, "We are not forgetting history. We were never told the proper history" (Brooke 1997). For both Mockler and legislative colleague Jeff Wasserburger, Philippine Ambassador Raul Rabe's presentation to the Cheyenne Rotary Club on the U.S. actions in the Philippines, and especially the video presentation of *Savage Acts,* proved a reeducation in American history in the Philippines. From the same presentation and video, representatives of the two sides had two diametrically opposing responses, both of which hinged on the viewers' perspectives on what constituted a legitimate exercise of American nationalism in the Philippines. For Wyoming veterans Sestak, Nab, and McCracken, such a portrayal of the American military in the Philippines as "rapists, murderers, and thieves" is both a betrayal of the U.S. national honor and an egregious indictment of soldiers simply doing their duty; therefore, the

Balangiga bells must stay where they are because to send them back is to rat-
ify such a repugnant characterization of the United States and its military
(Lloyd 1998). For others, such as Mockler and Wasserburger, Rabe's presenta-
tion/video, if not rewriting American history, radically enlarged it and called
upon sentiments based on national ideas such as democracy, fair play, and the
democratic precepts codified in the Declaration of Independence and the
Constitution; therefore, at least one of the Balangiga bells must go back, to
right a national wrong as well as to acknowledge the past and present Philippine-American alliance. To procompromise advocates, returning the bells is
not tantamount to condemning the United States; it is restoring it to its highest ideals—thus, once again recapitulating the anti-imperialists' arguments of
a century before.

A NEW MONUMENT?

As Cheyenne businessman Jim Helzer notes, "No one argues against a
memorial for our soldiers who died at Balangiga. At its heart, the issue is how
the inclusion of the looted bells of Balangiga in the [F. E. Warren] memorial
can possibly be appropriate. . . . We, in fact, dishonor the memory of those
soldiers by including [in the monument] bells whose taking was sacrilegious,
immoral and unlawful even in 1901" (Helzer 1998). A letter to the *Casper
Star-Tribune* agreed, stating, "Surely anyone with a sense of honor must question whether men's sacrifices are properly honored by stolen property" (de la
Cruz 1998). Helzer (2001) proposes that new, identical memorials be built,
one in Cheyenne and one in Balangiga, collaboratively designed by a Filipino
artist and an American artist—and not using the contested bells. Greg
Macabenta, a Daly City, California, businessman and community leader, also
advocates building a new memorial in Balangiga: "if the American Legion is
concerned with not doing due honor to soldiers, why not put up a memorial
in Balangiga, to honor soldiers on both sides and as a memorial to the futility
of war" (Chao 1998), and similar suggestions have been made in the Philippines (for example, Pennie Azarcon de la Cruz [1998] suggested, "Why not
even a joint memorial for those who perished in this war, people of both
countries who fought for what they thought was right?"). American veteran
Wayne Frisby supports changing the current memorial in Cheyenne: "The
right thing to do is to return both bells to the Philippines. A simple solution
is to build a new memorial with the names of all Wyoming fatalities of the
1898–1902 period. . . . When it is so easy to build a new memorial with the
names of all fatalities of the Spanish American [War]-Philippine Insurrection,
why not do so, and eliminate a memorial which will forever be a symbol of
an alleged atrocity ordered by an American general[?]" (Frisby 1999). Another
possibility is to recognize Company C on the memorial statue that already
stands in Cheyenne next to the state legislature building. This statue, erected

in memory of the soldiers who fought in the Spanish-American War, may be a fitting memorial for two reasons. First, its location on public ground would make the memorial more accessible; because the F. E. Warren memorial is part of a military base, public access is necessarily restricted. (In the days leading up to the Balangiga centennial on September 29, 2001, there was concern that civilians would not be allowed onto F. E. Warren at all, since all military bases were then on the highest alert level following the September 11 attacks two weeks earlier.) Second, since anti-return veterans and legislators take the position that the American military was in the Philippines in the wake of the Spanish-American War, one could argue that memorializing the men of Company C through the Spanish-American War memorial would be a fitting tribute.

In addition to suggesting that a new memorial to the Balangiga victims be erected, both Filipinos and Americans have suggested that the Congressional Medal of Honor be conferred posthumously on the men of Company C; such an action would commemorate the American soldiers, satisfy the American veterans and legislators who insist on honoring their memories, and presumably ameliorate the importance of the bells' residence in Wyoming, paving the way for their return. However, the U.S. government repeatedly has refused to grant the Medal of Honor to the men of Company C. As Rolando Borrinaga notes, "Three attempts were made in the 1930s to consider granting the Congressional Medal of Honor to the American survivors [of] Balangiga," but the U.S. government refused, although, "ironically, two American Marine officers were awarded Congressional Medals of Honor for their roles during the one-sided savagery operation in Samar," and a total of eighty-six Medals of Honor were awarded to American soldiers for their actions during what the U.S. Army Center of Military History calls the "Philippine Insurrection" (Borrinaga 1998b; see also Taylor 1931, 42).[21] "The War Department repeatedly opposed efforts to award [the men of Company C] medals, arguing in a 1928 memo that: 'No record has been found to show that any individual member of the company performed an act of gallantry beyond the call of duty,'" writes Robert Tomsho (1997, 6). In fact, the U.S. government did not acknowledge that American soldiers were actually fighting a war in the Philippines; for instance, "the War Department did not grant combat pay to [American] soldiers, claiming there was no war there!" (Kolb 1999a, 26).[22] Years after the unacknowledged war concluded, the U.S. government continued to deny military recognition to American veterans of the Philippine campaigns. James Taylor's *The Massacre of Balangiga* was compiled not only to honor the men of Company C; it also had a more practical goal: to lobby for pensions and government recognition of the men (see Taylor 1931, "Explanatory," 18, 42). While both pro- and anticompromise advocates have utilized diplomatic and legislative channels on both the Philippine and American sides all the way

30. Cheyenne Spanish-American War memorial. Photo courtesy of Sylvester Salcedo.

from the local (Wyoming state legislature) to the national (both U.S. and Philippine Senates) to the executive (U.S. President Bill Clinton and Philippine President Fidel Ramos) levels to redress the issue of the Balangiga bells in the present (through the building of a new Balangiga memorial and/or the proposed "sharing" compromise), the U.S. government has continued to refuse to redress the issue in the past by conferring posthumous awards on the men of Company C. Like the anti-return veterans, the U.S. government is loath to rewrite its official history in the Philippines. But perhaps it doesn't matter. Even if the government were to grant the Medal of Honor to the men of Company C, such historical revisionism would not likely change U.S. veterans' entrenched position on the disposition of the bells in Wyoming. If the fact that at least one (if not both) of the bells currently on display at F. E. Warren Trophy Park is not from Balangiga does not alter the veterans' position, then the conferral of the Medal of Honor on the Balangiga dead is not likely to make a difference either.

But the American veterans are not the only ones selectively crafting the Balangiga bells' national historical significance, and Filipinos have been just as entrenched in their position on the bells—even in the face of historical inaccuracies surrounding both the conventional history of the Balangiga incident and the questionable provenance of the Wyoming bells. If the Philippines had regained the bells by June 12, 1998, it would have posed an interesting question for the Philippine National Centennial Commission to decide where the bells rang in the Philippine centennial: in Balangiga or at the Philippine government's official commemoration ceremony at Emilio Aguinaldo's house in Kawit? The Balangiga bells did not have any part in the June 12, 1898, Kawit declaration. The vast majority of the Philippines' political, diplomatic, and cultural dignitaries attended the Kawit commemoration, so if the Balangiga bells had been rung in Balangiga, which would have been more historically accurate, very few people would have heard the historic pealing. If the bells had been rung at Kawit, it would have been historically anomalous. The Philippine National Centennial Commission's plan to ring in the June 12, 1998, centennial by pealing the Balangiga bells demonstrates the bells' symbolic significance to Filipinos: more like the U.S. Declaration of Independence than its Liberty Bell, the Balangiga bells have come to symbolize the aspiration of Philippine independence—a declaration of intention as important as the actual attainment of political sovereignty. In fact, for Filipinos, because of the U.S. preemption and co-optation of Philippine independence, the recognition of Philippine independence nearly a half century later, and the continuing debates and doubts about Philippine cultural, political, and economic sovereignty, perhaps the bells' symbolic declaration of the Filipino determination to be independent is more significant than the official recognition of Philippine independence. As discussed in chapter 4 of this book, the two ostensible dates signifying Philippine independence are both undermined by the United States: June 12, 1898, is questionable because the *declaration* of independence did not lead directly to its political reality, while July 4, 1946, is questionable because, understandably, Filipinos resent having their political sovereignty conferred as a gift after fighting to gain it in their own right. If June 12, 1898, and July 4, 1946, are, then, irreconcilably problematic dates for commemorating the attainment of Philippine independence, September 28, 1901, the date on which Filipinos initiated and won an attack against a much better armed foe, and drove them, even if briefly and ultimately at great cost, from their home, might be a better candidate.

Ultimately, both sides continue to fight for their version of the history of the Philippine-American War. In *America's Wars in Asia: A Cultural Approach to History and Memory,* Philip West, Steven Levine, and Jackie Hiltz comment on the complexity of the relationship between history and memory, observing that "historical memory is almost always contested, often as hotly as the blood-soaked ground of a major battle" (West, Levine, and Hiltz 1998, 5). The controversy over the Balangiga bells demonstrates this convergence of the figurative and literal battleground of history, as both Americans and Filipinos contend for the bells as symbols of a national past that casts its influence into the present. The bells' historical significance—their symbolization of the rectitude of the Philippines' and United States' role in the Philippine-American War—produces their overdetermination as national(ist) artifacts. This nationalist overdetermination exists for both sides, as revealed on the American side by veterans' refusal to return the bells, when even the most conservative representatives admit that at least one of the bells did not come from the Balangiga church, and as revealed on the Philippine side by the National Centennial Commission's plan to ring in the centennial by pealing the bells, when the bells have no strict historical relevance for June 12, 1898. For both Filipinos and (pro- and anticompromise) Americans, what is really being contested is each country's role in the Philippine-American War and its implications for national sovereignty on the Philippine side and moral rectitude on the American side. The figurative battle over nationalism continues to smolder, and, as the Balangiga bells controversy reveals, occasionally to erupt. As Palmer Cox revealed with his Brownies exploring the half-submerged wreckage from Dewey's spectacular victory in Manila Bay, residual tensions over the Philippine-American War are "full of mischief yet," and the continuing skirmishes over the Balangiga bells reveal the conflicts just below the ostensibly calm surface of Philippine-American friendship.

Notes

Introduction

1. For just a few recent examples, see Walsh (2002), Mallaby (2002), and Francia (2003).
2. For details of the debates and negotiations over the U.S. bases in the Philippines, see Bengzon and Rodrigo (1997) and Castro-Guevara (1997).
3. These military exercises have been conducted under the aegis of the Visiting Forces Agreement (VFA), which allows for short-term, noncombat, bilateral military ventures in the Philippines. Satchell (2000, 30) translates Balikatan as "Tagalog for 'shouldering the load together,'" while Francia (2002) translates Balikatan as "shoulder-to-shoulder," emphasizing the collaborative character of the bilateral military project.

    The Abu Sayyaf has a history of kidnapping for ransom, as it did in the recent kidnapping incident involving two American citizens, Martin and Gracia Burham. As Francia (2002) reports, the Abu Sayyaf "made no political or ideological demands," so the motive in its kidnappings appears to be economic rather than political. Francia notes that the group has made kidnapping "a highly lucrative enterprise, having made in its previous kidnappings between $10 million and $25 million, enough to purchase sophisticated weaponry."
4. In addition, the Bush administration displayed its preferential treatment of the Philippines in diplomatic terms; Macapagal-Arroyo's state visit to the United States was her only state visit in 2003, and it was one of only "three state visits under the Bush Administration" (Lopez 2003).
5. For Congressman John C. Bell's comments, see the *Congressional Record,* 1899, 32, pt. 2:2114.
6. See Sen. William Stuart's comments on the similarity between American Indians and Filipinos vis-à-vis the consent of the governed doctrine in the *Congressional Record,* 1900, vol. 33, pt. 2, p. 1866. However, William Jennings Bryan rebutted imperialists' invocation of Jefferson to support the forcible annexation of foreign territories. "The advocates of imperialism have sought to support their position by appealing to the authority of Jefferson . . . [but] Jefferson was emphatically opposed [to imperialism]," Bryan argued. "In a [1791] letter . . . [Jefferson] said: 'If there be one principle more deeply written than any other in the mind of every American, it is that we should have nothing to do with conquest'" (Bryan 1898).
7. Interestingly, pro-imperialists seldom cited either Jefferson or Washington's explicit predictions of the United States' future as one of the world's imperial powers. In 1873 Washington referred to the United States as "a 'rising empire,'" and three years later he said: '. . . [T]here will assuredly come a day, when this country will have some weight in the scale of Empires'" (Zimmerman 2002, 6–7). Thomas Jefferson also anticipated the U.S. rise as an imperial power in his April 1809 "empire for liberty" letter to James Madison.

8. As Katherine Verdery points out, nations traditionally have been conceptualized as a collective anthropomorphization of the national "we": "nations are conceived—like individuals—as historical actors, having spirits or souls, missions, wills, geniuses; they have places of origin/birth (cradles, often, in the national myth) and lineages (usually *patri*-lineages), as well as life cycles that include birth, periods of blossoming and decay, and fears of death; they have as their physical referent territories that are bounded like human bodies" (Verdery 1996, 229).
9. Roosevelt cited in Curtis (1904, 402).
10. From Recto (1960).
11. See, for example Constantino (1978, 1990, 1991, 1994, 1997), Constantino and Constantino (1978), and Ocampo (1998, 1990).
12. For example, Quezon supported a literacy requirement before the Philippines could petition the United States for absolute independence, because he thought that "the literacy requirement would not be reached until perhaps the next generation" (Constantino 1994, 330–31).
13. In addition to Benedict (1996) and Breuilly (1982), I used the following theorizations on nationalism: Bhabha (1990a, 1990b), Brennan (1990), Brubaker (1996), Constantino (1991), Gellner (1983), Handler (1988), Lloyd (1997), Mann (1996), Renan (1882), Shafer (1972), Smith (1996), and Verdery (1996). For useful essay collections on nationalism, which provided the source for several of the above articles, see Balakrishnan (1996) and Bhabha (1990b). For a rich online website on nationalism, see the Nationalism Project at http://www.nationalismproject.org/.
14. I am grateful to Tim Raguso for his help with developing this schema.
15. Anderson writes,

    I propose the following definition of the nation: it is an imagined political community—and imagined as both inherently limited and sovereign.

    It is *imagined* because the members of even the smallest nation will never know most of their fellow-members, meet them, or even hear of them, yet in the minds of each lives the image of their communion. . . .The nation is imagined as *limited* because even the largest of them, encompassing perhaps a billion living human beings, has finite, if elastic, boundaries, beyond which lie other nations. No nation imagines itself coterminous with mankind. . . .

    [I]t is imagined as a *community,* because, regardless of the actual inequality and exploitation that may prevail in each, the nation is always conceived as a deep, horizontal comradeship. Ultimately it is this fraternity that makes it possible, over the past two centuries, for so many millions of people, not so much to kill, as willingly to die for such limited imaginings. (Anderson 1991, 6–7)

CHAPTER 1

1. *Filipinas* refers to the Philippine archipelago in a politicized sense. It is used as an invocation of Philippine nationalism, not as a generic term referring to female Filipinos (as *Latina* is the feminine version of *Latino*).
2. For example, Rizal wrote to Ferdinand Blumentritt on January 26, 1887, "under the present circumstances, we do not want separation from Spain. All that we ask is greater attention, better education . . . one or two representatives and greater security of our persons and property" (Constantino 1969b, 19). As Austin Coates notes, the constitutional right to representation in the Cortes, the Spanish parliament, was enjoyed by Puerto Rico and Cuba, "but not by the Philippines, which had no representation of any kind" (Coates 1992, 71). Rizal's "assimilationist" policy rested on

his hope that the Philippines' situation would be improved if it could gain representation in the Cortes. See also Rafael (1995, 137).

3. From the December 28, 1946, *Free Press* account of the Philippine Commission meeting on selecting a national hero.

4. From Smith (1976, 283).

5. From Forbes (1928, 495).

6. From Friend (1965, 16).

7. Friar Lucio y Bustamante's comment about Indios' attempts to humanize themselves through clothing had specific relevance to the Philippine natives, who were required to publicize their inferior status by wearing their shirts outside their pants (i.e., untucked). Of course, the Spanish sumptuary decree, which required Indios to visibly identify themselves through dress, reveals the anxiety Friar Lucio y Bustamante's virulent statement manifests: the Indios were required to wear their shirts long precisely because, dressed in "shirt and trousers," Indios might be mistaken for peninsulares or insulare "Filipinos." The *barong tagalog,* a shirt worn long and untucked at the waist, evolved out of the Spanish colonial sumptuary laws. To this day, Filipino men often wear the barong tagalog for business or social occasions. Formal barong tagalogs, made of piña cloth woven from pineapple fiber and exquisitely embroidered, can cost thousands of pesos.

8. Austin Coates notes of José Rizal during his continental travels that "the [Spanish] colonial might not like what he saw, for Rizal was himself unconsciously a silent statement of racial equality. . . . As those Spaniards who spoke to him quickly discovered, he might be an indio, but he expressed himself like a European" (Coates 1992, 66). Thus Rizal was an example of an Indio "passing" as a European—exactly what Friar Lucio y Bustamante had denounced.

9. The word *propaganda* here has none of the negative connotation that the word generally carries in the United States. The Filipino Propaganda movement and its advocates, the Propagandists, refer solely to propagating in the literal sense the political goal of reforming Spanish colonial policy in the Philippines.

10. For example, analyzing Rizal's ideas of "national sentiment," a precursor of nationalism, Cesar Adib Majul writes that Rizal's "establishment of La Liga Filipina was Rizal's contribution on the organizational level and in the sphere of political action to the cause of building the Filipino nation" (Majul 1961a, 270). According to E. San Juan Jr., "Rizal's founding of the Liga Filipina was the prime catalyst for the mobilization of the Katipunan led by Andres Bonifacio and other separatists" (San Juan 1997, xv). See also Majul (1960, 3–4; 1961b, 54–55).

11. Richard White compares the Wild West and Turner's frontier thesis slightly differently than I but comes to a similar conclusion. See White (1994, 9).

12. White notes that the myth of Indian aggression lasted long after Native Americans were conquered, even after they had been contained in reservations; see White (1994, 27–29).

13. For example, in 1889, the same year Rizal saw the Wild West show in Paris, Thomas Jefferson Morgan, a commissioner of Indian affairs, affirmed, "Indians must conform to 'the white man's ways,' peaceably if they will, forcibly if they must. . . . This civilization may not be the best possible, but it is the best the Indians can get. They cannot escape it, and must either conform to it or be crushed by it" (Moses 1996, 74; originally from the *Fifty-eighth Annual Report of the Commissioner of Indian Affairs to the Secretary of the Interior,* 1889).

14. The "show Indians" developed their own star power: Sioux chief Sitting Bull's participation in the Wild West was an audience draw in and of itself, so much so that Cody wrote to William "Doc" Carver on February 11, 1883, "if we can manage to get [Sitting Bull], our everlasting fortune is made" (Kasson 2000, 170).

15. William Cody and his Wild West partner Nate Salsbury bruited the show's putative realism. For example, Salsbury claimed that "the historian on horseback has Truth for his amanuensis" and histrionically described the Wild West as "the grandest and most cosmopolitan Object Teacher ever projected by the exceptional experience and executive genius of man, scrupulously truthful in every respect . . . every historical and personal reference authentic, and every narrative, endorsement and criticism correct in spirit, context and application, as regards incident, person, time and location. It presents, with a colossal perfection and verisimilitude utterly impossible under any other management, living spectacles of heroic deeds of patriotic devotion and savage resistance" (Kasson 2000, 252). Journalists affirmed the show's historical authenticity. In 1886, Brick Pomeroy declared that the Wild West was "not a show. It is a resurrection . . . of honest features of wild Western life" (61).

16. From the *New York Dispatch,* July 18, 1886.

17. From *The (New York) World,* April 3, 1898.

18. From the *New York Times,* February 22, [1900?].

19. Other U.S. military leaders, including Brig. Gen. Arthur MacArthur and Gen. Samuel Young, also utilized reconcentrados during the Philippine-American War (Zimmerman 2002, 407). Pratt notes that "of greater consequence than the effect of the [Cuban] rebellion on U.S. economic interests was [the] effect on humanitarian sentiment in the United States, which deplored the misery and death among the reconcentrados" (Pratt 1993, 398C). The journalistic response to Butcher Weyler's reconcentrado policy versus Samuel Bell's reconcentrado policy is telling; see the *Boston Journal's* comment (ca. 1902) that Bell's implementation of concentration camps in the Philippines would be a hygienic blessing by destroying unsanitary native housing. In contrast, another American newspaper emphasized the sadistic brutality of Weyler's reconcentrado policy in Cuba a few years earlier: "Blood on the roadsides, blood on the fields, blood on the doorsteps, blood, blood, blood" (Miller 1982, 9; *New York World,* May 17, [1896?]). "Butcher Weyler" was Valeriano Weyler y Nicolau, governor-general of Cuba, who had previously served as governor-general of the Philippines (1888–91).

CHAPTER 2

1. William Cody chose the World's Columbian Exposition in Chicago (1893) as the site for the Wild West's domestic premier following the show's acclaimed European tour. Although the Wild West was not officially a part of the exposition, its arena was located just outside the exposition's gates and attracted many of the exposition's visitors. Frederick Jackson Turner gave his famous speech on "The Significance of the Frontier in American History" at the exposition, a fitting tribute to the exposition's commemoration of the four-hundredth anniversary of Columbus's discovery of the New World. As discussed in the previous chapter, the Wild West and Turner advocated slightly different readings of the method of conquering the frontier (Turner affirming an ostensibly peaceful conquest by Anglo farmers and settlers, the Wild West highlighting white scouts' defense of those farmers). Their result, however, was the same: U.S. nationhood achieved by Manifest Destiny.

2. Corbey notes that by 1890 "world fairs quickly became inseparable from imperialism and nationalism," increasingly emphasizing "political and imperialistic propaganda" until "science, commerce, and imperialism went hand in hand" (Corbey 1993, 357, 339, 356). Corbey's article on ethnographic showcases usefully puts U.S. world fairs in context with their international counterparts. For more specific analyses of U.S. photography and imperialism in the 1904 St. Louis World's Fair, see Breitbart (1997), Rydell (1984), Vergara (1995), and Wexler (2000).

3. The Filipinos constituted half of the entire number of "native peoples" at the St. Louis Fair (Breitbart 1997, 51).
4. Other colonial officials also participated actively in the construction of the St. Louis Philippine exhibits. Clarence R. Edwards, chief of the Bureau of Insular Affairs; Albert E. Jenks, head of the War Department's Ethnological Survey of the Philippine Islands; Daniel Folkmar, lieutenant-governor in charge of the Philippine civil service; and Pedro A. Paterno, president of the Philippine senate, all helped in the construction of the exhibit (Rydell 1984, 169).
5. Benito Vergara gives a detailed analysis of the significance of the "savage scowl" in American imperial ideology (see Vergara 1995, chap. 5).
6. For example, see Edwards (1992), Pinney (1992), and Banta (1986) on anthropology/photography in general. For studies of how anthropology/photography worked specifically in the American colonial program, see Breitbart (1997), Rafael (2000), Vergara (1995), and Wexler (2000).
7. For Susan Sontag quotation, see Sontag (1984, 7).
8. See Wexler (2000, chap. 7).
9. Cox had a handful of operational rules for his Brownies, to which he strictly adhered. The Brownies
   1. never allowed themselves to be seen by mortals;
   2. neither did harm to others nor could suffer serious harm themselves, although their adventures often entailed mishaps that inflicted scrapes, falls, and embarrassment;
   3. did good for its own sake, not for reward, profit, or approbation;
   4. could never get out of a predicament by means they had previously employed; and
   5. appeared in books which always totaled 150 pages. ("Palmer Cox Dead" 1924; "Father of the Brownies" 1924)
10. Cox did not explicitly name any of the Brownies. Individual Brownies, such as the "Dude" or the "Red Indian," came to be known by specific names by popular consensus among Cox's readers and critics of the time. To my knowledge, the Brownie "Photographer" was never specifically known as such. In *Brownies in the Philippines* the same Brownie throughout carries a Brownie Box–like camera and appears to have the job of photographing the band's exploits. I have dubbed this character the "Photographer" for ease of reference, not because it is a name that readers of the time, or even critics today, would instantly recognize.
11. Fannie Ratti explains, "The Brownie wearing the crown is not the king, Mr. Cox is often called upon to explain. He merely took the crown from one of the palaces they visited, and has worn it ever since; but it gives him no authority, as their government is strictly republican" (Ratti 1894, 240). The Brownie king does not appear in *Brownies in the Philippines.*
12. As Laura Wexler notes, "It would be astonishing how quickly th[e] rhetoric of the 'little brown brother' who needed American guidance and discipline was put in place were it not for the analogies offered by a reserve of racial understandings inherited from American slavery and Indian wars" (Wexler 2000, 44).
13. For a detailed discussion of American ethnic stereotyping of Filipinos during the early colonial era, especially the "wild" versus "civilized" tribes, see Vergara (1995).
14. The Rough Rider Brownie plays a central role in both the comic strip and book versions of Brownies in the Philippines, and he is the agent for American expansionism in the Brownies' Philippine adventures. Brownie egalitarianism ostensibly precludes any individual Brownie from assuming a dominant position in the band, but the Rough Rider Brownie is the most commonly depicted character in Brownies in the Philippines and usually is depicted centrally within individual illustrations.

The prominence of the Rough Rider Brownie, and particularly his centrality in the illustrations, demonstrates the perceived necessity for unambiguous assertions of American military prowess in the otherwise overwhelming wilderness of the Philippine political landscape. Whether demonstrating his skills as a superior marksman or taming a wild timarau, the Rough Rider showcases the "strenuous" masculinity Teddy Roosevelt and other imperialists equated with robust U.S. nationalism. The Rough Rider's unofficial leadership of the Brownie band in their Philippine adventures is demonstrated in the book's third chapter, where the Brownies confront a "torrent deep" on Mindanao. Determined to cross, the Brownies solicit "a leader . . . [w]ho has the courage to proceed." The Rough Rider immediately steps forward, announcing, "In thinking who that one should be, / Your eyes may rightly rest on me" (Cox 1904, 15–16). The Rough Rider heroically swims across the river with a rope, which he ties at the opposite end to form a tightrope for the other Brownies to cross. He alludes to Roosevelt's experience in triumphing over "outlaws" by means of his mastery with rope:

> Of ropes indeed I something know;
> Both how to tie, and how to throw:
> I've lived where they in daily use
> Did much the outlaws to reduce. (Cox 1904, 16)

"Outlaws" here refers to insurgents in the Spanish-American War, and the Rough Rider's oblique reference works to link the Philippine landscape to Cuban "outlaws," whom the United States had already subdued. Uncle Sam is one of the four Brownies featured crossing the river on the rope. The Rough Rider provides the means for Uncle Sam to penetrate the Philippine frontier.

15. One might be tempted to read the Rombloños' actions here as evidence of Cox's sympathy for Filipino anticolonial sentiments, but this is not the case. Cox describe the dead rats as one of the "things laid by / To make a wedding-dinner pie" (Cox 1904, 29). By specifying that the dead rats were part of the recipe for "a wedding-dinner pie," Cox undermined the Rombloños' fundamental humanity/civilization, for what reader would not be revolted by the idea of a dead rat as an ingredient for a wedding dinner? The Rombloños' misinterpretation of the Brownies' serenade as an insult as well as their disgusting retaliatory shower confirms at least the natives' savagery, if not their very inhumanity, thus indicating that here, as elsewhere through *Brownies in the Philippines,* Cox's sympathies lie with the Brownies/United States, not with Filipinos.

16. Critics of the American military's tactics during the Philippine-American War might raise an ironic brow at Durston's denigration of the "Igorrotes'" living in tiny huts "scarcely larger than good-sized dog kennels" and dying "in droves whenever any contagious disease attacks them." During the Philippine-American War, Jacob "Hell Roaring Jake" Smith, infamous for the order to his soldiers to kill Filipinos above the age of ten and his determination to turn Samar into a "howling wilderness" in retaliation for the Balangiga massacre, had experimented with torture by overcrowding. Smith had cells measuring 15 × 30 × 6 feet and crammed up to fifty prisoners into them, "with no toilet facilities . . . for months at a time." Stuart Creighton Miller notes that "Colonel Smith was so proud of these cages that he posed in front of them for a press photographer and gladly gave out grim statistics on the death rate in his 'cattle pen'" (Miller 1982, 238).

17. In both the book and newspaper versions, the Brownies decide to capture some monkeys for profit, not in the interest of science, thereby violating Cox's rule that the Brownies never had monetary motivations (e.g., the Brownies assert, "For money naught we care" [Cox 1904, 62]).

18. From an interview with Joyce Kilmer, originally published in "Palmer Cox of Brownie Caster Comes to Town," *New York Times Magazine,* January 16, 1916.

19. Originally published in "The Brownie Man's Hammer and Tongs," *San Francisco Examiner,* December 21, 1896.

CHAPTER 3

1. As a condition for the cease-fire of the continuous bombardment of the belea-guered Filipinos and Americans left on Corregidor, Japanese commander of the Philippines Masaharu Homma demanded the surrender of the entire Philippines. Thus Gen. Johnathan Wainwright's capitulation at Corregidor represented "the fall of the Philippines" (Zich 1977, 100). For accounts of the desperate defense of Bataan and Corregidor, see Agoncillo (1990, 393–94) and Zich (1977, 91–100). For a perspective critical of the American heroizing of the Bataan and Corregidor campaigns, see Constantino and Constantino (1978, 43–51).

2. For descriptions of the Japanese prisoner-of-war camps, the diseases and starvation suffered by the American and Filipino prisoners, and a detailed account of the U.S./Filipino liberation of the Cabanatuan prisoners, see Sides (2001).

3. The majority of film reviews cited here are collected in the *Back to Bataan* review file in the Academy of Motion Picture Arts and Sciences Margaret Herrick Library (AMPAS), Beverly Hills, Calif.

4. For a full discussion of the political allegories in nineteenth-century Filipino nationalist popular drama, see Rafael (1993, 185–218).

5. In her broadcasts Delgado implores, "Why do you fight? This is not your war. Americans brought you into it. . . . America has abandoned you. What good is lib-erty to the dead? . . . Look toward the sea where your [Japanese] liberators come to restore your homes and loved ones. . . . Filipinos, why do you fight?. . . . Filipinos, lay down your guns." In another of *Back to Bataan*'s characteristic ironies, in her radio broadcasts Delgado, while seeming to be collaborating with the enemy Japa-nese, is actually acting as a Filipino nationalist double agent. But much of her speeches ring true: at that point in the film America had seemingly abandoned Fil-ipinos; even Madden could not confidently assure Bonifacio that America would carry through its promises of military support.

6. In *Back to Bataan* Madden is a hardy, middle-aged man. Born in 1907, John Wayne was thirty-eight when the movie was filmed. Considering *Back to Bataan* portrays events in 1945, and the Philippine-American War occurred 1898–1902, even if Madden had been a boy solider of sixteen during his putative action in the Philip-pine-American War, he would have been at least sixty-three in the film's time frame.

7. It is widely believed that it was Filipinos' allegiance to the Americans during World War II and Filipino soldiers' brave fighting to liberate the Philippines from Japanese Occupation that finally ameliorated Americans' outright or lingering racism against Filipinos.

   The political importance of the Filipino-American alliance during World War II continues to this day; even now, both Filipino and American leaders cite World War II as the "crucible" of Filipino-American friendship. At the fiftieth anniversary of the July 4, 1946, granting of Philippine independence, American President Bill Clinton's "Message to the Filipino People," read at the independence commemora-tion on July 4, 1996, declared that "in the crucible of World War II, we forged bonds that went far beyond mere political links—bonds built on a common belief in the freedom of the individual and the strength of democracy" (Clinton 1996). President Fidel V. Ramos specifically commemorated the 1945 liberation of the Philippines as "a victory we owe to the American Armed forces, alongside whom Filipino soldiers and guerrillas bravely fought" (Ramos 1996).

8. The U.S. press repeatedly used the need to "teach" Filipinos the "lesson" of their subjugation as a rationalization for U.S. brutality during the Philippine-American

War. For example, in 1899 the *Omaha Bee* opined that Filipinos "had to be whipped into respectful submission. . . . [T]he Filipinos will love us later, for the fullness of the lesson we taught them" (Miller 1982, 77). Similarly, Pvt. William Christner reported that the men of his unit had shot a Filipino woman and child on January 23, 1899, commenting, "We killed a few [Filipinos] to learn them a lesson and you bet they learned it" (Miller 1982, 59).

9. For details of the early American educational policy, see Bernad (1981, 146) and de la Costa (1965, 221).

10. In *Gunfighter Nation,* Richard Slotkin notes that the developing genre of war films "worked as rituals of vicarious initiation into war. Hollywood . . . abandon[ed] the grand historical scale of the 'epic,' focusing instead on the intimate scene of small-unit combat, . . . making initiation a central theme of the narrative" (Slotkin 1992, 315). In *Back to Bataan* the initiation process is more ideological than military, especially with the pseudo-enlistment of Maximo, Dalisay Delgado, and Miss Barnes. Slotkin's formula of initiation into the combat unit applies most closely with Andres Bonifacio Jr., but Bonifacio's case is less a case of initiation into the unit as recontainment in it.

11. In hindsight we now know that in April 1945 the balance of power in the Pacific theater had been decided, and it could be argued that at that point, the U.S. government had determined that the Allies would win the war in the Pacific. But the American populace did not know that; thus my basic argument remains solid, that from the perspective of the film's mainstream American audience the outcome of the war still hung in the balance. One of the film's objectives as propaganda was to sustain popular support for the American war effort.

12. *Back to Bataan* review file, AMPAS.

CHAPTER 4

1. For example, in *The Founding* Fred Barbash gives a detailed account of the political, economic, and logistical challenges facing the new American republic during the constitutional convention.

2. Macapagal made this point explicitly in his June 12 proclamation, noting "the celebration of independence refers to its proclamation rather than to the final establishment of the government. In the case of America, when independence was proclaimed on July 4, the American Government was still a confederation and it was much later when it finally became a federal government" (Macapagal 1998a, 77).

3. Some Filipinos advocate observing Philippine Independence sometime in August to commemorate the beginning of the Philippine revolution against Spain iconized by Andres Bonifacio and Katipunan's "Cry of Balintawak," but because of the historiographical controversies surrounding the "Cry of Balintawak," that too is problematic: there is considerable debate about both its date and location. Sometime between August 20 and August 25, 1896, Andres Bonifacio held a meeting of the Katipunan at Balintawak, in the outskirts of Manila. The Spaniards found out about the meeting, so the Katipuneros went to nearby Pugad Lawin instead. There Bonifacio led the Katipuneros in tearing up their *cedulas,* certificates symbolizing Spanish colonial oppression. As the Katipuneros tore their cedulas, they shouted, "Long live the Philippines!" This event became known as the "Cry of Balintawak," although the event itself did not actually take place at Balintawak (Agoncillo 1900, 171–72). Historians have not been able to agree on the exact date of the "Cry of Balintawak." For an overview of the controversy over the Cry of Balintawak date issue, see Guerrero, Encarnacion, and Villegas (1996).

4. The occlusion of the 1996 centennial has led some Filipinos to be unaware that there even was a Philippine centennial in 1996. Rina Jimenez-David (1996) writes,

"'By the way,' said a friend, at the tail end of a conversation about the centennial of Philippine Independence, 'by centennial I mean the 1896 Centennial, not the 1898 one.'" To which Jimenez-David's response was, "I didn't even know there were two of them."

5. From the *San Francisco Call*, 1899? Because Miller uses omnibus footnotes, it is sometimes difficult to ascertain the original source information.

6. In an interview with Negroponte, Ernesto Hilario of the *Sunday Chronicle* (Manila) specifically asked the ambassador to explain the current definition of the continuing "special relationship" between the Philippines and the United States. Negroponte explicitly configured the RP-US "special relationship" as a direct and continuing effect of the United States' colonial relationship with the Philippines:

    > [HILARIO:] The relationship between the Philippines and the United States has often been described in the past as a "special relationship." Is that still true today? How "special" is the present relationship?
    >
    > [NEGROPONTE:] I think it's still special. One reason is that we have shared a considerable amount of recent history together, because of the colonial experience, because of World War Two. The special character derives from the closeness between the two countries in terms of colonial history (Hilario 1996).

7. The Luneta, a large park spanning an area of metro Manila from Ermita to Fort Santiago, is roughly equivalent in nationalist significance to the Mall in Washington, D.C.

8. The "flag ceremony" photograph is often printed in Philippine history books and is reproduced on the one-hundred-peso bill. Thus the Filipino audience on July 4, 1996, would have recognized the significance of the photograph.

9. American business interests were determined to maintain trade balances that were favorable to American capital. During the extended debates on when the Philippines should receive independence, the Americans "who [were] most anxious to give [the Philippines] immediate independence [were] those interested in sugar, cigars, etc., in the American market [, who did] not wish to continue the advantages to the Filipinos which they [were] receiving in the American market" (Agoncillo 1990, 335).

10. Citizens of a country that experienced "benevolent assimilation" as war and that was forced to wait for half a century for independence from the country that touted itself as the global champion of freedom and independence might well question the United States' motivation in funding the airport in General Santos. Was it altruism that motivated such a generous grant or was it interest in the fabulous oil reserves rumored to be resting under Mindanao? Mobil Oil's felicitous establishment of its Manila office in 1898 comes again to mind. Coincident with the celebration of the 1996 centennial and the completion of the General Santos airport was news of President Ramos's negotiations with Nur Misuari, commander of the Muslim troops of Mindanao, for peaceful relations between the Muslims and Christians of Mindanao. If these negotiations were successful, it could mean the pacification of Mindanao Muslims, who have resisted colonial and governmental control ever since the Spaniards came to the Philippines in the sixteenth century. Pacification of Muslim Mindanao—and gerrymandering that would bring Muslim areas into Christian/governmental control—could facilitate the mineral exploitation of Mindanao, which could change the entire Philippine economy if Mindanao's oil resources bear out their rumored potential. The development of significant oil reserves in Mindanao could bring greater prosperity to the average Filipino. However, Fredric Jameson argues that "the greatest misfortune that can happen to a third-world country in our time, namely the discovery of vast amounts of oil resources—[is] something which as economists have shown us, far from representing salvation, at

once sinks them incalculably into foreign debts they can never dream of liquidating" (Jameson 1986, 82). The development of the Philippines' natural resources is more likely to benefit foreigners and a few Filipino elite than improve the standard of living for the Filipino *masa*.

11. Filipinos are keenly aware of the discrepancies in political "stature" between the Philippines and the United States. In *Kalutang: A Filipino in the World*, N.V.M. Gonzalez relates an anecdote that portrays Filipinos' awareness of their national lack of stature in the global political community. "The Philippines values highly its place in the United Nations," writes Gonzales, "and there is more character portraiture than humor (which must be attributed to the Filipino nation rather than to himself) in General Romulo's standing before the United Nations General Assembly as its president to deliver an inaugural propped up by a stack of New York City telephone books because he was simply too short for the lectern" (Gonzalez 1990, 25). The symbolism of this anecdote, like the symbolism of the Fourth of July's "Star-Entangled Banner," is irresistibly ironic. To speak in the United Nations, the Filipino representative must be propped up by stacks of American marketing, demographic, and bureaucratic indices. If the representative Filipino is to register as a political speaker in global congresses, his lack of stature must be supplied by the United States. The fact that Gonzales attributes the "humor" of this anecdote "to the Filipino nation" rather than Romulo as an individual indicates his interpretation of Romulo's lack of political stature as a reflection of the Philippine nation's status in the global political community rather than simply denoting Romulo's individual physical characteristics.

12. *Pinoy* is a term used to denote a Filipino or traits that are distinctively Filipino.

CHAPTER 5

1. In the prefatory poem "Canto del Viajero," Nick Joaquin translates *viajero* as *wanderer*. *Viajero* also can be translated as *traveler*. In choosing the translation *wanderer*, Joaquin emphasizes a diasporic connotation in the novel's title.

2. In *Viajero*, and indeed throughout the Rosales novels, Sionil José implicitly endorses as "true" or "authentic" Filipino nationalism what I am calling emergent-nationalism. For Sionil José, emergent-nationalism, following from postcolonial theorists and especially Fanon, has at its heart the socioeconomic betterment and, therefore, political empowerment of the *masa*. Redressing the historic imbalance of economic/political power between the *ilustrados* and the *masa*, emergent-nationalism explicitly opposes *ilustrado*/bourgeois nationalism, which Sionil José indicts for colluding with colonial powers and maintaining an exploitative power system. For Filipino theorists of emergent-nationalism, see works by Anne Marie Mabilangan, Priscelina Patajo-Legasto, and E. San Juan Jr., cited in the next note.

3. I am drawing here from a whole school of criticism, including, on a general level, Fanon (1963), Bhabha (1990a, 1990b, 1994), Jameson (1986), Said (1989), Anderson (1986), Franco (1975), and Harlow (1987). For various definitions of Filipino emergent literature, my main sources were Mabilangan (1993), San Juan (1991a, 1991b, 1993), and Patajo-Legasto (1993b).

4. The Rosales novels were not published in order of their internal narrative chronology. In terms of their narrative chronology, the novels are *Po-on* (1984), *Tree* (1978), *My Brother, My Executioner* (1973), *The Pretenders* (1962), *Mass* (1982).

5. Sionil José's recurrent use of *Filipinas* as a politicized term (as opposed to *the Philippines*) emphasizes the novel's focus on Filipino emergent-nationalism.

6. When Salvador dela Raza was a student at Berkeley, Wack gave dela Raza extracurricular tutoring in the significance of the elision of race as an acknowledged component in Western history. Wack told Salvador, "You know so much of history but

without a racial slant to it" (Sionil José 1993, 33). During a discussion on Spain's colonial rule of the Philippines, Dr. Wack made explicit the connection between imperialism's systematizing of racial domination in both the United States and the Philippines: "Don't forget, [the Spaniards] once had an empire . . . And in that empire, they looked down on the Indians. In South America, in the Philippines. . . . So then, all of us who are not white are imprisoned in the concepts that the white man made. It is not a just world where color marks you at birth for degradation" (56).

7. E.g., see Pepe Samson's statement quoted above: "I am a pessimist. . . . So we will get rid of Marcos, but will we also get rid of all the powerful Filipinos who have enslaved us? . . . when will Filipinos realize that it is themselves who are often their worst enemy[?]" (Sionil José 1993, 221).

CONCLUSION

1. This is Eastern Samar Rep. Marcelino Libanan's position, codified in Philippine House Resolution 145, "A Resolution Demanding from the Government of the USA for the Immediate Return of the Bells of Balangiga to the People of the RP [Republic of the Philippines]," which Libanan introduced to the Philippine national legislature in 1998.

2. As, for example, the U.S. Army Center of Military History, which designates the 1898 conflict the "Philippine Insurrection." See the U.S. Army Center of Military History website at http://www.1stcavmedic.com/CMH.htm.

3. Edward Linenthal's *Sacred Ground: Americans and Their Battlegrounds* is a brilliant analysis of the ideology of American military memorials. The U.S. veterans' objections to the return of the Balangiga bells follows the general rhetorical pattern Linenthal outlines in his book.

4. The alleged facts of the Balangiga incident, as well as the factors prior and subsequent to it, remain hotly contested. In a September 22, 2003, e-mail to the Balangiga Research Group, Bob Couttie noted that "unfortunately, much of what is said about Balangiga, and the aftermath, is horrendously out of date. Examples include the supposed 250 Filipino dead during the attack—untrue; the mass slaughter of Balangiga civilians carried out—untrue. The death of 50,000 Samareños—untrue. That water torture was carried out in Balangiga prior to the attack—untrue."

5. As Victor Nebrida observes, "today the Balangiga Massacre still means in American history books the killing of forty-eight Americans, not the killing of tens of thousands of Filipino civilians" (Nebrida 1997).

6. From Moore (1906, 7:189–90).

7. The bodies were identified thus so that they could be reclaimed one year later and "buri[ed] in 'God's Own Country,'" according to George Meyer (Taylor 1931, 16).

8. The "water cure" consisted of suspected *insurrectos* being held down, mouth forced open, forced to ingest water. Miller gives a description of the water cure from the April 16, 1902, edition of the *New York World*: "handfuls of salt [were] thrown in to make it more efficacious . . . forced down the throats of the patients until their bodies become distended to the point of bursting. . . . our soldiers then jump on the distended bodies . . . so that the treatment can begin all over again" (Miller 1982, 251). For another piece excoriating the water cure, see Stuntz (1902).

9. See U.S. Senate Document 213, 57th Cong, 2d sess., 3, 6–7, 9–17.

10. Imperial's source: *Annual Report War Dept.* 1902, 439–40, 442, 447.

11. Imperial (1998) writes,

> General Lukban had organized the Samareños to prepare them for the impending clash with the American forces. He deputized Eugenio Daza to consolidate the towns for the local elections. In this way, the general

formed a decentralized de facto revolutionary government in the province. . . . The Balangiganons paid taxes and war contributions to the revolutionary government. . . . The welcome accorded by the town president, local chief of police, and town priest to the company of American soldiers in Balangiga was a strategy to keep the unsuspecting occupation forces in the dark about the Balangiganons' plan to vanquish them.

Daza (1935) emphasized Balangiga's significance to the revolutionary effort, writing: The Philippine revolutionary army in the province of Samar under the command of General Vicente Lukban was the last to surrender to the American troops. . . . I was an Infantry Captain of the revolutionary army in charge of collecting money to support the revolution and provide food supply to my countrymen. . . . I conceived, then, a very daring plan to capture all the Americans together with their arms and ammunitions in the most practicable manner under the circumstances. . . . I reminded [the Balangiganons] of the duty which we had to perform . . . if we were to be real patriots fighting for our liberty and independence.

Note that Daza's account (1935) is roughly contemporaneous with the Company C men's accounts compiled in Taylor's book (1931), so both are open to accusations of ex post facto revisionism.

12. As Bob Couttie (2001c) notes:

Food has a very special role in the Filipino culture and psyche far beyond its sustenance. . . . Almost the worst thing one can do to a Filipino is take away his or her food, the most shameful act is to "break his rice bowl," whatever else you might do. It is difficult for a Westerner to connect with this, and Connell did not.

Such seizure would have been disturbing to the Filipinos in normal times, but these were not normal times. At the time of the seizures, the rainy season . . . was approaching. During this period there could be no harvesting or drying of rice and food fishing would be severely limited. For the four wet months they would be dependent upon the root crops growing around their houses, the very root crops that Connell ordered cut down. In brief, the people of Balangiga had a very real and substantive fear that they would be facing starvation.

13. In all the debates on both sides—American and Filipino, military and civilian—one aspect has received little attention. Every year, on September 28, a commemorative service is held in the Balangiga town church for both the American and Filipino dead (Couttie 1998a). By including the men of Company C in their annual remembrance service, Samareños already commemorate the United States' shared history with the Philippines.

14. It is important to note that not all veterans oppose the return of one or both bells. The controversy became so vociferous that it became an issue for both state and national veterans' organizations. "The state chapters of the American Legion, Veterans of Foreign Wars, United Veterans Council, Veterans Affairs Council and the Special Forces Association all . . . oppos[e] the compromise," relates Kerry Drake, but in October 1997 the National American Legion voted against the Wyoming state opposition to the bells compromise (Drake 1998; Evaristo-Dahmke 1997).

15. Lloyd's assertion that returning the bells to the Philippines is an affront to the Balangiga victims' survivors may be an overstatement. Jean Wall, daughter of Adolph Gamlin, the first man struck in the Balangiga attack, strongly advocates returning the bells, or at least one bell, to the Philippines. Wall wrote to retired Air Force Col. David McCracken, "If there are three bells of Balangiga, one of these bells should be returned, to ring out in all its glory on September 28th, for all men, of all races, for all past conflicts, and for those who have fought and died for their

beliefs and their country, lest the world and all generations to follow forget their forefathers and what they gave up to protect the freedom of those to follow" (Borrinaga 2001b).

16. S.1903/S.404, known as the "Thomas Bill," is supported by Sen. Jesse Helms, chairman of the foreign relations committee, and Sen. Strom Thurmond, chairman of the armed services committee, as well as Wyoming Sen. Michael Enzi and Rep. Barbara Cubin.

17. From Wyoming Delegation (1998).

18. This is a point of which Filipinos continue to be aware. As Virgilio Babay observed of American's praise for Filipinos who "embraced peace" during the American colonial period: "Peace? It was either peace on the enemy's terms or the peace of the graveyard" (Baybay 2001).

19. See Pérez (1998, chap. 5).

20. E.g., for a useful analysis of contested history embodied in George Armstrong Custer and the National Park Service memorial to the Little Bighorn, see Linenthal (1991, chap. 4).

21. For information on the Congressional Medal of Honor, see the U.S. Army Center of Military History website at http://www.1stcavmedic.com/CMH.htm. The website includes Army Regulation 600-8-22 on Military Awards, which describes the requirements for Medal of Honor conferral. The Medal of Honor is awarded "to a person who, while a member of the Army, distinguishes himself or herself conspicuously by gallantry and intrepidity at the risk of his or her life above and beyond the call of duty while engaged in an action against an enemy of the United States; [or] while engaged in military operations involving conflict with an opposing foreign force. . . . The deed performed must have been one of personal bravery or self-sacrifice so conspicuous as to clearly distinguish the individual above his comrades and must have involved risk of life" (http://www.1stcavmedic.com/CMH.htm). For a list of Medal of Honor recipients for the "Philippine Insurrection" see http://www.army.mil/cmh-pg/mohphil1.htm.

22. This presents an interesting contradiction. The fact that the U.S. government awarded Medals of Honor for the Samar campaign indicates that the government did acknowledge the Philippine-American War as an official war, since the Congressional Medal of Honor is reserved for recognizing military personnel/actions. This contradicts the government's refusal to grant combat status to soldiers fighting in the Philippines.

BIBLIOGRAPHY

Agoncillo, Teodoro A. 1990. *History of the Filipino People.* 8th ed. Quezon City: Garotech Publishing.

Aguinaldo, Emilio. 1898. "Act of Proclamation of Independence of the Filipino People" (June 12). In *June 12, 1898, and Related Documents,* 45–48. Manila: National Historical Institute.

"Ambassador Offers Bell Compromise." 1997. *Wyoming Tribune-Eagle,* October 6.

Ancheta, Celedonio A. 1998. "The Man Who Fathered June 12 for Our Independence Celebration." In *June 12, 1898, and Related Documents,* 84–86. Manila: National Historical Institute.

Anderson, Benedict. 1986. "Narrating the Nation." *Times Literary Supplement,* June 13.

———. 1991. *Imagined Communities: Reflections on the Origin and Spread of Nationalism.* New York: Verso.

———. 1996. "Introduction." In *Mapping the Nation,* ed. Gopal Balakrishnan, 1–16. New York: Verso.

Atwood, J. Brian. 1996. "Fourth of July Remarks." Given at the Philippine-American Day commemoration, Luneta, Manila, July 4. Reprinted in *Manila Bulletin,* July 5.

Balakrishnan, Gopal. 1996. *Mapping the Nation.* New York: Verso.

Balangiga Research Group. 2002. *Information Pack BB1a.* At http://numistrade.net/balangiga/bb1a.pdf.

Banta, Melissa, and Curtis Hinsley. 1986. *From Site to Sight: Anthropology, Photography and the Power of Imagery.* Cambridge, Mass.: Peabody Museum Press/Harvard University Press.

Barbash, Fred. 1987. *The Founding: A Dramatic Account of the Writing of the Constitution.* New York: Simon and Schuster.

Baybay, Virgilio V. 2001. "Awkward Historical Situation." *Philippine Daily Inquirer,* December 14.

Bengzon, Alfredo R. A., and Raul Rodrigo. 1997. *A Matter of Honor: The Story of the 1990–91 RP-US Bases Talks.* Manila: Anvil Books.

Bernad, Miguel A. 1981. "Philippine Literature in English: Some Sociological Considerations." In *Essays on Literature and Society in Southeast Asia: Political and Sociological Perspectives,* ed. Tham Seon Chee, 145–59. Singapore: Singapore University Press.

———. 1989. "The Problem of Integrity." In *From Cabugaw to Rosales: A Filipino's Journey to Justice and Nationhood: F. Sionil José and His Fiction,* ed. Alfredo T. Morales, 1–11. Quezon City: Vera-Reyes.

Bhabha, Homi. 1990a. "DissemiNation: Time, Narrative, and the Margins of the Modern Nation." In *Nation and Narration,* ed. Homi K. Bhabha, 291–322. London: Routledge.

———. 1990b. "Narrating the Nation." Introduction to *Nation and Narration,* ed. Homi K. Bhabha, 291–322. New York: Routledge.

————. 1994. "Introduction: Locations of Culture." In *Locations of Culture,* ed. Homi K. Bhabha, 1–18. New York: Routledge.

Boot, Max. 2002. *Savage Wars of Peace: Small Wars and the Rise of American Power.* New York: Basic Books.

Boradora, Norman, and Carlito Pablo. 2002. "U.S. Troops Covered by VFA, Says DOJ." *Philippine Daily Inquirer,* January 18.

Borrinaga, Rolando O. 1998a. "Balangiga Bells Update." *Freeman* (Cebu), April 12.

————. 1998b. "Balangiga: A Confluence of Advocacy Positions." At http://www.geocities.com/rolborr/balcon/html.

————. 2001a. "Balangiga History Not Clear As a Bell." *Philippine Daily Inquirer,* August 3.

————. 2001b. "Solving the Balangiga Bell Puzzle." *Philippine Daily Inquirer,* Visayas Section, August 11.

Breitbart, Eric. 1997. *A World on Display: Photographs from the St. Louis World's Fair, 1904.* Albuquerque: University of New Mexico Press.

Brennan, Timothy. 1990. "The National Longing for Form." In *Nation and Narration,* ed. Homi K. Bhabha, 44–70. New York: Routledge.

Breuilly, John. 1982. *Nationalism and the State.* New York: St. Martin's Press.

Brockden Brown, Charles. 1887. *Edgar Huntly, or Memoirs of a Sleepwalker.* Philadelphia: David McKay.

Brooke, James. 1997. "U.S.-Philippines History Entwined in War Booty." *New York Times,* December 1.

Brubaker, Rogers. 1996. *Nationalism Reframed: Nationhood and the National Question in the New Europe.* Cambridge: Cambridge University Press.

Bryan, William Jennings. 1898. "Jefferson Versus Imperialism." *New York Journal,* December 25. At http://www.boondocksnet.com/ai/ailtexts/bryan981255.html.

Burns, Gerald T. 1992. *Presenting America, Encountering the Philippines.* Quezon City: University of the Philippines Press.

Bush, George W. 2002a. "President Bush Salutes Veterans at White House Ceremony." Remarks by the president, November 11. At http://www.whitehouse.gov/news/releases/2002/11/print/20021111-2.html.

————. 2002b. State of the Union Address, January 29. At http://www.whitehouse.gov/news/releases/2002/01/print/20020129-11.html.

Cameron, Kate. 1945. "A Stirring War Film, This *Back to Bataan.*" *(New York) Daily Times,* September 13.

Campomanes, Oscar V. 1992. "Filipinos in the United States and Their Literature of Exile." In *Reading the Literatures of Asian America,* ed. Shirley Geok-Lin Lim and Amy Ling, 49–78. Philadelphia: Temple University Press.

Canceran, Delfo Cortina, and Rose Yaya. 1996. "We the People." *Manila Times,* July 4.

Castro, Jovita Ventura. 1992. *The Revolution by José Rizal.* English Translation. Manila: Nalandangan.

Castro-Guevara, Marita, ed. 1997. *The Bases Talks Reader: Key Documents of the 1990–91 Philippine-American Cooperation Talks.* Manila: Anvil Books.

Chao, Julie. 1998. "Filipinos Fight for Return of Two Bells." *San Francisco Examiner,* September 13.

Churchill, Bernardita Reyes, ed. 1997. *Determining the Truth: The Story of Andres Bonifacio.* Manila: Manila Studies Association, the National Commission for Culture and the Arts Committee on Historical Research, and the Philippine National Historical Society.

Churchill, Malcolm. 1997. "Exposing an Exposer: A Critical Look at Glenn May's *Inventing a Hero.*" In *Determining the Truth:The Story of Andres Bonifacio,* ed. Bernardita Reyes Churchill, 52–68. Manila: Manila Studies Association, the National Commission for Culture and the Arts Committee on Historical Research, and the Philippine National Historical Society.

Cleveland, L. D. 1998. "America Should Not Bow to Foreign Pressure." *Wyoming Tribune-Eagle,* April 1.

Clinton, Bill. 1996. "A Message to the Filipino People." *Manila Bulletin,* July 5.

Coates, Austin. 1992. *Rizal: Philippine Nationalist and Martyr.* Ermita, Manila: Solidaridad Publishing.

"Congressional Delegation Writes Bill to Protect Bells." 1998. *Wyoming Tribune-Eagle,* April 2.

Constantino, Renato. 1969a. *The Making of a Filipino:A Story of Philippine Colonial Politics.* Quezon City: Malaya Books.

———. 1969b. *Veneration without Understanding.* Third National Rizal Lecture, December 30. N.p.

———. 1978. *Neocolonial Identity and Counter-Consciousness: Essays on Cultural Decolonization.* London: Merlin Press.

———. 1986. *Vintage Recto: Memorable Speeches and Writings.* Quezon City: Foundation for Nationalist Studies.

———. 1990. *The Nationalist Alternative.* Rev. ed. Quezon City: Foundation for Nationalist Studies.

———. 1991. "A Sense of Nationhood." In *History: Myths and Reality,* Renato Constantino, 3–5. Quezon City: Karell.

———. 1994. *The Philippines:A Past Revisited.* Vol. 1, *Pre-Spanish 1941.* Quezon City: Foundation for Nationalist Studies.

———. 1997. *Insight and Foresight.* Ed. Luis R. Mauricio. Quezon City: Foundation for Nationalist Studies.

Constantino, Renato, and Letizia R. Constantino. 1978. *The Philippines:The Continuing Past.* Quezon City: Foundation for Nationalist Studies.

Corbey, Raymond. 1993. "Ethnographic Showcases, 1870–1930." *Cultural Anthropology* 8 (August): 338–69.

Couttie, Bob. 1998a. "Bell or No Bell, There's Always a Service in Balangiga." *Casper (Wyo.) Star-Tribune,* March 4.

———. 1998b. "Mutilation." At http://rcouttie.topcities.com/balangiga/mutilati.htm.

———. 2001a. "Balangiga and Bad Historians." At http://rcouttie.topcities.com/balangiga/badhistory.htm.

———. 2001b. "History of the Bells." At http://rcouttie.topcities.com/balangiga/histbell.htm.

———. 2001c. "What Went Wrong at Balangiga?" At http://rcouttie.topcities.com/balangiga/whatwent.htm.

Cox, Palmer. 1903. *Brownies in the Philippines.* New York: New York Herald Co.

———. 1904. *Brownies in the Philippines.* New York: Century Co.

Cristobal, Adrian. 1996. "Phil-Am Friendship Day?" *Philippine Daily Inquirer,* June 27.

Crooker, Joseph Henry. 1984. "The Menace to America." 1900. In *The Anti-Imperialist Reader:A Documentary History of Anti-Imperialism in the United States.* Vol. 1, ed. Philip S. Foner and Richard C. Winchester, 304–7. New York: Homes and Meier Publishers. Originally published in *Liberty Tract No. 12,* American Anti-Imperialist League.

Cummins, Roger W. 1973. *Humorous but Wholesome: A History of Palmer Cox and the Brownies.* Watkins Glen, N.Y.: Century House Americana Publishers.

Curtis, Francis. 1904. *The Republican Party, 1854–1904.* New York: G. P. Putnam's Sons.

David, Randy. 2002. "U.S. Troops in Mindanao." *Philippine Daily Inquirer,* January 12.

Daza, Eugenio. 1935. "Balangiga: Its History in the Revolution on 28 September 1901." At http://rcouttie.topcities.com/balangiga/Daza_%20English.htm.

de la Costa, Horacio. 1965. *Readings in Philippine History.* Manila: Bookmark.

de la Cruz, Pennie Azarcon. 1998. "Bringing Back the Bells of Balangiga." *Philippine Daily Inquirer,* June 12.

Deloria, Philip J. 1998. *Playing Indian.* New Haven: Yale University Press.

de Ocampo, Esteban A. 1971. "June 12 in the History of the Filipinos." In *June 12, 1898, and Related Documents,* 1–8. Manila: National Historical Institute.

de Quiros, Conrado. 2002. "In the Land of the Blind." *Philippine Daily Inquirer,* March 20.

de Souza, Dudley. 1988. "The Novels of F. Sionil José: Protagonists in Spiritual Exile." In *A Sense of Exile: Essays in the Literature of the Asia-Pacific Region,* ed. Bruce Bennet, 155–65. Nedlands, Western Australia: Centre for Studies in Australian Literature.

Donnelly, Thomas. 2002. "The Past as Prologue: An Imperial Manual." *Foreign Affairs* 81 (July–August): 165–70.

Doronila, Amando. 2001. "U.S. Attacks Call for New Interpretation of VFA." *Philippine Daily Inquirer,* September 30.

Drake, Kerry. 1997. "Bells Controversy Still in Discord." *Casper (Wyo.) Star-Tribune,* October 5.

———. 1998. "Vets Groups Oppose Resolution on Bells." *Casper (Wyo.) Star-Tribune,* March 12.

Drake, Kerry, and Tom Rea. 1998. "Lawmakers Sign on to Bells Compromise." *Casper (Wyo.) Star-Tribune,* February 19.

Drinnon, Richard. 1980. *Facing West: The Metaphysics of Indian-Hating and Empire-Building.* New York: Schocken Books.

Edwards, Elizabeth, ed. 1992. *Photography and Anthropology, 1860–1920.* New Haven: Yale University Press.

Elliot, Michael. 2002. "George W. Kipling." CNN.com, July 1. At http://www.cnn.com/2002/ALLPOLITICS/07/01/time.kipling.

Evaristo-Dahmke, Nelinda. 1997. "Chime in, Tell Them To Take One Bell." *Casper (Wyo.) Star-Tribune,* November 23.

Face, Karin. 1999. "Little People, Big Impact: The Palmer Cox Brownies." *Winterthur Magazine* (summer): 23–25.

Fanon, Frantz. 1963. *The Wretched of the Earth.* Trans. Constance Farrington. New York: Grove Press.

"The Father of the Brownies: Palmer Cox and the Elfin Kingdom That He Created." 1924. *Current Opinion* (September).

Flower, Benjamin O. 1902. "Is the Declaration of Independence a Treasonable Document That Menaces Modern Imperialistic Republicanism?" *Arena* 27 (May).

Foner, Philip S. 1986. *The Anti-Imperialist Reader: A Documentary History of Anti-Imperialism in the United States: The Literary Anti-Imperialists.* New York: Holmes and Meir Publishers.

"For a Meaningful Fourth of July." 1996. *Manila Chronicle,* July 4.

Forbes, Cameron. 1928. *The Philippine Islands.* Vol. 1. Boston: Houghton Mifflin.

"For Whom the Bells of Balangiga Toll." 2001. Philippines ABS-CBN News, September 26.

Francia, Luis H. 2002. "U.S. Troops in the Philippines." *Village Voice,* February 20–26.

———. 2003. "Brown Man's Burden." *Village Voice,* January 29–February 4.

Franco, Jean. 1975. "Dependency Theory and Literary History: The Case of Latin America." *Minnesota Review* 5 (fall): 65–80.

Friend, Theodore. 1965. *Between Two Empires.* New Haven: Yale University Press.

Frisby, Wayne L. 1999. "A Veteran's Viewpoint on the Bells of Balangiga." Typescript, Bishop Hart Collection, Cheyenne, Wyo.

Galdon, Joseph A. 1972. "Introduction." *Philippine Fiction: Essays from Philippine Studies, 1953–1972,* ed. Joseph A. Galdon, xi–xvii. Quezon City: Ateneo de Manila University Press.

Gellner, Ernest. 1983. *Nations and Nationalism.* Oxford: Basil Blackwell.

Gonzales, Stella O., and Rocky Nazareno. 1996. "Ramos Cites 'Unique' RP-US Friendship." *Philippine Daily Inquirer,* July 5.

Gonzalez, N.V.M. 1990. *Kalutang: A Filipino in the World.* Manila: Kalikasan Press.

Gostas, Theodore W. 1999. "In Search of the Bells of Balangiga." Typescript, Bishop Hart Collection, Cheyenne, Wyo.

Guerrero, Leon Maria. 1977. *The First Filipino: A Biography of José Rizal.* Manila: National Historical Institute.

———. 1984. "Our Choice of Heroes." In *We Filipinos,* by Leon Maria Guerrero, 67–71. Philippines: Daily Star Publishing Co.

Guerrero, Milagros C., Emmanuel N. Encarnacion, and Ramon N. Villegas. 1996. "Balintawak: The Cry for a Nationwide Revolution." *Sulyap Kultura Quarterly* (second quarter): 13–21. Quezon City: National Commission for Culture and the Arts.

Handler, Richard. 1988. *Nationalism and the Politics of Culture in Quebec.* Madison: University of Wisconsin Press.

Harlow, Barbara. 1987. *Resistance Literature.* New York: Methuen.

Hart, Joseph. 1998. "Balangiga Bells Are Not War Trophies." *Wyoming Tribune-Eagle,* March 22.

Hathaway, Stan. 1998. Letter to Craig Thomas, March 13.

Helzer, James A. 1997. "Time to Right Injustice of Balangiga." *Casper (Wyo.)-Star Tribune,* November 23.

———. 1998. "Taking the Bells of Balangiga Was Unlawful in 1901." *Wyoming Tribune-Eagle,* April 10.

———. 2001. Interview by author. Cheyenne, Wyo., September 27.

Herman, Marguerite. 1997. "Bells Signal Emotional Dispute." *Wyoming Catholic Register,* December.

Hilario, Ernesto M. 1996. "Interview with U.S. Ambassador John Negroponte. *Sunday Chronicle,* June 30.

Hoganson, Kristin L. 1998. *Fighting for American Manhood: How Gender Politics Provoked the Spanish-American and Philippine-American Wars.* New Haven: Yale University Press.

Howells, William Dean. 1899. "The Philippine Problem: How to Secure Peace—Views of William D. Howells." *New York Evening Post,* October 17.

Imperial, Reynaldo H. 1998. "Balangiga and After." At http://www.up.edu.ph/cids/chronicle/articles/chronv3n2/chron3n2_infocus09_pg1.html.

Jameson, Fredric. 1986. "Third-World Literature in the Era of Multinational Capitalism." *Social Text* (fall): 65–88.

Javellana, Juliet L., and Armand Nocum. 2001. "President Defends All-Out U.S. Support; Militants Disagree." *Philippine Daily Inquirer,* September 17.

Jefferson, Thomas. 1801. First Inaugural Address. At http://www.cs.indiana.edu/statecraft/jeffinaug.html.

———. 1809. Letter to James Madison, April 27. At http://www.loc.gov/exhibits/jefferson/149.html.

Jimenez-David, Rina. 1996. "Independence Day Reflections." *Philippine Daily Inquirer,* June 12.

Jones, Scott A. 2001. "Keep the Bells at F. E. Warren Air Force Base." *Wyoming Tribune-Eagle,* March 13.

Karnow, Stanley. 1989. *In Our Image: America's Empire in the Philippines.* New York: Ballantine Books.

Kasson, Joy S. 2000. *Buffalo Bill's Wild West: Celebrity, Memory, and Popular History.* New York: Hill and Wang.

Kelly, Ryan. 1997a. "U.S. Has Third Bell in Korea." *Wyoming Tribune-Eagle,* November 25.

———. 1997b. "Veterans, Filipinos Clamor Over Bells." *Wyoming Tribune-Eagle,* October 30.

Kintanar, Thelma B. 1989. "Coming Full Circle: The Rosales Novels of F. Sionil José." In *From Cabugaw to Rosales: A Filipino's Journey to Justice and Nationhood: F. Sionil José and His Fiction,* ed. Alfredo T. Morales, 18–30. Quezon City: Vera-Reyes.

Kolb, Richard K. 1999a. "'Bamboo Vets' Fought in Philippines." *VFW Magazine* 86 (February): 22–26.

———. 1999b. "Combat Chronology of Philippines War." *VFW Magazine* 86 (February): 32–35.

———. 2001. "Remember Balangiga!" *VFW Magazine* 89 (September): 40–42.

Kunzle, David. 1975. Review of *Cummins' Humorous but Wholesome: A History of Palmer Cox and the Brownies. Art Bulletin* 52 (September): 454–56.

Lamb, David. 1998. "For Whom the Bells Toll: America or the Philippines?" *Today* (Manila), May 10.

Langit, Richel B. 1998. "Balangiga Bells Won't Ring on June 12." *Manila Times,* May 28.

Laurel, Herman Tiu. 1996. "American 'Friendship' Day." *Today* (Manila), July 4.

Laybourn, Margaret. 1999. "Filipino Bishop Asks for Return of Bells." *Casper (Wyo.) Star-Tribune,* June 29.

Linenthal, Edward Tabor. 1991. *Sacred Ground: Americans and Their Battlegrounds.* Urbana: University of Illinois Press.

Lloyd, David. 1997. "Nationalisms against the State." In *The Politics of Culture in the Shadow of Capital,* ed. Lisa Lowe and David Lloyd, 173–97. Durham: Duke University Press.

Lloyd, Jim. 1998. "Can We Move on to Other Business?" *Cheyenne (Wyo.) Tribune Eagle,* April 30.

London, Josh. 2002. "The Unlikely Imperialists." *Policy Review* (August–September): 81–87.

Lopez, Sixto. 1900. "Sixto Lopez's Conciliatory Appeal." From *Sixto Lopez to the American People.* Boston: Philippine Information Society. At http://www.boondocksnet.com/ai/vof/s1000622.html.

Lopez, Tony. 2003. "GMA's State Visit." *Manila Times,* Internet edition, May 16.

Mabilangan, Anne Marie L. 1993. "Approaches to a Criticism of Emergent Literature." In *Philippine Post-Colonial Studies: Essays on Language and Literature,* ed. Cristina Pantoja Hidalgo and Priscelina Patajo-Legasto, 65–72. Quezon City: University of the Philippines Press.

Mabini, Apolinario. 1900. "In Response to General Bell." In *Gems in Philippine Literature*, ed. Corazon V. Balarbar, Karina A. Bolasco, and Danton R. Remoto, 294–98. Quezon City: National Book Store, 1989.

Macapagal, Diosdado. 1998a. "June 12 as Independence Day." In *June 12, 1898, and Related Documents*, 76–80. Manila: National Historical Institute.

————. 1998b. "By the President of the Philippines, Proclamation No. 28 Declaring June 12 as Independence Day." In *June 12, 1898, and Related Documents*, 81. Manila: National Historical Institute.

Magno, Alex. 1996. "Philippine-American Relations: From Mystical to Pragmatic." Paper presented at symposium on the fiftieth anniversary of Philippine-American Friendship Day, Philippine Department of Foreign Affairs, Manila.

Majul, Cesar Adib. 1960. "Rizal and the National Community." *Panorama* 12 (September): 3–12.

————. 1961a. "On the Concept of National Community." In *Himalay: Kalipunan ng mga Pag-aaral kay José Rizal*, ed. Patricia Melendrez-Cruz and Apolonio Bayani Chua, 264–75. Manila: Cultural Center of the Philippines. Originally published in *Data Papers of the International Congress on Rizal*, 173–185. Manila: José Rizal National Centennial Commission, n.d.

————. 1961b. "Rizal as Father of Filipino Nationalism." *Century Magazine* (November): 48–56.

Mallaby, Sebastian. 2002. "The Reluctant Imperialist." *Foreign Affairs* 81:2–7.

Mann, Michael. 1996. "Nation-States in Europe and Other Continents: Diversifying, Developing, Not Dying." In *Mapping the Nation*, ed. Gopal Balakrishnan, 295–316. New York: Verso.

May, Glenn. 1997. *Inventing a Hero: The Posthumous Re-creation of Andres Bonifacio.* Quezon City: New Day Publishers.

McDaniel, Rodger. 1998. "Issue Deeper than Possession of the Bells." *Wyoming Tribune-Eagle*, April 10.

Memmi, Albert. 1965. *The Colonizer and the Colonized.* Boston: Beacon Press.

Miller, Stuart Creighton. 1982. *"Benevolent Assimilation": The American Conquest of the Philippines, 1899–1903.* New Haven: Yale University Press.

Moore, John Basset. 1906. *A Digest of International Law.* Washington: Government Printing Office.

Morgan, Wayne. 1994. "Now, Brownies Seldom Idle Stand: Palmer Cox, the Brownies, and Curiosity." *Ephemera Journal* 7:25–37.

————. 1996. "Cox on the Box: Palmer Cox and the Brownies: The First Licensed Characters, the First Licensed Games." *Game Researchers' Notes* 23 (June): 5533–39.

Moses, L. G. 1996. *Wild West Shows and Images of American Indians 1883–1933.* Albuquerque: University of New Mexico Press.

Nakpil, Carmen Guerrero. 1998. "Mixed Feelings." In *Centennial Reader: Selected Essays*, 228–30. Quezon City: Insular Printing Corp.

Nationalism Project. At http://www.nationalismproject.org.

National Security Strategy of the United States of America (NSS). 2002. At http://www.whitehouse.gov/nsc/nss.pdf.

Nebrida, Victor. 1997. "The Balangiga Massacre: Getting Even." At http://www.bibingka.com/phg/balangiga/default.htm.

Negroponte, John D. 1996. "Independence Address." Reprinted Address of Paul V. McNutt, U.S. high commissioner to the Philippines, and U.S. President Harry S.

Truman, on the inauguration of the Philippine Republic, July 4, 1946. *Manila Bulletin,* July 5.

Netzorg, Morton J. "Jock." 1985. *Backward, Turn Backward: A Study of Books for Children in the Philippines: 1866 to 1945.* Manila: National Book Store.

Ocampo, Ambeth R. 1990. *Looking Back.* Manila: Anvil Publishing.

———. 1995. *Rizal without the Overcoat.* Rev. ed. Manila: Anvil Publishing.

———. 1998. *The Centennial Countdown.* Manila: Anvil Publishing.

———. 1999a. "Indios Bravos." *Philippine Daily Inquirer,* May 26.

———. 1999b. "Rizal in the U.S.: Quarantined in San Francisco." *Philippine Daily Inquirer,* July 2.

———. 1999c. "Rizal's American Tour." *Philippine Daily Inquirer,* July 7.

Orosa, Sixto Y. 1961. "Rizal's Place in Philippine Heroology." *Mobilways* 6:2–7.

Pinney, Christopher. 1992. "The Parallel Histories of Anthropology and Photography." In *Photography and Anthropology, 1860–1920,* 74–95. New Haven: Yale University Press.

"Palmer Cox." 1924. *New York Times,* editorial, July 25.

"Palmer Cox Dead, 'Brownies' Author." 1924. *New York Times,* July 25.

Parsons, Louella O. 1945. " 'Bataan' Fine Melodrama." *Los Angeles Examiner,* July 19.

Parungao, Rhowena, and Ernest Porcalla. 1996. "Tale of Two Snagged Flags at July 4 Rites." *Manila Chronicle,* July 5.

Patajo-Legasto, Prescelina. 1993a. "Introduction: Discourses of 'Worlding' and Philippine Post-Colonial Studies." In *Philippine Post-Colonial Studies: Essays on Language and Literature,* ed. Cristina Pantoja Hidalgo and Prescelina Patajo-Legasto, 1–15. Quezon City: University of the Philippines Press.

———. 1993b. "Literatures from the Margins: Reterritorializing Philippine Literary Studies." In *Philippine Post-Colonial Studies: Essays on Language and Literature,* ed. Cristina Pantoja Hidalgo and Priscelina Patajo-Legasto, 38–53. Quezon City: University of the Philippines Press.

Pérez Louis A., Jr. 1998. *The War of 1898: The United States and Cuba in History and Historiography.* Chapel Hill: University of North Carolina Press.

Peterson, Molly. 1998. "Clinton Clashed with Congressional Republicans over Bells of Balangiga." Legi-Slate News Service, April 6. At http://www.legislate.com/n/news/980406.htm#212000390.

Philippine Historical Association (PHA). 1960. "Resolution Petitioning the President and the Congress of the Philippines to Adopt and Declare June 12 of Every Year as 'Independence Day' for the Republic of the Philippines." In *June 12, 1898 and Related Documents,* 88–90. Manila: National Historical Institute.

Potmesil, Ruby. 1998. "Desecration: Taking Bells from a Church." *Casper (Wyo.) Star-Tribune,* April 5.

Pratt, Julius W. 1993. "Spanish-American War." *Collier's Encyclopedia.* Vol. 21, ed. Lauren S. Bahr and Bernard Johnston, 398B–398D, 399–401. New York: Collier.

Pratt, Mary Louise. 1992. *Imperial Eyes: Travel Writing and Transculturation.* New York: Routledge.

Rafael, Vicente. 1993. "White Love: Surveillance and National Resistance in the U.S. Colonization of the Philippines." In *Cultures of United States Imperialism,* ed. Amy Kaplan and Donald E. Pease, 185–218. Durham: Duke University Press.

———. 1995. "Nationalism, Imagery, and the Filipino Intelligentsia in the Nineteenth Century." In *Discrepant Histories: Translocal Essays on Filipino Cultures,* ed. Vicente L. Rafael, 133–58. Manila: Anvil Publishing.

————. 2000. *White Love and Other Events in Filipino History.* Durham: Duke University Press.

Ramos, Fidel V. 1996. July 3 Speech at Malacañang Palace. Reprinted in "Our Common Future in the Asia-Pacific," *Manila Bulletin,* July 4.

"Ramos to Call for Bells' Return on Official Visit." 1998. Philippine News Agency (PNA), April 5. At http://www.newprint.com/balangiga/news.htm.

Ratti, Fannie. 1894. "Palmer Cox and the Brownies." *St. Nicholas Magazine* 21 (January): 238–42.

Recto, Claro M. 1960. "Nationalism and Our Historic Past." Speech given to the National Laymen's Convention, February 27.

————. 1962. "A True Filipino Is a Rizalist." *Panorama* (October): 2–5.

"Renaming of Philippines to Rizal Pressed." 1996. *Manila Bulletin,* June 12.

Renan, Ernest. 1996. "What Is a Nation?" 1882. In *Becoming National: A Reader,* ed. Geoff Eley and Ronald Grigor Suny, 42–55. New York: Oxford University Press.

"Return Bells to Philippines." 1998. *Salt Lake Tribune,* May 1.

Richardson, Steve. 1997. "Bells of Balangiga: One for Booty; One for Liberty." *Casper (Wyo.) Star-Tribune,* November 2.

Rizal, José. 1992. "The Philippines a Century Hence" (Filipinas dentro de cien años). 1889–1890. In *José Rizal: Life, Works, and Writings,* by Gregorio F. Zaide. Manila: National Bookstore.

Rodis, Rodel E. 1997. "The Bells of Balangiga: Send Them Home." *San Francisco Examiner,* December 23.

Roosevelt, Theodore. 1926. "Manhood and Statehood." In *American Ideals: The Strenuous Life, Realizable Ideals: The Works of Theodore Roosevelt,* ed. Hermann Hagedorn. New York: Charles Scribner's Sons.

Roth, Russell. 1981. *Muddy Glory: America's "Indian Wars" in the Philippines, 1899–1935.* West Hanover, Mass.: Christopher Publishing House.

Rufio, Aries. 1996. "Flags Get Entangled, a Mirror of Love-Hate Ties?" *Manila Times,* July 5.

Rydell, Robert W. 1984. *All the World's a Fair: Visions of Empire at American International Expositions, 1876–1916.* Chicago: University of Chicago Press.

Said, Edward W. 1989. "Representing the Colonized: Anthropology's Interlocutors." *Critical Inquiry* 15 (winter): 205–25.

San Juan, E., Jr. 1991a. "Mapping the Boundaries: The Filipino Writer in the U.S.A." *Journal of Ethnic Studies* 19 (spring): 117–31.

————. 1991b. *Writing and National Liberation: Essays in Critical Practice.* Quezon City: University of the Philippines Press.

————. 1993. "Filipino Writing in the United States: Reclaiming Whose America?" *Philippine Studies* 41:141–66.

————. 1997. *Rizal in Our Time: Essays in Interpretation.* Pasig City, Philippines: Anvil Publishing.

Satchell, Michael. 2000. "Back to the Philippines." *U.S. News and World Report* 128 (January 24): 30–32.

Scherer, Joanna C. 1992. "The Photographic Document: Photographs as Primary Data in Anthropological Enquiry." In *Photography and Anthropology 1860–1920,* ed. Elizabeth Edwards, 32–41. New Haven: Yale University Press.

Selfa, Lance. 2002. "A New Colonial Age of Empire?" *International Socialist Review* 23 (May): 50–57.

Senick, Gerard, ed. 1991. "Palmer Cox." *Children's Literature Review* 24:65–83.

Sestak, Joseph. 1999a. "Bells of Balangiga Became Instruments of War." *Casper (Wyo.) Star-Tribune*, May 9.

————. 1999b. "Don't Dismantle Memorial." *Cheyenne (Wyo.) Star-Tribune*, October 31.

Sestak, Joseph, and Robert Nab. 1997. "Bells Should Stay in Cheyenne." *Wyoming Tribune-Eagle*, November 2.

Sguisag, Rene A. V. 2001. "The Bells of Balangiga." Philippines ABS-CBN News, September 28.

Shafer, Boyd C. 1972. *Faces of Nationalism: New Realities and Old Myths.* New York: Harcourt Brace Jovanovich.

Sicat, Ma. Teresa. 1995. "The Philippine Nation in Literary Discourse." In *Nationalist Literature: A Centennial Forum,* ed. Elmer A. Ordoñez, 420–33. Philippines: University of the Philippines Press and PANULAT/Philippine Writers Academy.

Sides, Hampton. 2001. *Ghost Soldiers: The Forgotten Epic Story of World War II's Most Dramatic Mission.* New York: Doubleday/Random House.

Sionil José, F. 1962. *The Pretenders.* Manila: Solidaridad Publishing.

————. 1984. *Po-on.* Manila: Solidaridad Publishing.

————. 1993. *Viajero: A Filipino Novel.* Manila: Solidaridad Publishing.

Sloan, Larry. 1945. "RKO's 'Back to Bataan' a Top War Film." *Citizen News,* July 17.

Slotkin, Richard. 1992. *Gunfighter Nation: The Myth of the Frontier in Twentieth-Century America.* New York: Harper Perennial/Harper Collins Publishers.

Smith, Anthony D. 1996. "Nationalism and the Historians." In *Mapping the Nation,* ed. Gopal Balakrishnan, 175–97. New York: Verso.

Smith, Joseph B. 1976. *Portrait of a Cold Warrior.* New York: J.P. Putnam's Sons.

"Soldiers' Letters: Being Materials for the History of a War of Criminal Aggression." 1899. In *The Anti-Imperialist Reader: A Documentary History of Anti-Imperialism in the United States, Vol. 1,* ed. Philip S. Foner and Richard C. Winchester, 316–26. New York: Holmes and Meier, 1984. Originally published as a pamphlet by the Anti-Imperialist League.

Sontag, Susan. 1984. *On Photography.* Harmondsworth: Penguin Books.

Spiegel, Sydney. 1999. "Mark Twain Would Give Both Bells Back." *Casper (Wyo.) Star-Tribune,* May 15.

Stevens, Walter B. 1903. *The Official Photographic Views of the Universal Exposition Held in Saint Louis, 1904.* Saint Louis: Thompson Publishing Co.

Stuntz, Homer C. 1902. "The 'Water Cure.'" Originally published in *(Kansas City, Mo.) Central Christian Advocate,* June 4. At http://www.boondocksnet.com/ai/ailtexts/watercure020611.html.

Susman, Tina. 2001. "Asking to Whom the Bells Should Go." *Denver Post,* September 3.

Swallow, John L. 1998. Letter to Fidel V. Ramos, April 7.

————. 1999. "There's Equality in Sharing the Bells." *Wyoming Tribune-Eagle,* February 4.

————. 2000. "Time to Resolve the Bells of Balangiga Issue." *Wyoming Tribune-Eagle,* September 28.

Taylor, James O., ed. 1931. *The Massacre of Balangiga: Being an Authentic Account by Several of the Few Survivors.* Joplin, Mo.: McCarn Printing Co.

Thomas, Craig. 1998a. Letter to Stan Hathaway, March 24.

————. 1998b. "The Thomas Bill." S. 1903, "A Bill to Prohibit the Return of Veterans Memorial Objects, Committee on Veterans Affairs." At http://www.newprint.com/balangiga/thomas.htm. Includes related materials.

Tomsho, Robert. 1997. "The Bells of Balangiga Have a Different Ring in Manila, Cheyenne." *Wall Street Journal,* November 19.

Turner, Frederick Jackson. 1893. "From the Significance of the Frontier in American History." At http://history.acusd.edu/gen/text/civ/turner.html.

Twain, Mark. 1992a. "'Thirty Thousand Killed a Million.'" *Atlantic Monthly* 269 (April): 52–65.

———. 1992b. "To the Person Sitting in Darkness." 1901. In *Mark Twain's Weapons of Satire: Anti-Imperialist Writings on the Philippine-American War*, ed. Jim Zwick, 22–39. Syracuse: Syracuse University Press.

Underwood, Robert A. 1998a. "Centennial Anniversary of the Spanish-American War." Congressional speech given February 5. At http://www.newprint.com/balangiga/bell.htm.

———. 1998b. "Office of Congressman Robert A. Underwood News Release: Congressman Underwood Speaks on the Bells of Balangiga." At http://www.house.gov/underwood/news-releases/bells.htm.

U.S. Army Center of Military History. 2002. "The Congressional Medal of Honor." At http://www.1stcavmedic.com/CMH.htm.

U.S. Army Center of Military History. 2002. "Philippine Insurrection Medal of Honor Recipients." At http://www.army.mil/cmh-pg/mohphil1.htm.

U.S. House. 1997. 105th Cong., 1st sess., H.R. 312. Robert Underwood, Rep. Guam, "Urging the [U.S.] president to authorize the transfer of ownership of one of the bells taken from the town of Balangiga on the island of Samar, Philippines, which are currently displayed at F. E. Warren Air Force Base, to the people of the Philippines." At http://www.newspring.com/balangiga/hr312.htm.

Vaughn, Timothy. 1998. "The 'Blame America' Crowd Is Growing." *Wyoming Tribune-Eagle,* May 10.

Verdery, Katherine. 1996. "Whither 'Nation' and 'Nationalism'?" In *Mapping the Nation*, ed. Gopal Balakrishnan, 226–34. New York: Verso.

Vergara, Benito M., Jr. 1995. *Displaying Filipinos: Photography and Colonialism in Early Twentieth Century Philippines.* Quezon City: University of the Philippines Press.

"VFW Strongly Opposes Compromise on Bells." 1997. *Sheridan Press,* December 9.

Villanueva, Marichu. 1996. "The Star-Entangled Banner." *Philippine Star,* July 5.

Walsh, Lynn. 2002. "A New Imperial Moment?" *Socialism Today* 69 (October). At http://www.socialistparty.net/pub/archive/antiwar-newimperial.htm.

Wasserburger, Jeff. 1997. "Letter to the Editor." *Casper (Wyo.) Star-Tribune,* n.d.

West, Philip, Steven Levine, and Jackie Hiltz, eds. 1998. *America's Wars in Asia: A Cultural Approach to History and Memory.* Armonk, N.Y.: M. E. Sharpe.

Wexler, Laura. 2000. *Tender Violence: Domestic Visions in an Age of U.S. Imperialism.* Chapel Hill: University of North Carolina Press.

White, Richard. 1994. "Frederick Jackson Turner and Buffalo Bill." In *The Frontier in American Culture,* by Richard White and Patricia Limerick, 7–64. Berkeley: University of California Press.

Williams, Walter L. 1980. "United States Indian Policy and the Debate over Philippine Annexation: Implications for the Origins of American Imperialism." *Journal of American History* 66 (March): 810–31.

Wright, Virginia. 1945. Untitled film review of *Back to Bataan.* N.p., February 16.

Wyoming Delegation (Sen. Craig Thomas, Sen. Michael Enzi, and Rep. Barbara Cubin). 1998. Letter to President Bill Clinton, January 9. In the Thomas Bill website, at http://www.newprint.com/balangiga/thomas.htm.

Yoder, Elizabeth. 1989. "Under the Balete Tree." In *From Cabugaw to Rosales: A Filipino's Journey to Justice and Nationhood: F. Sionil José and His Fiction,* ed. Alfredo T. Morales, 66–70. Quezon City: Vera-Reyes.

Zich, Arthur. 1977. *World War II: The Rising Sun.* Alexandria, Va.: Time-Life Books.

Zimmerman, Warren. 2002. *First Great Triumph: How Five Americans Made Their Country a World Power.* New York: Farrar, Straus and Giroux.

Zwick, Jim. 1995. "Protesting the Independence Day Colony: Fourth of July Symbolism in the Debate about Imperialism." At http://www.boondocksnet.com/ai/ail/july4.html.

Index

Philippine-American War, 104–105, 205–206n8; in *Viajero* (Sionil José), 142, 162, 166

Twain, Mark, 36–37, 82

Uncle Sam: Brownie character, *58*, 61, *62*, 70, 78–79, 80, *81*; and Juan de la Cruz, 137–140

USAID, 12, 120, 122, 135, 207–208n10

U.S. imperialism: contemporary, 2–4; and defensive war (U.S.), 17, 34, 85; and Pax Americana, 3; and Philippine resistance plays, 95–96, 205n4; and War on Terror, 2–4. *See also* tutelage

U.S. nationalism: and debates over imperialism, 6–9

U.S.-R.P. Relations: Bush (U.S.) and Macapagal-Arroyo (R.P.) administrations, 5, 199n4; economic relations during Philippine Commonwealth period, 134, 207n9; as "special relationship," 125, 140, 207n6

Viajero (Sionil José, F): and Aquino, Benigno and Corazon (fictionalized), 152–153, 160–161; and EDSA (fictionalized), 152–153; and emergent nationalism, 19, 142, 143–148, 150–152, 155, 160–166, 208nn2, 3; and exile/repatriate themes, 141–144, 146–149, 153–154, 155, 162–163, 208n1; and Marcos, Ferdinand (fictionalized), 146, 160, 209n7; and Indio/Indian theme, 163–166; and patriarchy, 150, 156–159; and tutelage, 142, 159, 162, 166; and U.S. neocolonial influence, 141, 158–159, 163

Visiting Forces Agreement (VFA), 2–3, 199n3

War on Terror: 2–4; and U.S. imperialism, 3–4

Washington, George, 186; on U.S. empire, 199n7

Water cure, 175–176, 209n8

White Man's Burden: and *Brownies in the Philippines*, 64, 66, 74; political cartoon (1899), 64, 66, *67*; and twentieth century foreign capitalism, 12; and U.S. imperialism, 5; and War on Terror, 3–4

Wild West show: Filipino performers, 37–38; and historical realism, 35, 202n15; as imaginative space, 48; Indian performers, 35–36, 201n14; as national narrative, 36–39; and Manifest Destiny, 29–31, 33–34, 36–38, 49, 202n1; and Rizal, José, 27, 28–29, 30–32; and Rough Riders, 37–38; and Spanish-American War, 37; and Turner, Frederick Jackson, 32–34, 36, 202n1

ABOUT THE AUTHOR

Sharon Delmendo is an associate professor of English at St. John Fisher College in Rochester, New York.